The Liberal Idea of Freedom

Books by David Spitz

Patterns of Anti-Democratic Thought
Democracy and the Challenge of Power
The Liberal Idea of Freedom

Essays in

The Liberal Idea of Freedom

David Spitz

THE UNIVERSITY OF ARIZONA PRESS
TUCSON

For Morris Watnick
who is a part of this book

CONTENTS

On the Crisis, So-Called, of Liberalism

When one speaks, as in certain quarters it is currently fashionable to do, of the crisis of liberalism, he refers, most commonly, to one or perhaps both of two things. He means doubts as to the validity of liberalism as a doctrine or idea, or he refers to the instability of states that allegedly rest upon the liberal principle.

If it is the first — doubts as to the idea of liberalism — I fail to see that the mere existence of such doubts constitutes a crisis. Every idea, from that of the nature and destiny of man to the latest panacea for world salvation, has always been challenged by some men; but to the believers this is no necessary sign of error or of crisis. And in the present instance it may signify nothing more than a certain confusion in the minds of those who call themselves or others liberals but who may, in fact, be using a common label to denote different things. Alternatively, it may call attention to a lack of popular support, in which case the problem is one of producing intellectual conviction or an appropriate visceral response. It is, so to say, a crisis in opinion or emotion. It may even, as in the case of a distraught John Stuart Mill who was driven almost to suicide when he came to question the tenets of his utilitarian faith, take the extreme form of a crisis in the mind and heart of an individual man. But it is not necessarily a crisis that reflects an inconsistency or other deficiency in the intrinsic merits of the doctrine. Such a deficiency, if it exists at all, must be established on independent grounds. But if I read the arguments of the critics correctly, and as I hope the essays collected in this volume will show, the indictment of liberalism fails to disclose any such independent deficiency.

Nevertheless, the critics are quite firm in their insistence that liberalism *is* in a state of crisis. This they hold to be so self-evident as hardly to require demonstration. They must refer, then, not to liberalism as an idea but to the preservation and perpetuation of so-called liberal states. This, however, requires demonstration on at least two preliminary grounds. They must show, first, that those states which are *labeled* liberal states are *in fact* liberal states, which presupposes an acceptable definition of liberalism itself. And they must show, secondly, that such

1

liberal states are in grave if not imminent danger of destruction — either through internal collapse, civil insurrection, or external aggression. In this second instance, they must demonstrate too that such collapse or civil war or foreign conquest is peculiarly the consequence of liberalism itself, that liberalism, so to say, carries within itself the seeds of its own annihilation.

Now, what is striking about the arguments of the critics in this connection is that they nowhere establish these things. True enough, they *assert* some of them — pointing, for example, to the alleged decline of confidence in liberalism and to the rise of totalitarian movements. But to assert obvious or near-obvious dangers is not to establish a causal relationship between them and the principle of liberalism, any more than to assert that cancer is a danger to good health is to prove that good health produces cancer. On the contrary, it can well be argued that the dangers to "liberal" states emerge out of the failure of such states fully to embody the liberal idea; that it is not their liberalism which is in crisis, but a lack of liberalism which produces the crisis of less-than-liberal "liberal" states.

However this may be, and I shall return to this point in a moment, what is disconcerting in the speeches and writings of those who maintain that liberalism is in crisis is their failure to draw and carefully to observe the necessary distinction between these two notions of liberalism: liberalism as an idea or doctrine or set of dogmas, on the one hand, and liberalism as a principle embodied in actual states, on the other. These quite different conceptions of liberalism are treated as if they were one and the same thing, and the implication is drawn that to attack the one is to attack the other. But this, of course, is in no sense necessarily the case. In the City of God liberal states — if the ideas of liberalism and of God are compatible — may realize the liberal idea; but in the City of Man the liberal state, along with every other actual state, can but hope to approximate the ideal. Hence, the crisis of which the critics speak may be less in the idea of liberalism than it is in the practices of more-or-less, and often it is less, liberal states; and the cause of that crisis may derive from their failure to live up to the requirements of the liberal idea.

This brings me to a second major difficulty in the conception of those who talk of liberalism in crisis. This is their curious and often inconsistent definitions of terms, in particular the diverse definitions they put forward in response to the question, What is liberalism? Here the critics are less than clear. Some impute to liberalism as a doctrine the notion of moral unity, of agreement on values; others insist that what is central to the idea of liberalism is moral autonomy, the flowering of individuality. Some affirm that liberalism implies social cohesion and cooperation, a feeling of solidarity; but others contend that liberalism means freedom of action, even equal liberty. Still others argue that liberalism meshes human freedom and social order; but along with this it is often said that what is vital to liberalism is not only moral freedom but the release of men's social energies.

I am not at all certain that I understand the meanings of these various terms, but I am quite sure — to the extent that I do understand them — that they are not all compatible with each other, and that some liberals at least reject some of them.

Consider, for example, the contention that liberalism implies moral unity, that it insists upon agreement on values. If John Stuart Mill was a liberal, and I believe that he was, this is surely the very opposite of his argument in *On Liberty* and *Representative Government*. And from Mill to R. M. MacIver,[1] Bertrand Russell,[2] and Morris R. Cohen[3] in our own day, there is a long and established tradition which holds that freedom of diversity in moral beliefs is an essential attribute of the liberal faith. Indeed, it is precisely because men do not, and are not likely to, agree on values that liberals insist on the right to hold and to express divergent views. Otherwise men must resort to mutual slaughter and to the authoritarian imposition of a particular set of values. It is true that if men are to live together peacefully they must at the very least agree to disagree; and if it is this sort of agreement that the critics of liberalism have in mind when they speak of agreement on values, I have no quarrel with their position. But I do not read them always to mean this. For while they identify liberalism with a respect for differences, they also argue that liberalism entails, or should entail, purposiveness in social life; they call for a "positive" liberalism, for a "proper" consensus.

Consider, again, the identification of liberalism with moral autonomy, as well as with freedom of action and equal liberty. If men are free to act, in the sense that they are subject to no external restraints, then clearly only the strong are free, but only until there is a stronger. If equal liberty is to be assured — and I take their use of Tocqueville's curious phrase to mean an equal right to certain recognized and constitutionally guaranteed liberties — it can only be assured by denying some men the freedom to act in some ways, in particular, to act in ways that would deny certain related or apposite liberties to others. In any case, it is difficult to see why the denial of some liberties to some men precludes the attainment of moral autonomy, or why some inequalities intrinsically deprive persons of their *opportunity* for moral autonomy. Unless moral autonomy is to be equated with Netschaiev's nihilism, it can only be achieved by a mature man cognizant of his real and always

3

unequal world. Always there are some inequalities — of talent, of wealth, of power, of prestige, and the like — and I fail to see that these, however unjust we may hold their particular distribution to be, make impossible the attainment of moral autonomy. Here, as everywhere in life, the mature man must come to terms with his environment; he must find his own salvation, his own autonomy, not in escaping from the world, but in living within it. And while I should not for one moment deny the desirability and importance of seeking to transform that world so as to remove existing injustices as far as we can perceive them, and as far as we can grasp and implement the measures appropriate to their correction, I would at the same time insist that outside the City of God some injustices, some inequalities, are likely always to remain. If moral autonomy is to be achieved, it must be achieved in the face of such inconvenient facts.

Consider, finally, the contention by the critics that liberalism means both the flowering of individuality and the release of men's social energies, and that, from these, liberalism affirms both freedom and order will emerge. One has only to ask, what if the development of my individuality impels or requires me to interfere with the development of my neighbor's? or, what if other men's social energies combine to impose upon me a pattern of behavior that I find both distasteful and destructive of my own individual growth? to see that this peculiar formulation raises more difficulties than it resolves. In fact, by giving an essential and presumably equal right to all these forces, the critics of liberalism effectively and conveniently deprive the liberal of any principle by which he might resolve conflicts among them. For this reason among others, the critics' imputation to liberalism of an apposition of human freedom and social order is unconvincing. The issue in fact is improperly, even deceptively, stated; for to the liberal it is not a matter of freedom *versus* order, or even of freedom *and* order. What the liberal argues instead is that, in every society, what is required is a never-ending resolution of conflicting and sometimes equally ultimate claims into a working complex of individual freedoms and their concomitant restraints. Always some freedoms are in conflict with others, and the determination of who is to enjoy which freedoms, under what circumstances, and to what degree, entails the imposition of certain restraints. All that liberalism can do is to offer a particular way of approaching this determination; it cannot, with one crucial exception, prescribe the specific hierarchy of freedoms and their corresponding restraints. That exception, of course, is liberty of opinion without which liberalism would itself be dethroned.

I come now to a third and final difficulty in the image of liberalism given us by the critics. This is their notion that liberalism is a philosophy rather than an attitude, a particular set of dogmas rather than a method. And it is largely because they entertain this idea of liberalism that they can speak of moral unity, of an agreement on values, as essential to the liberal principle.

Now, there is a sense in which liberalism has been historically identified with a particular dogma, e.g., the doctrines of John Locke or the naïve nineteenth-century Social Darwinism of Herbert Spencer. But the more useful and enduring application of the term is not to a specific doctrine or philosophy, but to the methods of rational inquiry. It is this which unites otherwise dissimilar men, e.g., Mill and Cohen, Russell and MacIver. From this standpoint, conservatives who look to a body of principles allegedly embodied in some remote or recent past and utopian radicals who look to a body of principles contained in some blueprint of the future are alike fanatical men. They both claim possession of the truth. They both claim to "know" what is right. Yet they are both impervious to the results of scientific inquiry, to the tests of reason. What distinguishes the liberal from the adherents of both these dogmatic and absolutistic camps is precisely his repudiation of such final truths. He recognizes, as the conservative and utopian radical do not, that man is born not stupid but infinitely ignorant; and that, however much he may learn in his short span of life, the things he does not know are always greater than the things he does know; and that, consequently, the beliefs he holds to be true today may be subject to correction tomorrow. For this reason the liberal demands that all claims to truth be heard. His commitment is to the method of rational inquiry, not to the specific results that may at any one time emerge from such inquiry.

Hence, his basic value is the value of free inquiry; his basic attitude, the skeptical, or at least the inquiring, mind.

And if this is the meaning of liberalism, as I believe it most commonly is, then I deny that there is a crisis of liberalism. I admit, as one is bound to admit, that not many adherents flock to its cause; for liberalism so understood offers no royal road to certainty, no cheap ticket to political salvation. But this constitutes a challenge, not a crisis; and it is to be faced and met both in the theoretical realm of human understanding and in the practical or political realm or human conduct. In the theoretical realm, there is really no contest; for as long as we adhere to the court of reason there is no sensible alternative to liberalism. But in the political sphere, there exists a real danger that vain and foolish men, hopelessly pursuing the fancied delights of power and the furtherance of their conceived (or misconceived) self-interest, will thrust decency and the liberal way of life into darkness.

This, however, is not a crisis of liberalism. It is a crisis of man.

In the essays that follow, I have brought together a number of papers that deal in various ways with the merits and problems of liberalism. In Part One, I address myself to some general questions of structure and process, to theoretical formulations that treat broadly of the nature of freedom and power and their interrelatedness. In Part Two, I am concerned more with specific issues of freedom, and in particular with the vindication of the liberal idea of, and approach to, freedom. In Part Three, I offer some reflections on the curious contemporary revival of what may loosely be called conservative thought and its attack on liberalism. Finally, by way of an Afterword, I append one from among a number of essays in which I have attempted to deal with the theory and practice of Soviet Communism; this may be sufficient, I trust, to indicate my belief that Communism, despite all its pretensions to the contrary, is in fact nothing less than the negation of liberalism.

All but four of the essays included here have been published previously, as noted in the Acknowledgments at the end of the volume. They span more than a decade of writing, and it would be presumptuous for me to pretend that were I to write them all anew I would write them in precisely the same way. Nevertheless, except for the integration of some shorter pieces into the essay that now constitutes Chapter 14, for the insertion of some lines omitted from the original publication of some of these essays for reasons of space, and for one or two slight changes in phraseology, I have thought it best to reprint them as they then appeared. This has the further disadvantage of producing an occasional repetition of argument, but not enough, I hope, to offset the more important advantage of retaining these essays as integral units. Since, moreover, a number of these essays have been cited, and some occasionally discussed, in the literature, it may avert confusion to leave them in their original form. One ought not, in any case, arbitrarily alter what is now a matter of record.

The dedication at the head of this volume but meagerly acknowledges my deep and continuing debt to the most selfless of friends, and one who is perhaps the ablest mind of my generation; were he to have written on these themes, the vindication of liberalism would have rested on far richer and sturdier a foundation than I have been able to give it here. I am no less indebted to the continuing forbearance and wise counsel of my wife, but of this it is useless, because impossible, to speak. Merely to note that one man should have been thus twice blessed is enough to invite the envy of the gods.

David Spitz

The Ohio State University
Columbus, Ohio
1964

Part One

FREEDOM AND DOMINATION

Chapter 1

The Myth of the Iron Law of Oligarchy

Short of death, there is no way to escape power. Men may bemoan some of the consequences of its possession, but possess it someone will. Joined to a good cause, power is a meritorious tool. Joined to a bad cause, power becomes an instrument of discomfort and even, perhaps, of tyranny. But power by itself is neutral; what matters is not the fact of power but its uses, and this becomes largely a problem of determining who controls whom, and for what purpose.

From the democratic point of view, the answer to this problem is that the use of power is least subject to abuse when those who wield it are chosen by and held constitutionally responsible to the people. But to this, organizational theorists have always had a stock reply. They argue that the principle of political responsibility, quite apart from the fact that it is bound to degenerate into rule by mediocrity, is actually impossible to achieve. In this view, history, not human will, determines the destiny of mankind; and history, as they read it, reveals the inescapable operation of certain political laws. Not least among these is the law that fatally reduces the masses of men to domination by a ruling class or elite. In the face of this law, they contend, the argument for democratic control of political power collapses.

A number of considerations, however, suggest that the so-called iron law of oligarchy is more lore than law. For one thing, it assumes that politics is a science in essentially the same sense as the more mechanical phases of physics constitute a science, i.e., a body of organized knowledge with distinctive axioms, laws, and patterns of predictable behavior. It also assumes that power is not, and cannot be made, responsible. Both of these assumptions are demonstrably false.

Politics as a Science

It is not difficult to understand why men have sought to reduce politics to the imperatives of a science, why political theory has generally been suspect as a tangled web of speculative thought far removed from reality. Its abstract formulations and sometimes esoteric terminology —

9

whether produced by the profundity of the subject or the realization that if one cannot be understood he cannot be refuted — have done little to appease the craving for absolute certainty characteristic of many students of government as well as of that imaginary individual, the average man. Men unaccustomed to serious reflection like to *know*. They seek assurance, even dogma, and tremble in the face of the unknown. What *is* or what *must be* offers greater comfort than dissident views as to what *should* be. Such men tend to seek, and generally to discover, political and historical laws.

Unfortunately, the course of human history does not readily accommodate itself to this view. Politics is only partly a science — I am tempted to say the least significant part. What we know of the conditions of revolution, of the structure and functioning of legislative assemblies and political parties and the like, is not only limited but far less crucial than the art and philosophy that government involves. By the art of government I mean, among other things, the ability to manipulate people so as to achieve desired results, and along with this to explore with a discerning and discriminating hand the undefined limits of popular tolerance so as to avoid expulsion from power. By the philosophy of government I refer to the ends, the purposive values, for which power is sought and employed. Concerning the art of government we know all too little. Of the philosophy of government we know only that views are many and diverse. Yet it is here — in the art and philosophy of government — that we find the substance of politics. What organized knowledge we have is important only as it illuminates this substance, as it helps us discover and apply necessary techniques to the attainment of a particular end.

This is not, of course, to deny the importance of scientific method. If we are to move by the torch of reason, we must recognize that we possess no absolute truth, that dissent is not necessarily arbitrary and spiteful rebellion but a sincerely held belief that a contrary position is not altogether unreasonable. If we are not to play God, we must persistently maintain the critical spirit of free inquiry, submit our findings to the test of available facts, and be prepared to revise our most cherished opinions when experience and logic expose them as superstitions. Politics can and should use scientific method; but the use of scientific method does not of itself make politics a science. We are still dealing with animate rather than inanimate objects; we have still to account for men's prejudices and ideals, their interests and their often unpredictable emotions. Men are not bound by chains, whether of flax or iron; history and politics do not evolve according to certain canons of inexorable behavior.

Science defined so as to deal with probabilities rather than certainties does, to be sure, admit the study of politics into its orbit. Not all the disciplines accepted as sciences enjoy the same degree of precision and predictability. Weather forecasters, for example, are considerably less impressive in their ability to prophesy than are scientists in certain phases of chemistry or physics, and perhaps no more effectual than our unhappy public opinion pollsters of recent date; yet no one seriously challenges the classification of meteorology as a science on the ground that the correlation between the "controlled guessing" of the forecasters and actual events is significantly less than plus one, any more than we would cite the errors of diagnosticians to argue that medicine is not a science. Similarly, in the political sphere, the vagaries of courts and lawyers appear at times so to neglect the elementary requirements of consistency in the law as to deny, and even to render absurd, the expectations of men who conceive law to be a coherent legal system; but unless we are prepared to maintain that law is completely chaotic we are forced to recognize that law *is* "more or less systematic and hence that the ideal of logical system is an operative demand or imperative in the process of lawmaking by courts, jurists, and to some extent even by legislators."[1] Provided our methodology is sound and our data sufficient, certain probability patterns may emerge on the basis of which we may hazard more or less intelligent, if not conclusive, guesses, even in the field of politics. What we then do is to weigh the various and conflicting probabilities against each other, searching not so much for laws as for tendencies deriving from certain features of social organization and human personality that we regard as basic. The problem then becomes one of determining the probability of counteracting those tendencies we deem undesirable, in terms of the historical context in which we find ourselves. In this sense society is an arena of conflicting laws, or more properly tendencies, contending for mastery, rather than a passive recipient of the inescapable impact of a single law.

But throughout this involved give-and-take of knowledge and near-knowledge, of probabilities and guesses, of tendencies and counter-tendencies, there move the uncertainties of the main actor, man — his hopes, fears, envies, ambitions, reason and irrationality — who has still, in the political field at least, the sovereign power of choice. So long as men are free to choose in some measure, so long as the complexities of human nature remain to a considerable degree in the vast shadowland of supposition, the play of political and social forces cannot unalterably fix, in simple cause-effect relationships, the paths of human history.

These considerations are set forth not to deny the *fact* of or *tendency* to oligarchy, but to suggest the invalidity of any *law* of oligarchy. However, a closer examination of the "iron law" and its alleged operation may enable us to test its second, and more decisive, claim — that power cannot be made responsible.

11

Elite and Mass: The Operation of the "Iron Law"

The crux of the iron law theory of oligarchy is the necessary division of mankind into elite and mass. According to the formulators of the iron law — Robert Michels, James Burnham, and others — the functional demands of organization separate men into the few who rule and the many who are ruled, the directors and the directed. The few, leaders by technical necessity, once having tasted the delights of power, seek to retain and extend it. The many, an apathetic mass, relieved of the difficult task of making decisions, rest happily in the indifference from which they emerge only briefly, if at all. Thus the demands of organization, reinforced by the psychology of domination, give the leaders actual control. Whatever the democratic pretension, the few rule and the many are ruled. Oligarchy prevails.

At least one item in this category of suppositions must go unchallenged — organization does compel a division into the many and the few. Always, in any organization — whether a social club, business, labor union, political party, or government — only a few actually exercise the reins of power. But this simple truth proves neither the fact nor the inevitability of oligarchy. What is crucial is the presence or absence of responsibility. If the leadership derives its power from the freely given and continuing assent of the ruled, and if the policies pursued by the leadership conform to the changing tides of public opinion, democracy exists. If the leadership cannot be removed, the government is oligarchic.

What is central to the theorists of the iron law is their fatalistic belief that the leadership can never, in fact, be held responsible; that the lust for power is a passion the elite will strive to gratify even at the sacrifice of every human ideal; *and that it will succeed.* It is thus not the fact but the responsibility of leadership that is at issue.

Are we destined forever to dwell under irresponsible elite rule?

I must confess at the outset that I have not yet been able to discover what the word "elite" means. My dictionary tells me it is "the best or choicest part"; but this not only begs the question — Who or what is the best? — it fails to demonstrate that the term "best" has a general rather than a specific application, that, for example, the best flagpole sitter or street-corner orator is also the best statesman. The more elite theorists write on the subject, the more they obscure the issue; for not only do they seem unable to delimit the term adequately for themselves, they employ the word so as to deny, in effect, the validity of the definitions offered by others. The books of Mosca, Pareto, and Lawrence Dennis are vivid cases in point.

This semantic difficulty, even when complicated by the inability of elite theorists to relate "elite" to a particular ruling *class,* is far less trouble-some than the elite-mass dichotomy on which they build. If by elite we mean broadly the few who lead or rule, we are confronted by the fact that there is not one but a multiplicity of elites, and that they are not divorced from, but intimately related to, the mass. One can, I suppose, speak of Truman and his government, or Attlee and his government, as elite; but to do so would be to ignore the palpitations of an out-elite struggling to become the in-elite.[2] Crucial to this struggle is the appeal of each elite to at least a segment of the mass, which means that the conflict aligns one elite and its mass following against another elite and its mass follow-ing. To win and to hold the allegiance of its supporters, the elite must seek to satisfy their expectations and demands. In this interaction between a group of leaders (elite) and their followers (mass), and the appeal of elite-mass amalgamations to majority opinion, we have the first condition of democracy.

The fragmentation of elites and their dependence on the mass is accentuated in economic power-organizations such as labor unions. Walter Reuther, for example, heads an elite within the United Auto Workers; but he does so only because he is successful in retaining the support of a majority of his union against the blandishments of the previously in-, now out-elite. However, even though he speaks for the entire union when he negotiates with the management of General Motors, his views do not necessarily prevail over those of the managerial elite. And the demonstrated inability of labor leaders to defeat the Taft-Hartley Law (or subsequent legislation on labor-management relations regarded by them as detrimental) gives evidence that domination in one segment of the economic sphere does not of itself establish political domination.

There are limits to what any elite can do. Even though an elite in power may seek to perpetuate and extend that power, there is no assurance that it will succeed in freeing itself of popular control. I think it true to say that some "elites" — those led by men as dissimilar as Herbert Hoover and Franklin Roosevelt, Winston Churchill and Léon Blum, for example — have not sought so great an aggrandizement of power as to transform the character of the state. But even for those elite groups to whom oligarchy is not distasteful, there is not only the opposi-tion of other elites; there is always the danger of rebellion by the mass.

This last consideration deserves emphasis. Michels was fascinated by the tendency to oligarchy and proved, in a remarkable book,[3] that the *tendency* exists. But apart from the fact that he unwarrantedly extended this tendency into a law, he ignored the counter-tendencies that check the impulse or movement to oligarchy; he ignored the tendency to democracy.[4]

Men do not relish slavery; nor are they long prone to tolerate the cruelties and stupidities of dictators and kings. What history teaches depends of course upon the textbooks we have occasion to read, but if there is any one lesson that I think can be universally derived from the experience of the past, it is that the thrust to democracy, and the existence of democracy, is the institutionalization of man's protest against the demonstrated incompetence of oligarchical rule. The fact that oligarchical theorists plead the necessity of force and deceit to corrupt and restrain the passions of the many is evidence only that without recourse to such weapons oligarchy cannot hope to prevail. The iron law theory is thus the expression of a prayer, not the description of a deed.

From this standpoint, it is not democracy but oligarchy that is a prisoner of iron laws. Caught between the lust for power, on the one hand, and the fear of rebellion, on the other, oligarchical elites press for order and stability, forgetting that the surest guarantee of stability is adaptation to change. There is a curious and awesome paradox here. Democracy, through the institutionalization of revolution, makes for peace; oligarchy, through the institutionalization of peace, makes for revolution. Democracy is flexible; it not only permits but demands the expression of dissent and popular action to produce change; it bends with the shifting winds of doctrine. Oligarchy is inflexible; it suppresses but does not eliminate the pressures for change; and because it only succeeds in suppression, it ensures that one day the forces that make for rebellion will escape the bands of restraint and explode with greater violence. Thus not democracy but oligarchy is the system to which we must look if we are to discover the rigid operations of the iron law.[5]

Power and Responsibility: The Future of the "Iron Law"

I do not wish to press this thesis too far. Oligarchy does exist, and there are tendencies in democracy that invite the transformation to irresponsible elite rule. Not least of these is the tendency of men in power to worship their offices, and ultimately themselves. Samuel Butler has explained the process in a familiar passage:

> Authority intoxicates,
> The fumes of it invade the brain,
> And make men giddy, proud, and vain.

And Lord Acton's felicitous epigram has made us conscious not only of the fact that power tends to corrupt, but that the greater the degree and irresponsibility of power, the greater the danger of corruption.[6]

We are back, once again, to the problem of responsibility. How are

14

we to control power so that those who have it will not abuse it, and more important will not extend it so greatly as to do away with democracy?

To this question four answers seem worthy of mention. One is the appeal to aristocracy. I have elsewhere[7] examined those theories that seek to control power by locating it in the hands of a select few who are allegedly "the best" — whether for racial, biological, natural, or functional reasons — and I will not take time to explore the specific arguments here. But I ought perhaps to note in passing that the appeal to aristocracy is a surrender to oligarchy in the name of escaping oligarchy. To trust to the beneficence of a sacred few, moreover, no matter who they may be, is to ignore the historical evidence that men tend to equate their own interests and values with the interests of all, which means that in seeking to do to others what they would have others do to them, they forget that others want different things. Toynbee's *Study of History* suffers from the usual oversimplifications that attend grand interpretations of history, but his analysis of the ways in which "creative minorities" are transformed into "dominant" and therefore tyrannical minorities carries an insight that justly merits the stamp of greatness.

A second approach to the control of power is the appeal to the right personality. We ought not, it is said, select cruel and vicious men in the hope that upon attaining power they will succumb to the father-instinct and become shepherds rather than wolves. We must choose men of inherent stability and gentleness. No doubt there is much to be said for this avenue to the control of power, provided we can agree on the definition of the right personality. But I am greatly disturbed by the lengths to which some of the theorists of personality are prepared to go. Harold Lasswell, for example, in some of his more recent utterances, urges us to create a National Personnel Assessment Board to psychoanalyze and test candidates for office and tell us if they meet the basic minimum standards of the proper personality type.[8] Apart from the fact that psychoanalysis is still as much a mystery as it is a science, I question the wisdom of relying on the well-adjusted man, who too often is the man who bores us, even from within. I would suggest that if we are to have a vigorous, changing society, we must cultivate to an even greater degree than we thus far have, the *ill-adjusted* man, the man who is sufficiently different — maladjusted if you will — to probe for new visions that will excite thought and capture the imagination. Surely it is an ignoble ideal to seek stagnation.

Martin Hillenbrand's recent book, *Power and Morals,* suggests a third possible approach to our problem. Hillenbrand would control power by giving it only to men who are committed to the right morality, in his case Roman Catholic morality, or the natural law. The difficulties with

Hillenbrand's aproach are, first, that not all men are prepared to abide by his morality, and second, that even natural law is so imprecise as to permit conflicting patterns of behavior. It is not enough to "do good and avoid evil"; we must agree on the meaning of the good. And when we add to these considerations the fact that even moral men, once in power, are likely to abuse that power and do immoral things, we realize that our trust in morality may leave us helpless indeed.

None of these proposals satisfactorily resolves the problem of controlling power.[9] In the final analysis, they all rest on faith — in a man or group of men, or in a body of "right" principles. What democracy does is not to deny faith but to insist that it is insufficient. In a realistic vein, democracy asserts that we can never *prevent* the abuse of power; we can, through the threat of removal, seek to mitigate it, and ultimately, through the act of removal, hope to correct it. This may, in a paricular historical situation, require the institutional controls of the modern democratic state — free elections, checks and balances, cultural diversity, and the like — and the fragmentation and diffusion of power so as to prevent the consequences of a particular abuse from being catastrophic. We must always remember, too, that there is a difference between what a government *can* do and what it *will* do. A democratic ethos molded into a living tradition is not the least enduring brake on the ambitions of predatory men.

The test of democracy, and of oligarchy, is the reality of responsibility. We serve no useful purpose by refusing to recognize the many oligarchical tendencies visible in our society : in the principle of hereditary monarchy that we call ownership of industry; in the maneuvers of a labor boss like John L. Lewis who appoints the officers of some local unions on the ground that the membership is not competent to choose those officers wisely; in the machinations of a political boss who controls his district with a rigid hand. But democracy is not completely absent. Despite all its difficulties, the political process in Britain and the United States, in Canada and Sweden, makes government responsible. Rulers are chosen and removed according to the verdict of public opinion; policy does respond to the shifting winds of doctrine. Co-operatives challenge the idea of absolutism in industry. A Reuther is not readily to be included in the authoritarian camp of a Lewis. We have not one but many exceptions to the law that oligarchy necessarily prevails; and exceptions, contrary to popular impression, disprove the rule.

I do not seek to urge that oligarchy is impossible. Not only would this be absurd in the face of modern dictatorships; it would commit in reverse the error of determinism in history. Indeed, if we deny the free play of conflicting ideas because of hysteria or the arrogant assumption that our views are unavoidably right; if we exclude from the political process a considerable segment of the population on the ground that those excluded are unfit for racial or religious or political reasons to share the elementary perquisites of citizenship; if we limit educational and occupational opportunities so as to advantage a special few, or even many; if we fail, no matter in what degree, to meet the demands of freedom, equality, and self-government that are central to democracy, then in that measure we play into the hands of the lovers of oligarchy.

The future rests, as always, on the alertness and courage of the people. Inevitably some men — aided by their temporary ascendancy into positions of organizational leadership — will seek to translate the compulsion to oligarchy into the reality of oligarchy. But ever since man climbed down from the trees and found it necessary to establish ground rules, there have also been men willing to fight to preserve the rules of the game. In human history there are no iron laws, only tendencies and guides; and the desire for freedom and mastery of one's own destiny is a pressure that impels men to, rather than from, democracy. This thrust to democracy will continue unabated; for only in democracy can men hope to be masters rather than slaves.

Chapter 2

Politics and the Dimensions of Power

In politics, as in Christian fable, there is a continuing quest for the Holy Grail — for a principle or an approach that will unify the several fields that now divide the discipline. Professor Loewenstein believes that power, or the ways in which power is gained, exercised, and controlled, constitutes that unifying principle. *Political Power and the Governmental Process*[1] is his effort to explicate this threefold dimension of power within the framework of the two major political systems of democracy and autocracy.

In this respect Loewenstein repudiates those schools of political thought which focus, instead, on the principle of justice. He is committed to the modern rather than to the classical tradition; consequently, he seeks to describe rather than to prescribe, to build on what men do rather than on what it may be thought they ought to do. Unfortunately, it is not at all clear that so clear-cut a dichotomy can be sustained; and it is one of the difficulties of Loewenstein's book that the normative and empirical aspects of politics are frequently confused. The bulk of his book, for example, is addressed not to the classification of governments but to the problem of the control of power, on the assumption that "uncontrolled power is evil as such" (p. 8). But this is a moral rather than a sociological precept; and it is interesting to note that Loewenstein asserts but does not attempt to establish the validity of this fundamental assumption.

(It ought not to go unobserved, too, that for an empiricist Loewenstein assumes a great many things: that every state is "controlled" by a managerial elite; that Rousseau was a totalitarian; that a political party is a group of people holding similar ideological beliefs; that sovereignty, even under a federal system such as we know it in the United States, is indivisible; that the Portugese dictator Salazar is an honest, efficient, and non-fascist ruler. These and similar judgments are at least questionable; but Loewenstein does not attempt seriously to sustain them.)

One other preliminary remark needs to be made. This is that Loewenstein is all too prone to indulge in that ambiguity of language which obscures rather than reveals his meaning. Take, for example, his definition of sovereignty as "nothing else, and nothing less, than the legal rationalization of power as the irrational element of politics" (p. 4). I have worried a good deal over this definition and have decided, reluctantly, that I do not know what it means. I have, to be sure, looked elsewhere in these pages to discover what Loewenstein might mean, but there was little to help me other than the suggestion that the sovereign is the ruler, or power-wielder, or decision-maker. But many who are not "rulers" wield power and make decisions; who then is sovereign? Loewenstein answers: "He who is legally entitled to exercise *or* who ultimately exercises political power in the state community" (p. 4; my italics). But since communities generally boast both a formal or legal ruler *and* an informal or actual ruler — e.g., Louis XIII and Richelieu — who in Loewenstein's terms is the sovereign? His definition tells us that it is one *or* the other, but not which one.

Let us turn now to Loewenstein's classification of governments or, as he prefers to call them, political systems. By a political system Loewenstein means patterns of government linked together by a similar ideology and the institutions corresponding to it. Of such systems he distinguishes two — autocracy and constitutional democracy — the difference between them turning on whether, in the various stages of the governmental process (i.e., gaining, exercising, and controlling power), political power is shared or concentrated. Within the system of concentrated political power (autocracy), he distinguishes three patterns of government — absolute monarchy, Napoleon's plebiscitary Caesarism, and Neopresidentialism. Within the system of shared political power (democracy), he locates six patterns — direct democracy, assembly government, parliamentarism, cabinet government, presidentialism, and directory government as in Switzerland. It will be noted that while Loewenstein's primary division into autocracy and democracy departs from the classical division that turns on number (i.e., whether it is a government of one, or of a few, or of many) and on virtue (i.e., whether the ruler acts in the interests of a part or of the whole), it is similar to R. M. MacIver's division between democracy and oligarchy, which turns on whether or not the few who rule are responsible to the many. It will also be noted that Loewenstein limits himself quite rigidly to an analysis and classification of *political* power; he minimizes or ignores the relations between political power and other forms of social power — e.g., the economic, the military, the religious. It is true that in his concluding chapter Loewenstein addresses himself to the interplay between the government and non-governmental power groups; at one point he even says that "the border lines between the economic and political interests have become obliterated" (p. 350); but in his system of classification such considerations are basically left aside. And nowhere does he examine seriously the merits or implications of those positions which hold that political power is either a subordinate element in the total scheme of power (e.g., the Marxists) or that it is at best a co-ordinate element (e.g., C. Wright Mills in his *Power Elite*). This is all the more surprising in view of Loewenstein's admonition that in classifying governments we must look at the realities of each situation. What Loewenstein means by realities, however, are the informal rather than the formal arrangements within *political* power systems; and while these are surely necessary they are not likely to be sufficient. A comparison of Loewenstein's analysis with MacIver's treatment of the pyramids of power in his *Web of Government* will make this abundantly clear.

Loewenstein's treatment of the control of power, by which in the first instance he means the control of political power, rests on the premise that uncontained power is destructive of rights. But Loewenstein does not explain what he means by rights; he does not distinguish natural rights from rights guaranteed under a constitution or rights held to be intrinsic to the principle of government itself. Consequently he does not make clear in what sense uncontrolled power may be said to be evil as such. Given his assumption and loose usage of the term rights, however, how does he propose to control political power? Primarily through the constitution, through built-in restraints that assure the sharing rather than the concentration of power. "Human nature being what it is," says Loewenstein, "such restraints cannot be expected to operate automatically; ... it cannot be expected that the power holder, or holders, by voluntary self-restraint, will protect the power addressees and themselves against the destructive use of power" (pp. 8, 123). But this assumes a theory of human nature which Loewenstein does not bother to articulate or defend; once again he is content to assert what needs to be established. This also rejects out of hand a long, and some would add distinguished, tradition which holds that power can be restrained not by other powers — for what then restrains the greater power? — but by seeing to it that power is entrusted to the right man (whether a philosopher-king or a democratic personality), or that the rulers are committed to the right morality (e.g., natural law), or that the social order is constructed on right principles of organization (e.g., socialism). All of these alternatives may in fact be quite inadequate (as I believe they are); my point is only that Loewenstein does not consider them, and his failure to do so cannot be convincing to those who hold such positions.

It seems to be enough for Loewenstein that power is shared. "Because it is shared, the exercise of power is *necessarily* controlled. It is an elementary truism that, if two minds have to make a decision, one mind alone cannot prevail" (p. 29, my italics; and see further p. 50). But is this a truism? Is power *necessarily* controlled when two minds are required to share in the decision-making process? In a formal sense, perhaps so; but this is surely to ignore the realities of power. For, on the one hand, deadlock may result, in which case no decision may ensue; and the absence of a political decision, far from controlling power, may have the effect of continuing the status quo, of perpetuating an already-existing power relationship. Thus, if the American Congress and the President cannot agree, a business corporation may remain free to abuse its employees, or a labor union to discriminate against certain minority groups. On the other hand, the two minds may be formally equal but actually unequal. One of the two may dominate the other, in which case the constitutional requirement is of little consequence. In either situation, I fail to see that the sharing of power as such is a sufficient bar to abuses of power. If it were, one would have to conclude that abuses of power do not exist in constitutional states; and this, if we regard the treatment of minority groups in the United States, for example, would surely be an absurd contention. Loewenstein comes close to admitting the inadequacy of institutional arrangements as a sufficient check on power when he asserts that the institutional apparatus of both autocracy and democracy has in our time become stereotyped to the point of identity, and that autocracies can and often do function under a constitution. In one place he even concludes from this that not institutions but the recognition and protection of fundamental liberties are the decisive element of distinction between the two systems (p. 317). But he does not ask what it is that then assures the maintenance of these liberties. For if it is not the functional arrangements of a society— not a system of checks and balances and the general dispersion of powers — the key to the control of power must lie elsewhere. But Loewenstein does not, and in his scheme of thought cannot, tell us where this is.

In his concluding chapter Loewenstein argues the necessity of public regulation to control the abuses of private powers — of socioeconomic groups as well as of political parties. In this respect he accepts the quite simple and traditional imputation of responsibility for abuses of power by private groups to government: for if private powers endanger individual rights it is said to be because government permits them to do so; hence the corrective is for the government to interfere with such private acts. But apart from the obvious consideration that this might produce a new and even more dangerous Leviathan — a danger that Loewenstein recognizes — it is noteworthy that Loewenstein does not inquire into the internal arrangements of socioeconomic groups; he does not explore the possibility of establishing democratic controls within private organizations. More than this, he does not take into account that in a democratic state the government may be constitutionally required to let many things alone, or that the climate of public opinion may be such as to prevent a government from interfering effectively even where the government might be so inclined. (The problem of desegregation in the American South is a case in point.) A democracy, that is to say, if it is not to commit suicide by becoming a totalitarian state, must be prepared to leave certain areas alone; and where some powers are free, or partially free, the likelihood that they will abuse the powers left to them is always present. In a word, it is highly questionable whether abuses of power can ever adequately be controlled. This is not to deny the possibility of controlling particular abuses of power in particular situations. It is only to suggest that we are not likely to get very far if we formulate the question as one of controlling abuses of power as a general phenomenon.

I have not attempted to deal here with the many perceptive observations that the reader will find in this book. I have sought rather to judge Professor Loewenstein's work in terms that he has set for himself — as a unifying work in political science. If I do not believe that he has succeeded in his enterprise, it is less because of what he has done than because of what he has failed to do: for power without justice is not only an insufficient principle on which to ground an ancient and still (I venture to think) architectonic discipline; it is not even a brutal principle; it is simply an impossible one. And power with justice can have relevance only where it is seen that the problems of power are both more than political and less than general.

Chapter 3

Socrates versus Hobbes on the Nature of Power

Hobbes defines power as a man's "present means to obtain some future apparent Good."[1]

Now, to deal properly with this idea of power, and thereby to understand why it merits our attention, we must look, I think, primarily to that part of his definition in which Hobbes employs the phrase "apparent Good," and only secondarily to that part of his definition that refers to "means." For no one who has dealt seriously with the problems of power has ever doubted that power involves the utilization by some person or persons of certain techniques or instruments or resources — be they political, economic, military, religious, or ideological — to attain some desired end or ends. What has been and remains vitally at issue is the explication of that end. In particular, men have differed, often quite sharply and bitterly, as to whether or not this desired end involves the *real* or the merely *apparent* good; they have even raised the question whether it need be associated with the idea of the good at all.

From this standpoint, it is a matter of but subordinate interest to debate the many derivative issues that have occupied so many political theorists over the centuries, issues that turn on such questions as these: whether the term power is to be applied to one's *capacity* to control the behavior of others or only to his actual *exercise* of that control; whether it should include *influence* over such behavior or be restricted to the narrower conception of *control;* whether, again, as influence or control, active or potential, it is to be related to *people* or to *things* or both. Those who would relate it to people, either as the sole or partial object of study, have differed, too, as to whether political analysis is then most fruitful when focused on power as a *motive* for conduct on the part of those who desire it, or on the *fact* that power once possessed enables its possessor to achieve certain results, be these the *production* of intended effects or the *deprivation* of certain values. And among those who would study power as a behavioral fact rather than a psychological motive, there is further disputation as to whether we should then concern ourselves with the *unilateral* application of the act of domination (assuming such a unilateral application can be isolated) or with the multi-faceted *relation* between the superordinate and subordinate individuals or groups or classes involved. All these and similar questions, important as they are, become important, however, only after the primary question has been settled. In fact, from the standpoint of at least one major tradition in political philosophy, until we resolve the question of the character of this desired end for which "power" is used, we may find that we have not been talking of power at all.

This last consideration, if I understand it correctly, is substantially the position of Socrates as set forth in the Platonic dialogues. In the *Gorgias,* for example, as in the *Republic,* Socrates attacks the vulgar view that esteems tyrants as men of great power and insists that tyrants have in fact "the least possible power in states . . .; for they do literally nothing which they will, but only what they think best."[2] Tyrants, however, are not philosophers; consequently what they think best is not really the good but only the apparent good. Yet tyrants are in one respect no different from other men; what they really will is what conduces to their good and not to their evil. The tragedy of tyranny, Socrates therefore argues, is that because of this disparity between their will to do good and their inability to perceive or to take the proper measures requisite to the attainment of the good, tyrants never succeed in achieving what they really want to achieve. Instead, they grow only more miserable and lead a worse life from the exercise of what is popularly, but erroneously, conceived to be their power; inevitably, they become the real slaves.[3]

To Polus, Socrates' antagonist in this portion of the dialogue, this argument appears wholly specious and absurd; though of course, since it is Plato who puts the words into his mouth, he is unable to offer an effective counter-argument. Applied to modern tyrants, the Socratic thesis would assert that Hitler and Stalin, Mussolini and Perón, and the host of other dictators who have plagued, and in too many cases continue to plague, mankind, did not in fact have power but were really miserable slaves. To the millions who have been stuffed into furnaces and gas chambers or who have been subjected to unspeakable indignities, this argument must appear not only ludicrous but dangerous. We can well understand, then, Polus' astonishment at hearing Socrates expound this view.

But if we grant that Socrates was not a stupid man, that he may even, perhaps, have been a wise man, we must look deeper into his peculiar and seemingly foolish argument. And if we do so, we will find, I think, that even if we do not agree with his reasoning, or concede the validity of his premises, we are not likely to dismiss his argument as altogether absurd.

What does Socrates maintain?

Briefly, he asserts as a general principle the dictum or axiom that every action aims at an end, and that every actual manifestation of power is consequently an action aimed at an end. He asserts, further, as a second axiom, that every end is conceived of by the agent as good, for no man, he believes, seeks to do what is evil but only what is good; consequently, every act of power is the act of an agent aiming at something he conceives to be good. If power, then, refers to the means to an end or ends, it follows that those instruments that are employed to control the behavior of others, but which do not or cannot serve to bring about the end or ends which are intended, are not in fact instruments of power. More than this, since what constitutes power is, in any given case, dependent not only on the proper relation between means and ends, but on the choice of the "right" end, which is the Good — for no man, let it be remembered, seeks what is evil — the question of whether or not power is actually being exercised turns on the answer to the prior question of the wisdom of the agent. If he chooses not the real good but the apparent good, he is, in Socrates' view, no more exercising power than he would be if he chose the wrong means to the right end; for in choosing the apparent good he is defeating his own purposes, he is acting against his own intentions. What distinguishes the tyrant from the philosopher, Socrates argues, is, among other things, the fact that the tyrant does not know what is really good; nor, generally, does he know what are the right instruments for attaining this real good. Consequently, the tyrant will never succeed in achieving his real intentions. His actions will, save by accident, always produce the wrong, unintended results. This is why the continued exercise of tyrannical "power" will lead only to disaster; and the tryant, far from exercising power — in the sense in which Socrates uses the term — is in fact the least powerful of men.

Now, one has only to think of the demise of tyrants brought about by actions taken by them in the conviction that those actions would produce a quite different result — e.g., the actions of Hitler and Mussolini — to perceive the element of validity in Socrates' argument.

The errors, or limitations, of this analysis, however, are at least twofold. In the first place, by relating the term power only to one's real will, Socrates deprives us both of a word to describe the actions of the actual will and of the desire to concern ourselves with such actions. In the second place, by assuming that we, or more strictly the philosopher — for to Socrates only the philosopher has knowledge as distinct from opinion — can know what is the real good for man, he restricts the analysis of power to the philosophical realm and takes it out of, or renders it but a secondary consideration for, the sociological realm.

It is the distinctive contribution, and therefore the significance, of Hobbes that he indicted Socrates on precisely these points; and by doing so he reintroduced, or with Machiavelli introduced, into political science an empirical dimension that had heretofore been lacking. He did this in part by exposing the verbal confusions in the Socratic argument. More importantly, he did it by emphasizing the fact that politics, and the problems of power which are central to politics, devolves more from what men do than from what it is conceived they ought to do. In both respects he broke sharply from the classical tradition in political philosophy and, along with Machiavelli, established the modern approach to politics.

For Hobbes, it ought never to be forgotten, denied categorically that there is such a thing as the real or ultimate good. There is no such thing, he said, as the *Summum Bonum* "as is spoken of in the Books of the old Morall Philosophers."[4] There is only an incessant succession of objects of desire; and the voluntary actions of men to secure these objects of their desire differ only in the way they proceed to secure them, such differences arising partly from the diversity of passions in diverse men and partly from the diversity in the knowledge, *or opinion,* that each man has of the causes which produce the effect desired. This is why Hobbes put "for a generall inclination of all mankind, a perpetuall and restlesse desire of Power after power, that ceaseth onely in Death."[5]

Now if there is no such thing as the *Summum Bonum* or ultimate good, the claim of the Socratic philosopher to know this good is a pretentious one. (Surely it is pretentious if not inconsistent for Socrates, whose claim to be the wisest of men rested on his claim to know nothing, to claim now that he did know something — that he not only knew that he knew nothing, which is of course both logically impossible and empirically untrue, nor even that he knew only the ultimate questions, but that he knew at least some of the ultimate answers, all devolving from his true knowledge of what is really good for man.) The Socratic philosopher, like all informed men, has *some* knowledge, but on the ultimate questions he too acts on the basis of his opinions about the nature of things. If all the actions of men, then, derive in part from knowledge and in part from opinion, the term power cannot legitimately be applied only to some actions that command the services of others and not to all such actions.

I shall not add here to the familiar and protracted debate over the terms "real will" and "actual will," and the consequences that flow from drawing this distinction, but will move instead to one other contribution of Hobbes. This is his insistence that, if power applies to all the actions of men, it must be studied at its instrumental level. In present-day language, we would express this as a concomitant of the distinction between instrumental ends and ultimate or intrinsic ends, instrumental ends in this context being essentially ends-in-view. From this standpoint, it makes sense to talk of tyrants like Hitler exercising power when he put people to death or interned them in concentration camps; for whatever his ultimate objective, his decision to act as he did in such an instance produced actions directed at the achievement of an end, even though this end was instrumental to another and more distant end.

I conclude, therefore, that whatever the limitations of Hobbes's own definition of power, the insight contained in that definition exceeds by far its few and essentially minor deficiencies.

Chapter 4

Montesquieu's Theory of Freedom

Montesquieu labored for twenty years to produce a remarkable book. Its central qualities are a vast erudition, a subtle terminology, and a judicious moderation. Its major reward is the realization that political structures and institutions are not universally ordained but are relative to the whole life and character of a people — to its customs and traditions, its modes of thought, its economic and geographic environment. Its greatest claim to fame rests, however, on the celebrated doctrine that freedom can be secured only through the dispersion or separation of powers. On the basis of these and other contributions *The Spirit of the Laws* has become a classic. It has been compressed and digested in the standard histories of political philosophy, though not infrequently with startling and disparate results; and a voluminous literature both laudatory and critical — even to the inclusion of Montesquieu's work in the Catholic Index of Forbidden Books — has elevated his name to a first rank in the annals of political thought. It has also suffered the fate of most classic writings in being more recited than read. This is unfortunate, for Montesquieu is rewarding far beyond the representations — or misrepresentations — of any summary.

There is need for a new evaluation of Montesquieu's contributions to political and legal philosophy. Not least important in this respect is a required re-examination of Montesquieu's idea of political liberty and its relation to law and power. In the remarks that follow I shall deal only with certain difficulties inherent in this aspect of Montesquieu's thought,[1] subject to the caveat, however, that Montesquieu is not to be understood unless his distaste for democracy and his attachment to aristocratic privileges are borne in mind.[2]

Freedom and Law

In Montesquieu's view "political liberty" does not mean the absence of restraints, the unlimited freedom to act as one may please.[3] Such a notion he assigns to people in democracies. "In governments, that is, in societies directed by laws," Montesquieu writes, "liberty can consist only in the power of doing what we ought to will, and in not being constrained to do what we ought not to will."[4]

28

Taken literally, this definition poses some perplexing questions. For, if the attributes of a free man include both a will and a knowledge by that will of its right purpose or morality, we must ask — apart from the vexing question of the existence and localization of the human will — Who is to tell, and by what standards, whether a will wills rightly or wrongly, whether it wills what it ought to will and not what it ought not to will?

Montesquieu's answer is unconvincing. He believes that some people — e.g., women, slaves, the poor — "are in so mean a situation as to be deemed to have no will of their own."[5] Consequently they are not competent to decide their proper purpose. But a reading of Montesquieu's book does not disclose a considered or substantiated ground for this judgment. It is clear that demeaned men and women have desires and opinions. To hold that those opinions cannot be expressions of a right morality — that they are inherently wrong or ill-founded or contrary to the best interests of their advocates — requires at the very least a standard in terms of which that judgment is to be validated. But Montesquieu advances no real criterion other than the law, which itself requires such a standard.

To declare, as Montesquieu elsewhere does, that "liberty is a right of doing whatever the laws permit,"[6] is to compound rather than to eliminate the difficulty. It is true that liberty so conceived is an important part of freedom, that Montesquieu is right in arguing that men are not free if they can be punished by a wilful act of the executive power, without recourse to independent law courts[7] and without proof of criminality. But the right to do what the laws permit still requires a principle on the basis of which we can determine what the laws are to permit; otherwise the right is at best arbitrary, if not useless. "In France, after the Revocation of the Edict of Nantes," to take an example offered by Bertrand Russell, "the exercise of the Protestant religion was illegal; it cannot therefore be said that the right to do what the laws permitted conferred any effective liberty upon French Protestants."[8] No less important, Montesquieu here[9] forgets that laws are not the only sources of restraint. To say that a man is free when the laws do not constrain him is to ignore the fact that he may be constrained by other than legal means — e.g., economic or physical duress. Unless law then interferes to remove that restraint, it is difficult to see how such a man can be termed free. Moreover, if the laws permit a man to do that which he should have no will to do, then he is both free and unfree, depending on whether or not he acts according to the law or to the dictates of his conscience; and this is an absurdity.

Montesquieu appears to recognize these difficulties when — despite his attempts to reconcile the natural with the positive law[10] — he admits that positive law is not always to be equated with justice. Indeed, he goes so far as to say that some laws have been "puerile, ridiculous, and foolish ... stuffed with rhetoric and void of sense."[11] On these terms the laws cannot reasonably be advanced as a valid criterion of what men ought to will. In fact, the laws may actually render men unfree by permitting them to do what they ought not to will.

We are thus forced to return to the question: How do we know what men ought to will? Montesquieu's reply is not easy to understand. He often looks to nature, arguing, for example, that we do best when we "follow the bent of our natural genius,"[12] and holding it a misfortune that legislators should sometimes enact laws "repugnant to the dictates of nature."[13] But it does not appear that Montesquieu takes the criterion of nature too seriously. For, in the very passage in which he urges the legislature to follow the spirit of the nation, he adds the qualification, "when it is not contrary to the principles of government."[14] But are the principles of government more "natural" than the spirit of a nation? If so, Montesquieu does not adduce the evidence. Again, Montesquieu, in speaking of the "natural" inequality of the sexes in hot climates, says: "It is natural ... when no law opposes it ... to have polygamy."[15] But if it is natural, it must be so irrespective of human law. And, if law opposes this dictate of nature, obedience to the law (which Montesquieu affirms to be freedom) involves disobedience to nature (which Montesquieu with equal fervor would regard as a denial of freedom).

In one place Montesquieu suggests that happiness rather than nature is the proper standard of value. Nature having made men equal, he writes, "reason could not render them dependent, except where it was necessary to their happiness."[16] This is strange doctrine. It postulates that men equal by nature can be made unequal by reason, but it does not tell us whose reason shall render some men subservient and why those men should accept that status. It would appear that Montesquieu can accept only the reason of aristocrats. "The lower class," he writes, "ought to be directed by those of higher rank, and restrained within bounds by the gravity of eminent personages."[17] But it is at least open to question whether those of higher rank enjoy a superior status because they are eminent or whether they are eminent because they enjoy a superior status. If it is true, as Montesquieu claims, that it is the very nature of the people to "act through passion."[18] it is equally true, by his own admission, that passion and prejudice govern "superior" men whose function it is to make the laws.[19] And, if passion rather than reason is the dominant force in men's lives, it is meaningless to say that reason can transcend the natural inequality of men in the interests of their happiness. Happiness, of course, is itself much too vague and general a criterion or justification of this process; for we are still bedeviled not only by the definition of that tortured term but by the inability of men to agree on the definers.

One is forced to conclude that Montesquieu has no real standard other than law itself by which men can know what they ought to will. Human laws, he observes, are "made to direct the will";[20] they are appointed for some good.[21] The "good," of course, remains ambiguous; phrases like "the moral goodness of men in general," or "the general welfare of society,"[22] beg rather than resolve the question. More important, however, is the fact that if laws are to direct the will, the will presumably ought not to direct the laws. Since this has no possible relevance to the real world, what Montesquieu must mean is that the wills of some men make the laws which are to direct the wills of other men.[23] Montesquieu believes that men so directed are free. The unstated yet underlying premise of Montesquieu's position — reflecting again (despite his repudiation of natural rights) his tendency to transfer the assumptions of natural law doctrine to the positive law — is that those exercising their will through positive law will act in conformity with the dictates of natural law. Stated differently, liberty in Montesquieu's view is secured through law if the will which enacts the law is not wilful or arbitrary. This explains why Montesquieu can argue that arrest and imprisonment leave the person "really free," since he is "subject only to the power of the law."[24] To the man outside observing the prisoner within, this may seem true; but it is doubtful that the prisoner would agree.

Despite Montesquieu, men are not free merely by virtue of the fact that they are "under the restraint of laws."[25] They are all too clearly restrained, at least in those things that the law forbids. Montesquieu might argue that they are thus rightly restrained, but that is another matter. It is also, unfortunately, a question on which Montesquieu sheds no great illumination.[26]

Freedom and Power

If freedom is ill-defined, it is difficult to see how one can meaningfully search in Montesquieu's scheme for a particular political system to secure it. If we take the simplest of Montesquieu's definitions of liberty — namely, the right to do whatever the laws permit — it is clear that every political system, even a despotism, secures liberty so defined. For every political system, in providing order, provides certain liberties: it constrains men in some things but is indulgent or indifferent to them in others. To the extent that this is so, even if only in slight degree, "liberty" as Montesquieu conceives it is secured, and we need inquire no further.

If we use Montesquieu's definition of freedom as the power of doing what we ought to will and equate this normative judgment with the judgment of the ruling group, we are caught in a similar tautology. For, if the laws formulated by the ruling group tell us what we ought to will, we are free wherever there are laws — i.e., in all states. If, on the other hand, the individual determines the ethical standard, judgments of a government will vary according to the values men attach to some freedoms as against others. Hence a government that secures "liberty" to some men is likely to be condemned for denying it to others.

Once again what is at the root of Montesquieu's trouble is his confusion of the postulates of natural law with those of positive law. In an apparent attempt to free Montesquieu's doctrine of these difficulties, Franz Neumann suggests that Montesquieu's idea of liberty be construed to mean "the freedom to act unless such act is prohibited by law."[27] This enables us to avoid a difficulty that turns on Montesquieu's use of the word "power" in one definition and the word "right" in the other. For freedom conceived in terms of power implies not only the absence of *all* restraints — political, economic, and social — but the positive possession of means necessary to the act. The right to act, on the other hand, may involve no more than a legal abstention; it may provide freedom from *legal* restraints but not necessarily from nonlegal restraints that the law might — and indeed ought, if the legal right is to be substantially achieved — remove. Montesquieu clearly is thinking of freedom only in the narrow legalistic sense, though his terminology abets confusion. Professor Neumann's reformulation is an aid to clarity, but it does not save Montesquieu; for it does not circumvent the fact that a legal prohibition is still a restraint. And men are not free merely because they are restrained and regardless of the source of the restraint. If we argue to the contrary, we are forced to the absurd conclusion that every government, in constraining men through law, thereby makes them free.

It remains true, of course, that a law which restrains one man may liberate another, that a law which prohibits a policeman, say, from searching a man's house without warrant provides a measure of personal freedom and security that the individual otherwise would not have. And among the freedoms that Montesquieu values is freedom from arbitrary power. He is anxious to secure a measure of certainty in the law, believing that one can have liberty only when the law is known and the individual is punishable only for offenses against it. In Montesquieu's view, "the political liberty of the subject (as distinct from the liberty of the constitution) is a tranquillity of mind arising from the opinion each person has of his safety. In order to have this liberty, it is requisite the government be so constituted as one man need not be afraid of another."[28] This can be achieved, Montesquieu believes, only in a government that realizes a separation of powers.[29]

Much has been written concerning this familiar principle.[30] It is generally asserted that Montesquieu was right for the wrong reasons — that his principle was sound but that his analysis of the structure of the English government of his day was incorrect. Yet the evidence suggests that Montesquieu was not altogether wrong in his reading of the structure of English government.[31] The crucial question, however, is not his reading of the empirical data but the validity of his principle; and this depends on the interpretation attached to it.

If it is taken as a rigid adherence to a particular threefold division or separation of powers, the principle is patently untenable. Bentham, Locke, and many others have convincingly shown that the business of the executive and judicial branches of government is to give effect to the wishes of the legislative power. And since the application of law is essentially a reduction of general principles to specific cases, the executive and judicial powers are, properly speaking, participants in an extended or protracted lawmaking function. There can be no real separation in the functional sense, though levels of legislative authority based on hierarchies of personnel and stages of lawmaking necessarily remain. The experiences of both the United States and England have demonstrated that the actual stratification of power resulting from these levels of authority bears little relation to the formal tripartite division that Montesquieu advanced.

If, however, we view Montesquieu's principle as being a general rule of the dispersion of political powers, however classified, it contains a very real and vital — though insufficient — truth. For what Montesquieu sought was a way to control power. "Political liberty," he argued, "is to be found only in moderate governments; and . . . there only when there is no abuse of power. But constant experience shows us that every man invested with power is apt to abuse it, and to carry his authority as far as it will go. . . . To prevent this abuse, it is necessary from the very nature of things that power should be a check to power."[32]

Now it is all too evident that a concentration of legislative, executive, and judicial powers in the hands of a single person or group is unlikely to secure the liberty for which Montesquieu constructed his principle. A monarch who sits in judgment on a man arrested by one of the monarch's minions as an evader of a tax due the monarch under one of the monarch's own laws would run counter to the whole oligarchic tradition were he, in adjudicating the case, to evidence a full measure of impartiality and a fine regard for the niceties of legal procedure; a Solomon by his rarity eloquently testifies to this truth. And in this sense a fragmentation and dispersion of powers is a precondition of freedom. But it is by no means clear that power conferred in one place is an adequate check on power

33

exercised elsewhere. If the powers agree, such a check does not enter; if they disagree, the greater power will have its way. This is particularly evident where the powers are unequal, but it is no less true where the powers are formally or seemingly equal. For if they are equal in fact, deadlock results; and power, far from checking power, simply checks a new or particular power that seeks to deal with an already existing power; the checking power, that is to say, maintains or creates a void in which an old and different power remains dominant. Thus, if the American Congress sought to check the abuses of a business corporation or of a labor union or of a religious power group but was restrained from doing so by the check of the executive, the power vacuum created by the inaction of political power would be filled by the nonpolitical (i.e., the economic or religious) power group. It is nonsense to say, as Montesquieu does, that the necessity for movement in human affairs will compel the legislative, executive, and judicial powers to move out of their natural state of repose or inaction and move in concert.[33] *A* power may be in a state of repose, but *all* powers are not. And the movement in concert may unite a nonpolitical power bloc with a branch of the legislative, or with the executive or judicial power, against the other political powers. There is no law that compels united political action.

Montesquieu's basic error is that he thought almost exclusively in terms of the dispersion of legal or political powers.[34] Now political power alone, even if primary, rarely exhausts the vast areas of social action; and never does it do so in "moderate" governments. But political power, if it is to have potency, cannot stand alone. To be an effective curb upon the activity of a rival political power group or institution, a political power unit must represent a significant social or economic interest. "It must," says Mosca, ". . . be the organized expression of a social influence and a social authority that has some standing in the community, as against the forces that are expressed in the political institution that is to be controlled."[35] Without such a substantial backing, legal power suffers a loss in its effectiveness.

Even if we examine Montesquieu's doctrine within the traditional limits of political power, we note that Montesquieu is on weak ground. For a system of separate powers generally involves a system of checks and balances; and this serves to connect and perhaps integrate as well as to divide and deadlock the fragmented power blocs.[36] Montesquieu is wrong, again, because he confuses the attempt to control power with the attempt to prevent its abuse: the former is conceivable, though not on Montesquieu's terms alone; the latter is a different and — men and temptation being what they are — perhaps an impossible task.

Yet Montesquieu's perception that a free society cannot survive without some sort of institutionalized fragmentation and dispersion of power remains a crucial and abiding truth. This is not the place to enlarge on this theme, but two things perhaps ought not to go unmentioned. One is that apolitical restraints, when constitutionally sanctioned, are doubly important; they hinder the power of the individual or group, but they limit also the power of the state. In this respect power outside the state — while it may and indeed generally does exert arbitrary and undemocratic controls over the lives of citizens even in a democracy, as the activities of the modern corporation and some labor unions, churches, and schools often make clear — is a deterrent, and, if sufficiently strong, a preventive, to excessive or totalitarian political controls. The other is that to concentrate in the same hands all the instruments of power within a particular field — religious, economic, military, cultural, and the like — is to confer on the ruling group within that field of power an undue measure of control. If this concentration occurs in the political field, the danger becomes overwhelming. And, where this political concentration is conjoined with a system in which apolitical restraints are essentially insignificant, the invitation to tyrannical rule is compulsive.

That Montesquieu failed to take adequate account of the role of such apolitical restraints constitutes his great and tragic failure. That he perceived the necessity for some form of restraints to absolute political power constitutes his enduring achievement.

Chapter 5

Politics as a Secular Theology:
The Aristocratic Theory of George Santayana

Despite his eminence as a moral philosopher, Santayana's reflections on government have rarely commended themselves to students of political theory. In part, this was attributable to the absence of a systematic treatise on the subject; fragmentary chapters in *The Life of Reason, Dialogues in Limbo,* and *Soliloquies in England,* revealing as they are, do not comprise a political philosophy. In part, it was the consequence of a cultivated detachment that sought insight and expression in poetic sentiment rather than in logical analysis and a knowledge of post-Hellenic history. And, in part, it was the unhappy fact that Santayana did not have very much to say; with minor modifications, his politics has been Plato's and his prejudices the orthodox contempts of the aristocrat. His new book, *Dominations and Powers*[1], does much to remove the first difficulty but little to correct the remaining two.

The theme of the work, pervaded by Santayana's naturalistic philosophy, is the relation, actual and ideal, between dominations and powers in the three orders of society: the Generative Order of growth, custom, and tradition; the Militant Order, which includes all voluntary associations, such as armies, political parties, and religious sects; and the Rational Order, which seeks to liberate all human interests, especially those that are ideal and harmless and, therefore, do not materially conflict with one another. By a "power" Santayana means any action resulting from the natural needs, passions, or interests of an animal organism seeking to develop itself within a particular environment. A "domination" is any power that deliberately and egotistically curbs or threatens this spontaneous life. The distinction between them is moral: a power is good, or at least morally neutral; a domination evil. The distinction is also subjective: a power from the standpoint of the interests of a given person or society is from another point of view a domination, i.e., a government that is a benign and useful power for one class may exercise a cruel domination over another.

Some preliminary difficulties might be noted. One is that some men, if certain psychologists are to be believed, "naturally" (and I beg here the question whether this nature is innate or contrived) seek to dominate others; consequently for them a power involves, indeed *is,* a domination; and the two, far from being distinguished, must be studied precisely at the point where they coincide. A second is that powers and dominations almost always operate as two aspects of a greater whole; where a power freely exercised by one man interferes with the exercise of a power by another and thus becomes a domination, a domination that restrains the interfering power releases, paradoxically, the other power. Dominations and powers are, accordingly, not necessarily opposed but generally complementary, and the moral judgment must be applied to the two together as part of a total situation, not to either in isolation. We cannot say, for example, as Santayana seems to imply, that to do good we may have to do evil; we must rather say that to do good we may have to inflict pain. But in Santayana's own doctrine the act of inflicting pain must then be right, not wrong. This is particularly true of political government which, by the very multiplicity and complexity of its acts, cannot be interpreted as a power *or* a domination but only as a system of powers *and* dominations in which some dominations limit or restrain certain powers in order that other powers might be free; and on these terms the dominations, since they are directed toward a concept of the good, are no longer dominations but powers. What is involved, clearly, is a question of values, of the proper primacy or hierarchy of powers; and this, despite Santayana's terminology, is but the ancient if still vexing political problem of reconciling freedom and authority, of discovering that combination of liberties and restraints that will best provide the conditions for the good life.

A third difficulty concerns the nature or definition of the "natural." How do we know when an action is natural, that is, a response to a "natural" need? Santayana tells us that from the standpoint of an organism striving toward its ideal fulfillment, a necessary action is morally neutral or good even if it involves the destruction of another power; thus a large fish properly swallows a small one. But Santayana as a naturalist also speaks of "the equal legitimacy of all existence." Why then is the large fish justified in consuming the small fish? It can only be that the large fish has a greater legitimacy. But wherein consists this greater claim? In his size, strength, interest? Suppose many small fish were to band together to destroy the single large one, or, as is more common among humans, large and small units variously combine to combat each other. Santayana would perhaps urge that they ought not to combat, that the life of reason dictates other forms of resolution. But if *any* action resulting from a natural need is a power, it cannot be condemned; while if only certain, i.e., necessary or natural, actions are proper, we need a criterion to determine necessity or naturalness. To complicate the problem further, there is the added consideration that an adult organism, if it is intelligent, will generally discover alternative ways of moving toward its ideal fulfillment. If each of these possible paths involves a particular kind of domination, on what basis shall we say that the choice of one rather than any of the others is natural rather than deliberately oppressive and perhaps even insincere? If the criterion is the interest of the subject, who is to determine that interest — the individual himself or, in a democratic state, the people? Santayana's low estimate of human nature in general and of democratic political systems in particular compels a negative answer. Where then are we to turn?

Concerning the fiirst of these general difficulties, Santayana is silent. He evidences no familiarity with the vast literature on the psychology of domination, from the technical studies of social psychologists and psychoanalysts through the more general treatises of men like Lasswell, Mannheim, Russell, and Max Weber, to the novels of Koestler and Orwell. Nor, apart from the customary opprobriums against communism, does he seem to have reflected on the totalitarian experience. What we are offered, as he candidly admits in his preface, is not historical investigation but intuition.

Reflections on the remaining difficulties, however, comprise the substance of his book and reveal his political theory. What Santayana has to say on freedom and authority may be subsumed under his doctrine of true or "vital liberty." His attempt to meet the problem of right government — to disentangle dominations from powers in accordance with his naturalistic morality — may be epitomized as a theory of oligarchy rooted in a secular theology.

Liberty is for Santayana a supreme good, but by liberty Santayana does not mean Hobbes's absence of restraints. This is rather "vacant freedom," the freedom to exist in a vacuum, to be shed of one's bonds as a slave would be freed of his fetters but to remain without purpose, unknowing of the form that true or vital liberty would take and that would alone make the rebel happy. Vacant freedom, indeed, implies a demand for protection from the dangers of a free life itself, from want and fear, and so leads to the contracting of freedom for the sake of security. It is not vital liberty but only a condition of vital liberty, which is, according to Santayana, "the exercise of powers and virtues native to oneself and to one's country" (p. 58). Vital liberty is thus not simply the freedom to live but the freedom to live well, to live in accordance with one's nature, so as to direct one's powers toward a right goal — happiness.

Now liberty is not, historically speaking, monogamous; and if Santayana wishes to wed it to the adjectives "true" and "vital" he has every license to do so. But if true liberty is itself to be understood only in terms of purpose, and purpose varies with nature as nature varies with person and country (which are not self-evidently coincident), we emerge with a pastiche, not a definition. Liberty as absence of restraint is understandable, even when in the real world this must be reduced to a system of liberties and restraints. But true or vital liberty limits this reduction to a *particular* system of liberties and restraints; and when one asks what this system is, the reply is only that it is in accord with one's purpose, which is happiness. But what if a man denies that purpose, or agrees to the purpose but accepts only his reading of it? Then his vital liberty may lead him to the exercise of powers which challenge, say, the instructions of his government. What is he then to do: disobey the law or surrender his version of what constitutes his right purpose?

Santayana's reply is curiously shallow and ambiguous, lacking in any of the insights or refinements that political philosophers have contributed to the resolution of this problem in the 2400 years since Plato grappled with it in the *Crito*. Santayana is convinced, as is appropriate to a man who loves order, that freedom is legitimate only when it does not usurp authority. "Spirit," he says, "loves and reveres the order from which it springs. It is consecrated to the defense of that order, and to its perfection" (p. 219). But he is no less firm in his belief that society suffocates liberty merely by existing, and that a government which seeks to impose its conception of good or perfect freedom on a people — on the pretense that it knows better than the people what freedom their natures crave — condemns them to a collective suicide.. Which master, accordingly, shall a man obey — society or the free play of mind? He cannot, says Santayana, obey both; yet he ought not, if I read Santayana correctly, obey either; for obedience to one impairs or destroys the primacy of the other. Santayana presents and pleads for them as alternative values, but nowhere does he clearly delineate their respective spheres. In his conclusion he wistfully suggests that a rational government would separate the two so that order would prevail where the conditions are known, and liberty where imagination makes its own laws. But this ignores the fact that a system of order implies a system of liberties; and it begs the questions: who is to know, who to imagine, and when are the known and the imagined "natural?"

Were Santayana less a speculative poet and more an observer of political realities, he might have escaped the never-never land of vital liberty and rational government (with his test of rationality here being circular) for a less schematic world of clashing impulses, freedoms, and powers, in which a government (rational or otherwise) necessarily limits or curbs *some* freedoms in order to assure or to maximize others. Whether the liberties thus secured are "vital" or "vacant" involves a value judgment, and a corresponding criterion, apart from the fact of freedom itself; for freedom does not cease to be freedom merely because the

39

liberated impulses are deemed to be wrong. And since, as Santayana insists, the moral judgment is subjective — "each man is autonomous, the only seat and absolute final judge of all judgments" (p. 368) — no man, not even Santayana, can say for another that a particular combination of freedoms and restraints liberates or binds his nature. Indeed, save for the most ruthless and discerning totalitarianism, there is no combination that does not liberate man's nature in some things and frustrate it in others.

Many of these difficulties would be removed — for the proper hierarchy of freedoms would be perceived — if we had before us a fairly unambiguous concept of the natural and of the government that embodies it. Concerning the natural, Santayana at times explicitly, often implicitly, looks to the naïve nineteenth-century naturalism of Darwin and Herbert Spencer; but he ultimately casts his lot with a secular theology that substitutes "nature" for "God" in the doctrine, "This is right because God intended it to be so." But if we abandon the cruel and demonstrably false theory of the Social Darwinists for the intentions of nature, we have still to discover and correctly transcribe nature's teachings.

Santayana's edition of this text is revealing. He approves as natural such institutions as the patriarchical family, with children and servants and duties "clearly imposed." But are duties clearly imposed because they are natural, or are they natural because they are imposed? Does Santayana approve servile status for some because nature decrees it, or is it so ordained because it is approved? Santayana holds it proper to segregate peoples for reasons of race, religion, or nationality. But is racial discrimination natural because Negroes, say, are morally or intellectually "different" (i.e., inferior), or are they different in these things because of the discrimination? So to catalogue Santayana's findings — in defense of monarchy, the subordination of women, the elimination by government of "political vermin" (i.e., men who are odious, infected, deformed, and beastly), etc. — is to make clear that what we are dealing with is little more than sanctimonious prejudice. There is no rational demonstration that these are "natural" rather than arbitrary preferences.

This secular theology permeates Santayana's considerations on government. For him, good government is one which secures "the true good" of its people, and *true* good refers to ultimate rather than accidental aims. Now the criterion by which to judge the true good of a people or of an individual lies, Santayana has repeatedly said, within that individual or people, and not in a source outside of them. But if true good involves the recognition of one's fundamental needs and capacities, and not mere consciousness of one's casual desires, then the expressed will of a person or people may not be the true Will — Santayana uses the capital to distinguish real or true Will from incidental will — and a good government must see, or instinctively pursue, that true Will even when the stated or popular will is opposed to it. Thus Santayana disingenuously abandons, even as he seemingly affirms, the absolute finality of subjective moral judgments, and embraces instead the ghosts of Rousseau, Hegel, and Bosanquet; for on such terms a theological ("naturalistic?") standard is provided whereby man, when coerced by right government, is nonetheless rendered both good and free.

It is not altogether clear from Santayana's discussion whether such coercion is a "domination" or a "power," but it is allegedly "rational" and therefore right. All that remains, consequently, is to locate that government which perceives, "or instinctively pursues," the real Will.

Ideally, this is ideal monarchy.

> Government being an art, . . . only one Will and one intelligence can plan and conduct it. . . . So if the mind and heart of a monarch could share all the demands of his people, reason and goodness in him would automatically dispose all things for the best. . . . He would appreciate equally all other men's aims and possibilities, and would see clearly and follow faithfully the best possible path in the given labyrinth [pp. 107-108].

Santayana knows that such sympathy and impartiality are an ideal not realized in any mortal, but he hopes that with respect to a special function it may be approached, as a father may guide and judge the interests of his children better than they can. Aristotle's caution that a family is not a state ought not, however, to be forgotten; and when we add to this the vices and stupidities of kings and of the courtiers who surround them, we see that there can be no relation in the real world to the pious hierarchy of offices and emoluments that Santayana visualizes. His insistence that careers in such an order of distinct classes be open to talent ill accords with his sentiment that "it is natural and pleasant that sons should adopt their father's profession" (p. 110). His suggestion that this ideal monarch be selected not by hereditary right but by designation of his predecessor or "some council rich in experience," begs the question of the initial selection of either, as it avoids telling us how long this designated "best" remains the best. And his citation of the Catholic Church as model for this ideal arrangement conveniently ignores the sordid phases of that body's history. In brief, until Santayana is God and men are clay, his ideal polity can have no relevance to "natural" society.

The rational alternative to ideal monarchy is not, for Santayana, democracy; for this satisfies desires when it should satisfy needs. In a surprisingly realistic vein he argues that "it is the people's business to get as much good out of their government as they can" (p. 427), but he does not think the people are competent to judge their best interests or good. "In the political field," he writes, "the ordinary man thinks little and gets that little wrong" (p. 185); hence reason dictates that public opinion give way to private opinion. Private judgments, even of experienced and competent men, may of course be partial, but it is only through the institutionalization of their convictions that we can hope to produce a government that is morally representative and therefore more truly a guardian of all natural interests. Such a government might exercise at least a modicum of control over temporal impulses and preserve the ideals of liberty and justice. The rulers and managers of this government "would be selected, not by popular elections, but by co-option among the members of each branch of the service, as promotion normally ensues in armies, banking-houses, universities, or ecclesiastical hierarchies" (p. 382). In this way, Santayana believes, a world in which good government has never existed and perhaps can never exist would be made tolerable, and the interests of the people secured.

The assumptions and fallacies involved in this complex of ideas are many, and some have been noted and commented upon elsewhere. I shall address my remarks here to only two: Santayana's misconception of democracy and his self-defeating theory of "natural aristocracy."

In Santayana's view, modern democracy is a government in which power is exercised by the incompetent proletariat — "an ugly modern word for an ugly thing" — for its own benefit; and this means a socialistic majority seeking "to organise, equalise, and train everybody, making them all unanimous" (pp. 348, 288). If this were true and not the straw man it obviously is, Santayana's harsh judgments would still be largely indefensible; for in his theory it is precisely its own benefit that the "proletariat" should seek. But Santayana's reading of democracy is unrealistic. Democracy does not identify public opinion with the opinion of the ordinary man, nor does democracy require that opinion to decide the specific issues that daily confront governments. In a democracy, public opinion (which is a collective judgment involving all — including "exceptional" — men) is called upon only to select the rulers and thereby determine the *general ends* of public policy. With respect to this function, the evidence by no means disproves the competence of the people to judge their own interests. Nor does democracy imply a uniform leveling that denies difference or distinction. On the contrary, democracy, by insisting upon cultural freedom and the free play of ideas, provides a method whereby the inequalities of power and privilege that always exist will reflect the true or "natural" differences among men. For this reason not equality but certain kinds of equality — of citizenship and of opportunity — are the necessary conditions of "natural" or democratic inequality.

Santayana recognizes the need for equality of opportunity but argues that his "right" oligarchy will alone secure it. This is difficult to reconcile with his frequent condemnations of past aristocracies as artificial, and with the fact that every oligarchy — whose first concern, Santayana admits, is always to preserve its own life — is insensibly corrupted by power. Santayana argues, however, that what corrupts is not power but power that envelops a mediocrity; power "in those born or fitted to exercise it" can be trusted (p. 389). This is a large assumption, requiring in turn a demonstration that such men can not only be found and put in power, but that democracy prevents the attainment of such a government while some other system secures it.

Santayana's method of "co-option" is not in this regard convincing. In the first place, it is not one method but many: men do not normally advance in universities for the same reasons that they do in armies, or in banking-houses as in the Catholic hierarchy, except as we recognize that promotions depend upon a variety of factors all or almost all of which can be found in any hierarchical system. In the second place, it assumes, as established, the conclusion that the men initially at the top are there because of merit and not because someone, perhaps themselves, put them there. Finally, if power does tend to corrupt even good men (and it is revealing that Santayana does not consider that nonpower also corrupts, in the sense that it destroys responsibility and drives men into other, perhaps illegal or revolutionary, channels), a self-perpetuating "aristocracy" would end by denying equal opportunity and access to positions of power, and would thereby cease to be an aristocracy. On the record, certainly, no nondemocratic system secures the "best." And in logic as well as in history, democratic government when properly institutionalized furthers, indeed alone makes possible, the rise of "natural" eminence. For this reason men who sincerely believe in natural aristocracy have been compelled, like Jefferson, to argue for democracy.

Nearly half a century separates Santayana from the man he was when he wrote *The Life of Reason,* but the passing years do not seem to have increased his political sophistication or his compassion. He remains aloof, contemptuous of the "common" man. He clings to his prejudices, cavalierly ignoring the requirements of logic and the intrusions of inconvenient facts. Yet the play of his imaginative mind on a multitude of problems and ideas will continue to attract, and in some measure reward, serious readers. As a contribution to political philosophy, however, this book is likely to be read for the prominence of its author, not the author for the significance of the book.

Chapter 6

Freedom and Domination:
The Political Theory of R. M. MacIver

I

Ever since Machiavelli, political theorists have understood, even if they have not always observed, the necessary distinction between political behavior in the positivistic sense and the ethical values by which such behavior is judged. It is the strength of Robert M. MacIver as a political thinker that he has utilized still another dimension in the study of politics; he has shown, along with Max Weber, that men's conceptions of what they ought to do are themselves determinants of what they actually do, and that, in turn, what men do or can do tends effectively to limit the range of their ethical obligations.[1]

So understood, political behavior and ethical values are neither divorced nor unilaterally related. Ideals move men even as men move toward the realization of their goals. Values thus become motives that govern as well as principles that explain human behavior. Yet in politics as in other areas of social action, MacIver has reminded us, the actual range of historical possibilities places outer limits on what may be allowed as the attainable moral desiderata of political behavior. Hence, theories of what government should or should not do must properly be rooted in the objective realities of the social situation.

If the political theorist, then, is to apprehend the nature and direction of the state — that is, the state in its historical activity, sociological relationships, and ultimate purposes — he must avoid, so far as he can, those arbitrary and subjective interpretations which accord with his own ethical tradition. But he ought not on that account — as in fact he cannot — rule out considerations of human ideals; he must enter imaginatively into the realm of values and relate social institutions to human intentions and their consequences. For the state is an agency of human purpose, and if it is true that its character changes as its purpose changes, it is no less true that its purpose tends to be revealed and linked to the possible as human intelligence and human will mold or influence the structure itself. We are thus enabled to see the importance of MacIver's insistence that, while an "objective" understanding of the character of the state is the necessary foundation for an appreciation of its ethical value, the latter is equally necessary to give meaning to the political structure.

In this respect, the business of the political theorist is not, in MacIver's view, to validate an ethical philosophy, for an ethic cannot possibly carry its own authentication and those who reject it can offer no *proof* that it is wrong. Instead, his task is to take the entire complex of incorporated values that we call culture as a datum of his study and relate it to the utilitarian or instrumental systems that sustain the culture. The latter— comprising the political, economic, and technological systems — make up the huge apparatus known as civilization; they constitute a complex of means, not ends. And from this point of view the state or the political system is essentially a mechanism for the manipulation of means, differing from the economic system (which also controls means) in that it is the authoritative ordainment for the social regulation of the basic technology. The state is of course more. It is an association established by the community for the regulation of the universal external conditions of social order — for example, codes of behavior. But it is not coterminous with the social order; nor is it, as the Hegelians insist, the embodiment of a transcendant purpose which the social order exists to fulfill. Consequently a theory of the state is a theory of an association within a more inclusive unity; it is a theory about means, not ends, and it takes account of ends only insofar as they determine the character and uses of the means.

This implies that political theory is social theory brought to bear on one agency of social existence, the state; and that to understand the state as it is and as it changes, one must first grasp the meaning of community and of the structures and processes of society. Accordingly MacIver as political theorist has been concerned with general sociology as well as with its application to the life of the state. He has sought to classify the types of political situations, seeking an understandable order of things out of the vast complexity and variety of political patterns. He has not been unaware of the risk of the "ideal type" approach — as evidenced, for example, in Max Weber's treatment of the Protestant ethic — in discounting or ignoring the tendencies to change already present in the situation. But even though the "ideal type" does not fully correspond with reality it remains, in MacIver's view, an indispensable instrument of understanding. For it enables us to grasp the political situation, the historical moment, the social system, as something coherent, as somehow a unity of elements. And, although individuals and groups only approximate these typical ways of behaving, these generally accepted norms of action, they tend in the main to act in accordance with them.

Consider, in these terms, his classification of the forms of government.[2] Traditionally, such classifications have accepted the tripartite division into monarchy, aristocracy, and democracy, and have been based on political factors alone. But a moment's reflection will make clear that this distinction is more a formal than a substantial one, resting on much too narrow a ground to encompass a full measure of reality. No government is ever a mere monarchy, for the one who titularly rules is nearly always the representative or symbol of an associated class, clique, party, or group of some kind. And in the strict sense the many, or the people, never *rule;* for the actual business of ruling is always in the hands of the few. Hence, the real as well as constitutional question concerns the relation of the few who rule to the many who are ruled. If the few are responsible to the many, the system is democratic; if they are not responsible, it is oligarchic. Aristocracy, MacIver argues, is a question-begging expression since no method has ever been devised to assure that the best qualified persons preside over the state, or indeed to determine who are the persons best qualified for that role. Consequently the constitutional basis of classification must be a bipartite one, its major categories being democracy and oligarchy. MacIver's classification takes account of the variations within each of these categories — subsuming monarchy, dictatorship, theocracy, and plural rulership under oligarchy, and limited monarchy and republic under democracy. But no less significant is his extension of the bases for the classification of governments to include economic and communal differences and the sovereignty structure. Thus the various types of government can be separated according to their feudal or capitalistic or socialistic economy, or with respect to their tribal or national basis, or as they form a unitary or federal state or empire. By means of criteria other than that supplied by the traditional constitutional taxonomy, a more adequate classification of political forms becomes possible.[3]

But government is not to be understood if it is confined to a study of political forms alone. What is required is a more comprehensive analysis of social power, of the graduated orders of command and obedience, of the characteristic and distinctive pyramids of power that exist in every type of society and weigh heavily or lightly upon men in varying stations of life. From among the wealth of types and their endless variations, MacIver has outlined three broadly differentiated types of the pyramid of power. One is the caste pyramid, characterized by virtually impenetrable barriers separating the different levels of the pyramid and a marked inverse relation between the power and the size of each stratum. This "ideal type" — of which the Indian caste system is an illustration — is approximated only under conditions of primitive technology, the vast masses of the population being both illiterate and poverty-stricken. The second broad type — the oligarchical pyramid — differs from the first in that, although the main classes of the population are still anchored to their assigned social status and are still clearly demarcated by cultural differences as well as by the ranges of opportunity and of power at their disposal, individuals nevertheless have some chance to rise from one level to another, there being somewhat greater differentiation within each level, and a less distinct differentiation between levels. The slope of the pyramid is less abrupt and the middle class is proportionately greater than it is in the first type. The later stages of feudalism and the oligarchical centralized states that have emerged out of feudalism approximate to this type. The third broad type — to which Canada, the United States of America, and the Scandinavian countries, among others, belong — is the democratic pyramid, characterized by a breakdown of the corporate character of the class structure and a greater mobility within and between the various levels of the pyramid. Status, position, and power no longer coincide, and groups disadvantaged by class or wealth may accordingly move to power through organization.

MacIver does not, of course, advance these power pyramids as categories into which political or power systems are to be forced; they are rather analytical tools, instruments that enable us to comprehend the nature of a system and, within that system, to relate social institutions to human values. For what the political theorist must seek as the basis for his formulations is the order within society, the nature of the species as well as of the individual members of a species. Without such perception, without insight into the character and types of structures and processes, the theorist cannot hope to understand, or to contribute to an understanding of, the causal nexus itself. He cannot interpret the dependence of one phenomenon on another, and that greater interdependence of them all which constitutes at each moment the changing social and political equilibrium; he cannot see how in the intricate complex of conditions every change that is introduced reacts, or might react, upon a whole situation. He cannot, in a word, construct a valid political theory.

II

Although the political theorist must use a correct methodology, methodology alone cannot produce a political philosophy. For methodology remains incidental to the formulation of doctrine; it is useful only as it aids or confirms insight, only as it contributes to our knowledge of the principles that govern, or ought to govern, political and social systems.[4] What makes MacIver's work so significant is that he has understood and kept constantly in mind the proper relation of analysis to doctrine. His search for and discovery of political facts — that is, the myths or value-systems that men live by or live for, and the techniques or ways of knowing that enable them to control objects, including persons as objects — has led to the revision of old and, because imperfectly understood, partly erroneous concepts so as to vest them with a new meaning and a new validity. His perception of the unity of community and of the relations of institutions to values has enabled him to reintegrate into a new theoretical unity a body of doctrine that explains not only what the state *is* but what it ought or ought not to do. MacIver's reinterpretation of the general will may serve to illustrate the former of these contributions. His theories of federalism and democracy, and within democracy of freedom, power, and political obligation, will be used to indicate his sense of the community and his scheme of values.

MacIver's use of the general will derives, of course, from Rousseau. It is a principle that builds on the recognition that society is an integral unity and that the consciousness of unity emerges out of the sense of common interest or welfare. And to the extent that Rousseau affirms the general will to be the true sovereign and ultimate authority in a state, he shares, with MacIver, the democratic thesis that the people are politically sovereign. But when Rousseau goes on to argue that the general will is not to be equated with the will *of* the people but is the will *for* the general good, and that the necessary political sovereignty of the people is identical with a moral sovereignty, he creates insuperable difficulties. Although it may be insisted that the sovereign cannot err, this is only an expression of a legal truth. Legality cannot transcend law but morality obviously can. To hold otherwise is to confound the actual with the ideal; it is also to deny the necessary distinction between the state and the community, between the bonds of law and the moral sanctions that keep a society together. And while it may be to the general interest or good that the general will should be fulfilled, it does not follow, as MacIver has shown, that the general will is the will for the general good; for what is general in Rousseau's sense is the interest, not the will; and this may be willed by one or by a few, in which case the will is not that of the body of the people but of only a fraction of the population. But which will is it that wills the general will? Clearly there is no positive standard in Rousseau's theory according to which this can be determined. When Rousseau therefore turns to a majority will determined through a balance or cancellation of pluses and minuses, he accepts a political principle that is useful and perhaps alone practical, but one that nevertheless bears no necessary relation to the general will as he understands it.

By avoiding Rousseau's identification of the political with the social order, MacIver has given the general will a new and more realistic application. In his construction, the general will is not the will *of* the state but the will *for* the state, that is, the will to maintain it. It is not the will that directs or determines policy, that, as Rousseau believed, continuously and directly legislates; it is rather the will that sustains the community in the face of differences among men and groups as to what that policy shall be. It is the will of the person to be a citizen, to accept the decision of a majority or of a constituted government even if it does not win his approval. It is the will for political unity and is therefore logically prior to and more universal than the will of the political association, which is never more than a partial and evanescent will. This latter will, conceived of as the will *of* the state, is the majority or policy-directing will. It is, in MacIver's theory, the true ultimate sovereign which sets up and pulls down governments and which dictates the contours of their policy. In no state, least of all in a democratic state, is the active government the choice of all the citizens; the "will of the people" is rarely, if ever, the will of all the people. The government in power is at most sustained by the will of a fluctuating majority, a sovereign neither one and indivisible but elusive and inconstant. But it is a sovereign that, through its incessant rejection of alternatives, can alone give direction, can alone move through difference to the policy of the hour. Since, however, common action cannot proceed simultaneously from a great number of autonomous wills, however common their interest, the political as every other association must have a center or focus of action. Here MacIver finds his third kind or stage of common will, which he terms the government or legislative sovereign. The majority will or ultimate sovereign makes (and unmakes) the government, but it is the government or legislative sovereign that has the exclusive right, during the term assigned to it by the ultimate sovereign, to make laws of universal validity within its own sphere, together with the right to the exercise of force in the maintenance of such laws and of the machinery for their enforcement. But this right accrues to the government only because it is the guardian of the constitution, the executor of the laws — laws which it enforces but which it too must obey. The government does not have this power in its own right; its power is not legitimate outside the realm of law.

Thus the will of the community is revealed in the maintenance of the state; and the will of the state is manifested in its laws. This explains why the law is obeyed by those who oppose as well as by those who support it. Political theorists who ascribe obedience to the fact that the majority has also the greater force fail to perceive that there is a will more ultimate than the will of the state, and that is the will to maintain it. Consequently, states in which the general will is not active must be regarded as imperfect forms; and the state *qua* state — the state as an organ of the community — must be a democracy, understanding by democracy not necessarily the rule of the many but the active functioning of the general will, giving direct support, and not merely passive acquiescence, to a government chosen by itself.[5] More explicitly, MacIver means by democracy a form of state in which (*a*) the distinction between the state and the community is constitutionally drawn, and (*b*) both the composition and the policies of government are determined through the free operation of conflicting opinions. The first of these criteria implies, among other things, the existence of constitutional guarantees and civil rights which the government is not empowered to abrogate. It is a way of making power responsible by confirming and strengthening the distinction between government as an agent and the people as the principal who holds it to account; it is a way of establishing the formal superiority of the community over the state. The second criterion implies, among other things, a system under which any major trend or change of public opinion can constitutionally register itself in the character and policies of government. It is not a way of governing, whether by majority or otherwise, but primarily a way of determining who shall govern and, broadly, to what ends. It is consequently the meaning of democracy that the political system is one form of the organization of the community, limited to the ends that meet with major approval of that community, and that force is never directed against opinion as such.

In these terms, federalism becomes the necessary principle for the coordination of community, and democracy the necessary principle for the control of power and the protection of freedom. MacIver here employs the term federalism in its wider meaning to refer to the general relation of local to national autonomy; it is the attempt to reconcile the nearer specialized claim with the more universal claim, to transcend the multiplicity of allegiances rather than to reduce all allegiances to one. As a pluralist, MacIver seeks to retain not only the numerous likenesses but also the differences among social groups; he respects and wants to preserve the diversity of interests within the wider community. He argues, indeed, that the small community need not and should not be completely absorbed within the great community, since the small community fulfills a unique and valuable service — the realization of intimate loyalties and personal relationships, and of the specific traditions and memories of everyday life. On the other hand, the growth of common interests has made the institution of war between nations both irrational and vain; hence the coordination of community into some permanent form of international federation with appropriate sanctions is indicated. The principle, if not the application, of federalism thus becomes clear: so far as common interest extends, so far ought a federation also to extend, with narrower and wider circles of community duly corresponding to narrower and wider needs.

What sustains a federation, in MacIver's conception, is the general will; and what distinguishes a federation from, say, an empire, is that the general will is as broad as the federation (except, of course, in a time of civil war), whereas empire rests on a far narrower basis of will. A federal state thus presents an important problem of reconciling sovereignty with the requirements of coordination. For in a true federation each of the constituent units has a certain autonomy, a partial sovereignty, recognized in the articles of union through a definition of the respective powers of the federal state and of its constituent states. It would then seem to follow that no change in the relation of the unit to the whole can legitimately be forced upon the constituent unit by a majority outside itself, that, apart from the conditions it has accepted in entering the federation or at any later time, the constituent unit remains in the position of a free state.

Its jurisdiction and power thus limited, the federal state should not, in MacIver's view, attempt to exercise compulsion over the communities organized into constituent states. It is rather the latter which should prevail as against the federation, when on some issue they are overwhelmingly and bitterly opposed to a principle or policy accepted by the rest.. The alternative is to risk disruption of the federation. In this way, MacIver believes, the coordination of the community, once achieved, is maintained; and the general will is able to override, though not to remove, the interests that divide men.[6]

Federalism is the form a state must take if it is to act as a unifying agent, but it can act in this way only if it has itself undergone evolution toward democracy. Although no institutions are secure, those which rest on the sustaining power of the conscious cooperation and participation of the community are, in MacIver's judgment, the strongest. The institutions are then not alien to the people but are the people's own. A people can overthrow any form of government, but what reasonable alternative is there to overthrowing one that is uniquely its own? Clearly democracy would be foolish to restore the class-ruled state — a state historically identified with the interests of a ruler or ruling caste, military or landed or financial oligarchy — as against a state directed toward the interests of the whole. The democratic state, even when only partially realized, reveals in striking form the transition from a power-system to a welfare-system. In an oligarchy the holders of power may profess the general welfare, but they are rarely, if ever, committed to it; nor are they constitutionally responsible for their failure to move from verbal profession to actual deed. But if power is an instrument and welfare a goal, the ultimate and crucial distinction is between a system maintained for the welfare of a class and one maintained for the welfare of the whole. Since democracy alone makes the state responsive to the dominant desires of the people, since indeed it is the only kind of government that explicitly rests on the constitutional exercise of the will of the people, it is of all political systems the least likely to deny the welfare of the whole. And it is by the same token the system most likely to realize the general will.

It is true, of course, that citizens in a democracy do not always set the common welfare above their special interests. This gives greater urgency to the task of the state, which is to strengthen the sense of common interest by promoting the common good. By providing equality of citizenship and of opportunity, and by extending power and assuring certain primary liberties to all the people, the democratic state can emerge as the guardian of the whole. Thus only can the regard for personality — which is in MacIver's political theory the only intrinsic value, the highest end — be secured, and only then can freedom and power be so reconciled as to achieve this value for all men.

By freedom MacIver means an ordered system of liberties and restraints. By power he means the capacity to control the behavior of others, whether directly by fiat or indirectly by the manipulation of available instrumentalities. Since power is social and not merely political, the determination of what freedoms shall exist is made by those who have economic, religious, military, and other forms of power as well as by those who control the state. This produces unending conflict between, and in a multi-group society within, the various power centers; for each of the power groups, in seeking to advance its own interests, attempts to restrain the activities of those that impede it. Since, however, political power remains under all conditions the final lever of control of the social order, most apolitical power groups have generally sought to attach to themselves the power of the state. At all times the state has been a primary object of the ceaseless struggle for power.

To make the state the instrument of the whole and to prevent abuse of the power of the state by special groups, the community must set limits to the power of the state — even a democratic state. Fundamentally, these limits are set by certain civil and political liberties which the state may not transgress. Such liberties, MacIver is aware, do not cover all the liberties that men prize, and there are other things besides their liberties that men prize, most notably economic security. This suggests to MacIver that the state may properly assume the additional function of supervising the economic order. In the interests of the community, the state should, among other things, control the restraints imposed by power organizations such as business corporations and labor unions, ensure a basic standard of well-being, assure to the worker a social position as a partner in enterprise rather than as a mere item of cost, and sustain, where the system itself proves incapable of doing so, the economic equilibrium.[7] Another task of the state is defined by the area of culture. There are certain functions — in particular those which sustain and equip the arts of living (for example, museums, libraries, and public parks) and which provide opportunities for the citizen to share the cultural heritage of mankind (such as education) — that properly, although not exclusively, fall within the domain of the state. But where one group of people can practice its particular code without entailing outward consequences that directly impede or prevent other groups from practicing in equal liberty their own ways, the state should not attempt to invoke coercive sanctions against the group code. What, in these terms, the state can properly do and what it should or must leave to others cannot be settled merely by the establishment of broad principles. There remains always a large debatable area, where experience alone can be an adequate guide and where the lines of interference should be adjusted to the needs of the time, changing standards of private and public morality, and advances in the art of government itself.

Through such transformations and expansions of its functions, the state fulfills and increasingly reveals its true nature as the guardian of the community, wielding its power in the interests of the general welfare. And this is achieved, MacIver maintains, precisely because the state is a democratic state; for only in democracy is government rooted in the active and freely expressed will of the people.

But the will of the people, as we noted earlier, is seldom, and perhaps never, the will of all the people. Almost always dissenters will oppose the policy of the government. Almost always there will be those who do not *will* the law. Why, then, should they obey? Traditionally, MacIver observes, the obligation to obey has been justified on two main grounds. One is the legitimacy of the source from which law emanates, that is, the right ascribed to the law-making authority. The other is the rationality of content, the intrinsic merit of the law itself. Whether these are conjoined or distinguished, the answers thus far given remain, in MacIver's judgment, inadequate; for, even if the legitimacy of the source is acknowledged, there are other authorities and other obligations, with whose demands the law of the state may be in conflict. To which shall we yield the prior obligation — state or church, state or labor union, state or political party, state or family? On a question such as this, MacIver is convinced, there is no hope of consensus; the answers given will differ with the kind of government under contemplation as well as with the value-system of the respondent. In general, however, MacIver holds that obedience is obligatory except when, in the considered judgment of the citizen, disobedience promotes the greater welfare of the whole society in which he lives. Where the law of the state denies or overrides other claims, it has no sure foundations; the firmament of order is not likely to be sustained. Hence a wise state will not seek unnecessarily to impose laws that clash with the customs, beliefs, or traditions of any important sector of the people. It will endeavor instead to recognize and, so far as is possible, to accommodate within its legal framework the various loyalties of men. Thus only, in MacIver's view, can we approach a truly universal general will.

III

A political theory can be criticized on a variety of grounds, and MacIver's effort — like any comprehensive system of theory — has already been subjected to a critical scrutiny of some of its first principles of methodology and value.[8] In what follows, I shall confine myself to the terms of the system itself, accepting (for the moment) its values and presuppositions, and seek instead to explore some of the difficulties which follow from their application. This will make it possible to focus on the two difficulties that attend all formulations of theory and bedevil all political philosophers irrespective of the "truth" of their values or the "rightness" of their principles. One is the reduction of right principles to right conduct. The other and more serious difficulty involves the reconciliation of conflicting principles. In all such conflicts one of three solutions is open. If one principle takes precedence over the other, we sacrifice the lesser, in which case no real problem can be said to exist. If the conflicting principles are relatively equal in value, we may look to a standard or value transcending either of them in terms of which the resolution can be made. Or if the conflicting principles are relatively equal but no consensus can be reached concerning a greater or more comprehensive principle, we may look to a method such as democracy and the principle of majority rule — in place, say, of force or divine intervention — as a necessary expedient rather than an eternally "true" solution.

These difficulties, and MacIver's resolution of them, can best be demonstrated as they emerge from his applications of his broad principles. I shall restrict my examination here to two instances in which MacIver's reduction and reconciliation of conflicting principles do not, in terms of his own theory, exhaust the possible alternatives — where, indeed, the political and moral elements of that theory suggest a contrary solution. These are, first, the clash between the principles of federalism and of political obligation; and second, the conflict between the values of freedom, order, and political obligation with respect to the treatment of those who advocate the overthrow of democratic government by force.

(1) *Federalism and Political Obligation.* It is easy to see how these principles may come into conflict. Federalism urges, as a necessary principle of unity, that the greater power abstain from coercing the constituent states on matters concerning which the latter feel deeply and uncompromisingly. But federalism does not limit, any more than does any other political arrangement, the action of the greater state to instances where it obtains unanimous agreement. It is the first axiom of political obligation, as MacIver understands it, that the minority must, for the sake of the common good realized through the association, accept and carry out the decision of the majority. This, for him, is the established rule of all associations; it is part of the sociality of the civilized man. He admits, however, that the policy of the majority may on occasion seem to the minority to be destructive of the general good. In this event, he argues, the minority *must* secede and form a new association. And where, because of the thoroughgoing character of state power, secession is impossible, disobedience is the remaining and proper alternative. The individual and the group must choose what seems to them the greater loyalty; and since the act of disobedience depends on the same sense of obligation which alone justifies enforcement of the law, it cannot be condemned.[9] In the interests of the community, therefore, MacIver contends that "in spite of the verdict of the American Civil War, it may be generally better for the federation as a whole to suffer the inconveniences and hindrances resulting from the concomitant operation of contrary principles than to enforce its majority-rule against the determinate opposition of a real community."[10]

Now it is by no means clear that MacIver's conclusion follows from the terms of his argument. Where a constituent state represents a fairly homogeneous set of interests motivating the great bulk of its population, his case for pure or extreme federalism is readily sustained. For under such conditions, a conflict of values between the constituent state and the federal government would involve distinct sets of interests clearly opposed and embodied in the respective political units : the constituent state would stand for one set of interests, the federal state for another. But if, as is quite generally the case, there are divisions or conflicts within the constituent state no less strong or important than those that applied in the first illustration, then pure federalism, pushed to an extreme, merely serves to promote the special interests of the group that happens to be in power, that controls the government of the constituent state. MacIver's principle would thus lead to the defense of a fictional geographic interest and the sacrifice of a real and perhaps overriding economic or social interest of the bulk of the total population.

How can secession in the latter case be held to promote MacIver's greater principle, the general good? And if a resolution of the conflict is not to be made in terms of a superior standard or value, how can one reconcile secession with the alternative principle of majority rule? How reconcile the ensuing state with the principle of the general will; for if the basis of the state is the general will, whose will is it that in this circumstance wills the withdrawal of the constituent state? These considerations are all the more relevant when a cleavage within the constituent state follows the lines of rigid stratification, as in the American South before the Civil War. For then, in the face of a dual community, the free adjustment of differences is clearly precluded.

The conflicts of principle are thus multiple and weave bewildering patterns. On the one hand, a dissenting constituent state is, in MacIver's theory, entitled to disobey the will of the greater majority. But a minority within the constituent state is also entitled to disobey. Now, however, disobedience by the latter against the majority-will of the dominant group involves, or might involve, obedience to the majority-will of the total community. Thus the disruption of the greater community does not assure the unity of the lesser community; while compulsion of the constituent state may make possible the creation of a new unity between the minority within the constituent state and the national majority. Which community shall the federal state seek to serve? Which obligation shall it recognize? If we take personality as the ultimate value, the standard against which we shall measure these conflicting claims, can we legitimately say, as MacIver seems to imply, that the personalities of the rulers within the constituent state have a greater claim to fulfillment than the personalities of the dissenters? If we adopt the alternative method of resolution, the majority process as it operates in democracy, shall we say that this shall prevail only at the level of the constituent state but not at the level of the federal state? The principle of federalism is but one of many values, and I am unable to see why, in MacIver's own terms, it carries an inherently superior claim, why it necessarily compels the conclusion to which MacIver was led.

(2) *Freedom, Order, and Political Obligation.* "To establish order and to respect personality — these are the essential tasks positive and negative of the state."[11] This is the central principle by which MacIver seeks to delineate the limits of state action. What, however, does it mean to establish order? Obviously MacIver does not have in mind the order of a concentration camp. He means a particular kind of order, an order conducive to the general welfare which, in his view, is not only a proper aim but the sole justification of government. It is an order that establishes certain liberties and concomitant restraints which make for the develop-

ment of the free personality. And foremost among such liberties MacIver puts freedom of opinion. Whatever else the state may or may not do, it should not, MacIver argues, seek to control opinion, *no matter what the opinion may be.* But to this underscored principle a crucial exception is immediately entered: the state may take cognizance of incitements to break its laws or defy its authority. MacIver does not imply by this that the citizen in a democracy may not voice his belief that an existing law is pernicious, or that an act of authority is illegitimate, or even that the constitution is misguided; the citizen can, indeed, go further and seek by peaceful persuasion and all constitutional methods to change the law and the constitution. But to urge law-breaking is to attack the fundamental order, the establishment and maintenance of which is the first business of the state. Here, MacIver insists, the state must have the right to take whatever steps it deems necessary to assure the very object of it existence. Particularly is this true where the incitement is itself an attempt to subvert the rule of free opinion, where an individual or group advocates the overthrow of government by force.

But if, as MacIver also contends, opinion can be fought only by opinion, if force is pitifully irrelevant in the control of ideas, why should not the advocacy — as against the utilization — of force be countered by opinion? Why resort in this instance to force? To suppress the advocacy of force by force does not make what is advocated untrue. Indeed, as MacIver recognizes, to use force is to snatch from truth its only means of victory. It is itself a blasphemy against truth.

What is at issue, among other things, is the distinction between the word and the deed, between what men say and what men do. "Order" can tolerate many things that men might say, for even the strongest words become virtually impotent in certain situations — a truth to which Hyde Park and Columbus Circle orators will readily attest. It is the context in which the word is uttered that is most relevant, and here I must still follow the "clear and present danger" precept of Justice Holmes. MacIver himself seems to share this position when he remarks that the state has authority over action but not authority over thought and opinion, and again when he asserts that a democratic system does not, in principle, deny the right of the citizens to advocate anti-democratic ideas or even the complete abandonment of democracy.[12] But he remains fundamentally committed to the broader restraint. Repeatedly he returns to the principle that when an individual in a democratic system approves the resort to force for the furtherance of any cause, or when, in pleading this cause, he identifies himself with any group or party that accepts this method, he rules himself out from the sufferance of democracy.[13]

MacIver thus takes the position that the free play of ideas is, in effect, a principle that does not apply to its own domain. Unlike ideas per se, the free play of ideas is but a method through which ideas are judged; it is pre-eminently the rule by which the political game shall be played. But one can affirm the instrumental superiority of this method only if he is prepared to accept whatever policy decisions may emerge from it. It does not, *as a method,* carry an intrinsic value that is beyond attack. For those whose sense of personality forbids acceptance of a method that might lead the state to adopt what is in their view a wrong policy, democracy commends itself but poorly. For such men the supreme value is another ethic or principle; and democracy is valid to them only as it conduces to the achievement of that value. It is easy enough for one who believes in democracy to say — and to say truly — that the method permits of self-correction; but what if the necessary corrections are not made? What if men of rigid conscience, what if revolutionaries, of whatever orthodoxy, find that they cannot achieve their objectives through the democratic framework, and further, that there is no hope of winning popular support for a constitutional change in the structure itself? Then clearly their only alternative, as MacIver recognized in another connection, is secession or rebellion. But if MacIver admits the right of political disobedience and rebellion when the citizen is convinced that by such action he is promoting the general welfare, why should he repudiate that principle when the citizen merely seeks greater support for his cause by the oral or written expression of his ideas?

Once again we are confronted by a conflict of principles — the claims of order *versus* the claims of civil disobedience. If MacIver's philosophy of political obligation has merit, I cannot see why the individual must in principle accept as final the state's denial of his freedom to advocate the revolutionary overthrow of the government. No state, it is true, can as a matter of policy admit this right; but neither can a state admit any claim to disobedience. This, however, is a legal and not an ethical principle; and in point of fact states do concede the right of men to refuse obedience in certain instances, as in the case of those who profess a conscientious objection to military service. From the point of view of the individual, the moral issue is not essentially different. In both cases he is confronted by a law he cannot accept; in both cases he disobeys, knowing full well that certain consequences will attend his refusal to abide by the law. If MacIver vindicates an act of disobedience in the one case, it is difficult to grasp the principle that precludes vindication in the other.

It may even be argued that in this respect the cause of order is advanced rather than obstructed by the recognition of such a freedom; for it is easier for a state to protect itself against those who openly urge its destruction than it is to guard itself against those who disobey. What, for example, would the state do if, in the face of the Taft-Hartley Law which the labor unions vehemently oppose, labor were to put down its tools in a general stoppage of work? Would it be easier for the democratic state to sustain the social order under such conditions than it would be to protect it from the constantly known, because openly affirmed, advocates of revolutionary overthrow? "In the last resort," MacIver once said, "character needs to employ force only against the stupidity which relies on force."[14] It does not appear to me that the democratic state must operate as if it were *always* driven to the last resort. The faith and intelligence of men committed to a right principle, when conjoined with a fundamental respect for personality — of all men, not merely of themselves — can maintain a social order even in the face of violent dissents. The general will is not destroyed by the extreme pleadings of a recalcitrant few.

IV

These reflections articulate certain difficulties in MacIver's political theory, but they are the difficulties inherent in all philosophies that do not rest on closed systems. In the absence of absolute truth, of the kind of conviction that is indistinguishable from dogma, men cannot "solve" what MacIver knows to be an irreducible ethical conflict, the conflict of principles. MacIver has failed to reconcile these conflicts not because he has been unaware of them, but because, as a democrat, he respects personality and recognizes that men will always differ in their sense of right and wrong. Enlightenment, no matter how close it may lead men to the abandonment of their innumerable petty difference-breeding bigotries, will always vary from person to person; conflicting interests are in any case always powerful in shaping ethical judgments. Thus the conflict can never cease.

The political problem is then to resolve the conflict in ways that will not disrupt the community. It is to discover not a solution but a means to a solution, a means at once consistent with the ultimate value of personality and with the maintenance of the social order. This is the central principle of democracy. In this principle alone, MacIver is convinced, can such a resolution be secured. For no other principle builds on the diversity in man. No other system respects man's individuality and seeks to bind him to the social order not by demanding a total and exclusive loyalty but by an allegiance that transcends, and therefore absorbs, the multiplicity of loyalties intrinsic to his nature.

In the elaboration of this principle, MacIver has made his primary contribution. He has grasped the meaning of democracy and related it to human values and the sense of community. He has analyzed the structures and processes of human action to show how democracy can employ its utilitarian or instrumental systems to achieve and sustain the values that constitute culture. If his approach has been at times a pragmatic one, it is because the very nature of social life does not admit of mathematical reduction; always there are vast areas in which experience is the only guide, in which the establishment of broad principles cannot settle concrete problems. What democracy can do is to supply the form of solution, but the application of it is a task that has no end.

Much may be said to dispute some of MacIver's concepts, such as the theory of the general will, and to point to certain shortcomings or inadequacies of analysis, such as his failure to treat the nature and problems of horizontal mobility in the same systematic fashion that he examined vertical mobility in the pyramids of power. Nor is his system without certain difficulties when his principles are applied and at times come into conflict, as I have tried to indicate above.

But when all this has been said, it remains clear that MacIver has contributed an important and searching body of doctrine to political theory. His influence has already been manifested in the works of contemporary theorists, not least that of G. D. H. Cole, although MacIver would not, I think, subscribe to the conclusions to which Cole was led. His elucidation of terms such as community, association, institution, state, and the like, has made for greater clarity in political and sociological analysis. His own incisive and systematic analysis of social causation and social controls, of the state as an association of community, of theory as a methodological tool, and of the relations between political structures and processes on the one hand, and human values on the other, between the actual and the ideal — these are contributions that have profoundly affected the course of political thought. MacIver owes much, of course, to the thinkers who have preceded him, particularly to such German sociologists as Tönnies and Alfred and Max Weber. But in the depth and richness of his own formulations, and in the lines of exploration he has suggestively advanced, he has laid a groundwork on which future theorists can in turn firmly stand.

Part Two

THE LIBERAL IDEA OF FREEDOM

Chapter 7

Democracy and the Problem of Civil Disobedience

I

If Sophocles were alive today to recast the dilemma of Antigone in contemporary, if less sanguine, terms, he might well seize on the problem of the citizen who refuses to answer questions put to him by a congressional investigating committee. Antigone, you will recall, was torn between two loyalties. Her religion commanded her to bury the body of her brother, while her state commanded that his body be left, unburied and unmourned, to be eaten by dogs and vultures on the open plain outside the city walls. As a loyal citizen, Antigone was required to yield her conscience to the state, to guide her conduct not by her rational moral knowledge but by the precepts of the law. As a person bound to her kin by the dictates of her religion, she was required to subordinate the instructions of Creon the king to those of her faith. She chose to obey her conscience and paid the penalty. Socrates, who — according to a traditional interpretation of the *Crito*[1] — would doubtless have counseled otherwise, was also executed by the state. Thoreau, who at a critical moment followed what has scornfully been termed "the primitive attitude of Antigone, rather than the mature comprehension of Socrates,"[2] found that refusal to obey a law resulted not in loss of life but in temporary loss of physical freedom. This moderation of punishment from ancient Greece to mid-nineteenth century America, though not a steady historical trend, reveals a greater tolerance on the part of the state toward manifestations of civil disobedience, but the state's adamance still remains, and with it the essential dimensions of the problem.

Governments and people still contend over these old and fundamental problems of political obligation. Now as before, there are those who categorically assert that it is the duty of the citizen always to obey the law, while others insist that a citizen owes his primary obligation to his own conscience. Since it is my general conviction, with Aristotle, that "in all disputes upon government each party says something that is just,"[3] I propose to consider here those principles which, in a democratic state at least, appear to me to render valid *some* claims to the right of civil disobedience.[4]

Of such appeals to the right of civil disobedience I shall restrict myself in this paper to three: (1) the claim that the democratic state has no moral authority to make any demands on the individual because the political system (or the social order maintained by that system) is, in principle, unjust; (2) the claim that the system ideally conceived is just but that the particular state is a perverted form of democracy and is therefore unjust, and that consequently, as in the first instance, it lacks authority; (3) the claim that while the social order and the institutionalized form of democracy that seeks to maintain it are just, the particular law (or laws) is unjust in that it constitutes an attack on and a repudiation of that ideal, and that consequently disobedience to the law in question is, in the particular instance, calculated to achieve a greater good — the preservation of the system itself — than is likely to be achieved by compliance.

Since the resolution of a problem requires first that the problem be understood, it may be well to state at the outset what I conceive to be the underlying questions emerging from the present conflict over the principles of political obligation.

II

When a citizen today is summoned by a congressional investigating committee to answer questions he regards as morally reprehensible — questions, for example, that call upon him to state his political beliefs or to be an informer — he finds himself in a grave dilemma. If he answers the questions, he obeys the law but violates his moral code, and may, in addition, expose himself to certain non-legal consequences of his legal action — e.g., the loss of his job. If he refuses to answer on moral grounds, he satisfies his conscience but denies his obligation to the law, and thereby, if we are to believe certain conservative thinkers from Socrates' day to our own,[5] endangers as well the very foundations of the social order. His personal risks in such a course are even greater, entailing possible imprisonment, and his only consolation would be the knowledge that he had displayed the virtue of courage, or, with Thoreau, the thought that "under a government which imprisons any unjustly, the true place for a just man is also a prison."[6]

If, however, he resorts to a legal instrument — e.g., the self-incrimination clause of the Fifth Amendment to the Constitution — which will enable him both to satisfy his conscience and by invoking another law to stay out of jail, he invites a further dilemma. For if he invokes the Fifth Amendment knowing that it does not strictly apply to his case — e.g., if he seeks to protect someone else, although under the self-incrimination clause he is not entitled to do so — he does not tell the truth and may thereby dishonor his moral code. Nor can he enjoy the consolation of having been courageous, if he now seeks to escape the consequences of a refusal to answer based solely on moral grounds. On the other hand, if he is convinced that a lie is necessary to achieve a greater good, he may find it difficult to understand why one who acts rightly should be expected to invite wrongful punishment. To one who believes that a lie is always wrong, such conduct is inexcusable. But to men sensitive to the fact that moral dilemmas arise precisely because a particular situation offers no clearcut distinction between right and wrong, and that it is sometimes impossible to do that which is good without doing or suffering something that is bad, the performance of what under other circumstances might be evil is then right, not wrong. Moral rules are often in conflict, and a moral man may have to choose between telling the truth or lying to do good. If the greater good is right, the lie — otherwise bad but now necessary to the good — is also right. It is at least questionable whether an ambassador (or a spy) who lies, when necessary, for the good of his country, merits moral censure.

The gravity of the dilemma is compounded (a) by the failure of law, in general, to protect men from the non-legal consequences of legal action, and (b) by the deliberate use of the law, on occasion, to expose men to non-legal sanctions against actions heretofore beyond the pale of legal penalty.

Appeal to the Fifth Amendment may protect a man from certain legal penalties ensuing from his refusal to answer questions that might tend to incriminate him, but it provides no legal protection against the economic or social consequences of his refusal. Thus a man who invokes the Fifth Amendment may find himself without a job and with little likelihood of obtaining one, at least in his established field of endeavor. He may find himself and his family ostracized as well as impoverished. He may discover that his reputation and good name have been sacrificed on the altar of conscience. He may begin then to understand the element of truth in Machiavelli's cynical advice to one who would win popular approval and support — that it is often better to *seem* good than to *be* good. And he may learn, perhaps when it is too late, the awful significance of the words of Sophocles' Chorus:

> Tomorrow and for all time to come,
> As in the past,
> This law is immutable:
> For mortals greatly to live is greatly to suffer.[7]

Since it is the rare man who is willing to suffer greatly, the dire non-legal consequences of permissible legal action impose pressures that make difficult a right resolution of the moral dilemma. The citizen may obey the law not because he conceives it right to obey but because he

65

fears the consequences of disobedience. This introduces a new element into the problem, namely, the question of the moral obligation of the state to protect a citizen from social punishment when certain legal authorities or *private* powers disapprove his act, however unobjectionable it may be on strictly legal grounds. Does the state have an obligation to guarantee to a citizen not merely the constitutional right to refuse to answer questions with an incriminating bias, but also the legal right to protection from non-legal sanctions attendant upon such refusal?

It would be futile to deny that an affirmative answer to this last question leads into patent (and perhaps insuperable) difficulties, not the least of these being the dangers involved in unduly extending the sphere of state intervention. But the question of the state's obligation is not for this reason to be avoided. For if the Constitution is the final legal norm from which all subsidiary law derives its validity, then the protection of the Constitution must be made real and not simply formal. This can be achieved only when (a) the Constitution is applied not merely against *de jure* governments but against citizens and groups who comprise *de facto* or private governments that proclaim "laws" and impose sanctions, and (b) the laws of the state and the actions of governmental authorities conform both to the letter and to the spirit of the Constitution, i.e., they avoid so maltreating men as to expose them to non-legal sanctions where no legal punishments are or have been intended.

These principles, especially the former, may appear at first blush to embody a revolutionary proposal. Clearly, they require distinctions which are not likely to admit of mathematically precise application. On the one hand, there are certain social and economic consequences of lawful action which the state cannot prevent or eliminate even if it seeks to do so — e.g., the suspicion in the minds of some people that a man acquitted of a charge of rape or murder is nonetheless guilty.[8] On the other hand, there are certain cases in which the state should not intervene even if it could do so — e.g., the dismissal from the police force of an officer who refuses, despite the direct and obvious nexus between the information sought and the responsibilities of his position, to testify even before a non-legal but properly constituted tribunal of his superior officers concerning his alleged collaboration with dope-peddlers. But between these two extremes there still remains a vast intermediate range of instances in which governments may properly undertake to protect men from non-legal sanctions which in effect invalidate a constitutional or legal right. In line with this principle — a principle long grasped by some of our more perceptive legal and political thinkers[9] and incorporated in considerable measure into American constitutional law by the decision of the Supreme Court in *United States* v. *Classic*[10] more than a decade ago — governments have in fact sponsored legislation which, like the Wagner Act, prevented an employer from dismissing an employee for joining a labor union, or which, like fair employment practices acts, seeks to curb certain discriminatory practices by private powers. And it is in line with this same principle that governments might well prevent a university from dismissing a member of its faculty if his sole offense is that he has invoked the protection of the Constitution in refusing to answer questions put to him by a legislative investigating committee. I do not mean to imply by this that a refusal to testify under protection of the Fifth Amendment is necessarily to be condoned. But it ought not to be automatically condemned; for a decision not to testify may involve profound and complex ethical as well as legal considerations to which automatic condemnation and consequent social punishment are blind, not to mention the fact that they violate the spirit of the constitutional amendment itself.

Similar considerations support the proposition that legal authorities are to be condemned when they circumvent, and indeed violate, the Constitution in employing indirect (non-legal) sanctions to coerce an individual in cases where the law itself does not give them that power. Consider, for example, the not infrequent behavior of a congressional investigating committee. If the primary purpose of — and warrant for — such a committee is to gather information as a basis for recommending legislation, then a private or closed hearing would normally enable it to achieve this end without exposing the citizen to non-legal penalties. If the committee is not only indifferent to this last consideration but, through a second and open hearing that adds nothing but publicity to answers already vouchsafed or refused by the witness, deliberately contrives a situation that brings social and economic sanctions into play, it in effect converts such non-legal sanctions into indirect forms of legal action. This all too common effect of the sustained congressional investigations into the loyalty of university professors and others is a calculated perversion of power that raises serious questions concerning the justice of governmental behavior.

What is involved, consequently, is not only the obligation of the citizen to the state but also the responsibility of the state — certainly, at least, of a constitutional state — to the citizen.

The dilemma of the citizen, then, may derive not simply from a conflict between the commands of the state and the dictates of his conscience. It may emerge as well from the incompatibility of an enacted law or of the acts of governmental authorities or of private powers with the constitution of the state, understanding by the constitution not simply the written rules that comprise a revered document but the logic or underlying principle of the system which the Constitution (written and unwritten) is supposed to represent. In this circumstance the dilemma of the citizen takes another, and perhaps more aggravated, form than Antigone's moral problem; for the citizen here believes that he is being loyal to the Constitution in rejecting the obligation to obey the law (or the bidding of a legal authority). He is not pitting simply his conscience against the law but also the law against the Constitution. He is asserting that in defending the fundamental law he is being more loyal than those who would compel him to violate it. He invokes not (or not merely) the Fifth but the First Amendment, which, while thus far rejected by the courts in such cases, nevertheless appears to him the proper ground on which to take his stand.[11]

It is easy to say, and to say rightly, that there are legal mechanisms for the resolution of a conflict between an enacted law (or the bidding of a legal authority) and the Constitution, and that it is not the business of the citizen to displace such mechanisms by self-arrogation. But such mechanisms — e.g., the Supreme Court — do not always restrict social or economic or religious power groups from attaching severe penalties to action that is legally right. What is legally right may be deemed socially or economically or morally wrong. Consequently, the moral question for the citizen remains, all the more so since there is no legal machinery to prevent coercive action by non-legal power groups, by *private* governments.

III

What, then, is the citizen to do? If he obeys the law, he may violate his conscience. If he obeys his conscience, he may violate the law. If he obeys his conscience and seeks to vindicate his alleged disobedience by invoking the protection of the Constitution, he exposes himself to social or economic sanctions that are sometimes more powerful than the legal penalties that might have been applied had he not claimed that protection. The state, where it is not itself the deliberate *provocateur,* is indifferent to his fate in this last circumstance. Should he then be indifferent to the state?

The answer of the state, at least, is clear. It is no. There can be no law to which obedience is optional, no command to which the state attaches an "if you please." Consequently, there can be no legal right to disobey the law. Nor will the state, customarily, recognize a moral claim to disobedience. It may be urged that conscientious objectors often escape the prescribed legal punishments by appealing to a higher law. But this is only half true. For they escape such consequences only because a court or a statute admits such a claim as a legal one. The state, so to speak, incorporates the higher law into the positive law; it proclaims that in such cases it is lawful for some men to follow a certain course of action denied to the populace at large.

The state, then, demands obedience to its laws; and while it employs (or can employ) a number of different arguments to vindicate this claim,[12] its primary justification is the ground that such obedience is essential to the maintenance of the social order. Order, it is said, is better than disorder; and if men are free to set aside the laws of the state whenever they find them in conflict with their private interests, particular religion, or individual sense of morality, anarchy will result. Disobedience to the laws, therefore, involves an attack on the state itself. It is an act of rebellion, an attempt to subvert the foundations of the entire system of order which it is the business of the state to secure. This is why Socrates rejected Crito's suggestion that he flee to escape execution. What reply could he make, Socrates asked Crito, if the Athenian government should come to him and say:

> Tell us, Socrates, . . . what are you about? are you not going by an act of yours to overturn us — the laws, and the whole state, as far as in you lies? Do you imagine that a state can subsist and not be overthrown, in which the decisions of law have no power, but are set aside and trampled upon by individuals? . . . Tell us, — What complaint have you to make against us which justifies you in attempting to destroy us and the state? . . . And because we think right to destroy you, do you think that you have any right to destroy us in return, and your country as far as in you lies?[13]

He could, Crito admitted, make no answer. Since by his failure to emigrate Socrates had agreed to abide by the laws, he could not now disavow that covenant. He could not through disobedience seek to overthrow the state.[14]

Clearly there is merit in this position. Order is a necessary condition to the achievement of larger values; and if order is to be maintained there must be power, and a general readiness on the part of men to abide by the commands of power. But the merit is a relative one. Order in itself is not a *sufficient* condition for the realization of those values, and a government which merely secures order without, or at the expense of, those larger values, lacks moral vindication. Under such circumstances, it might well be argued that anarchy or disorder is to be preferred — not for its own sake but for the opportunity it provides to recreate the requisite conditions for a better human existence. Thus, while order is good, it is not necessarily the highest good. We must still distinguish the just or the decent order; we must still recognize that order is but a means to some larger end.[15] Epictetus may command our sympathy when he observes: "Did heaven owe me perfect parents? — No; it owed me parents." But, as Aristotle reminded Plato, it is surely a shallow philosophy that ignores the vast difference between a family and a state. And if we are to adhere to the principle of democracy, then not order but a certain kind of order — one based on opinion, on consent — constitutes the necessary framework of justice.

This being so, it is hard to see what absolute moral claim democracy can make on those who withhold their fundamental consent. Anarchists, communists, fascists, and others who deny — not through revolutionary action but through civil disobedience — the authority of the social order which democracy seeks to maintain, appeal instead to some alternative principle of justice. If they obey the laws of democracy, they do so for reasons of expediency, not of principle. It is true that fascists like Lawrence Dennis who affirm fidelity to the notion that might makes right are by this standard logically committed to the acceptance of democracy where it prevails; for democracy by virtue of the fact that it prevails has might and is therefore "right."[16] But democracy is not responsible for the confused arguments of its opponents. Nor can it without denying its very essence stand on any principle other than that of generalized consent. Consequently, democracy must recognize that for men who reject its values and refuse their assent to its system of order the dictates of democratic government appear as the commands of an illegitimate power. And where that power can be defied, especially with some expectation of success, opponents of democracy will claim a moral right to do so. In this regard they claim no more, on purely formalistic grounds, with respect to democratic systems than democrats do with respect to oligarchical systems. Hence the problem for democracy is not that of validating its own claim to their obedience, but that of allowing them that degree of civil disobedience which will balance the need for its own institutional preservation with its ultimate values, especially the provision for maximum free play for the individual conscience. Democracy can, to be sure, offer an opposing value judgment; but it cannot — without invoking intuition or divine or natural sanction or the proposition that might makes right — *prove* that its value system is truly best. Consequently, while democracy must, in defense of its own values, reject the scheme of justice proposed by the anti-democrats, it must at the same time face the uncomfortable fact that on intrinsic grounds it lacks an absolute moral standard in terms of which it can justly disavow the right of civil disobedience to those who deny the validity of the social order.[17]

It may of course be argued that men who reject democracy should leave the state, that if they stay, as Socrates stayed, they assume the obligation to obey its laws.[18] And we have, in point of fact, instances in our time in which the right of egress has been exercised — e.g., T. S.

Eliot, George Santayana, and Ezra Pound; even, perhaps, Alexander Berkman and Emma Goldman, who rejoiced when they arrived (albeit after an unintended and involuntary voyage) in Lenin's Russia. But apart from the practical objections that the state does not always grant the right of egress and that there may not be another state which embodies the "right" political system and social order — witness the tragic tale of Emma Goldman's disenchantment with Russia[19] — I fail to comprehend the moral character of this solution. I recognize that while on intrinsic grounds democracy affirms that each man's conscience is "right," it must set instrumental limits on this "right"; that, operationally speaking, the notion that each man is entitled to have any conscience he wants does not imply that he has a right to subordinate the laws to his conscience. Nevertheless, if democracy insists that all men are subject to the laws, it must also insist that all men are protected by the laws, that all men have an equal right (say) to life and liberty. A majority under this principle has no absolute moral justification to limit this right except where it has secured the consent of the governed — not, of course, in the sense that consent is given to each particular law, but in the sense that generalized consent or consensus is accorded the system under which that majority has come to power. This being so, what moral principle justifies a democracy in going outside the area of consent to deny the right of civil disobedience to a recalcitrant individual or minority? What principle other than force gives a democratic people the right to exclude those who reject democracy from that portion of the earth possessed by the democrats? Clearly, the argument asserts only that the bulk of the people regard a particular system as just, and that those who do not accept this valuation shall nonetheless be required to submit.[20] But if consent is acknowledged to be the ultimate source of authority, the appeal to force leaves unanswered (where it does not negate) the question of justice — whether that system is good or, indeed, best. This is not to deny that even the *best* system may depend on a measure of force to maintain itself; it is only to affirm that the resort to force, even when successful, cannot of itself establish that a system is best.

I return, therefore, to the position that where consent is withheld from the entire system of order itself, democracy's claim to obedience with respect to such dissidents rests on power, not on a universal morality. Consequently, democracy cannot insist, without denying its own framework of justice — the principle of consent — that such individuals or groups obey the law. In such cases it can only resort to the rule of expediency referred to above — namely, that of disallowing only that expression of the individual conscience which is incompatible with democracy's own ultimate values and institutional preservation.[21]

71

IV

Of those who accept democracy as the theoretically or practically best political order, yet contemplate disobedience to the law, two classes of citizens must, I think, be distinguished. One denies the intrinsic merit or rationality of the law itself; the other challenges as well the claim of the particular form of state enacting the law to be called a democracy.

For this latter group, democracy is good but the state is not democratic; hence with respect to the principle of political obligation their attitude toward the political order is not essentially different from that of those who accept the state as democratic but deny that democracy is good. They not only argue, with Aristotle,[22] that a government democratic in form may be oligarchical in fact; they insist further that a careful examination of the American political system discloses it to be formally insufficient as well. From their point of view, the American Senate (based on a quota system that does violence to the principle of popular representation), the Supreme Court (with its power of judicial review), the system of staggered elections (which not infrequently prevents a popular majority from becoming a legal or controlling majority), the involved apparatus that separates and checks powers so as to deadlock no less than to balance them, the amending clause (which puts the Constitution itself beyond the reach of normal majorities) — all these and more (e.g., suffrage restrictions, gerrymandering, and the like) are but devices to hinder and at times effectively to block the translation of public opinion into public policy. Even the sacred rules of the game may be changed by the group in power when those rules no longer operate to that group's advantage. This is amply evidenced by the history of the Supreme Court with respect, for example, to the Fourteenth Amendment.

Knowing these things (or feeling this way), a citizen confronted by what he conceives to be a morally reprehensible law (or an action under that law) has difficulty in accepting the argument that he should express his disapproval not through civil disobedience but through the regular legal and political channels available to him. In his view, it is simply not true that these legal and political channels *are* available to him, that is, available in the way that democracy ideally requires. Such a citizen might agree that all human contrivances are imperfect. He might admit, too, that it is great folly, if not fanaticism, to insist on the perfectibility of political institutions regardless of consequences. Nevertheless, if it is not simply to evoke his blind acquiescence, a democratic system must above all be democratic; it must embody to a major degree elements of that just political order which it purportedly represents. If it falls so far short of this ideal as to foreclose any real possibility of correcting legislative evils by (say) normal majorities, if the political mechanism obstructs public opinion by institutionalizing various forms of minority control, it is in fact not a democracy at all. It is a perverted form of democratic government and, as such, it is bound to rely on unjust laws.[23]

To the extent that there is substance in this view — in the sense that the indictment of institutional arrangements is sound — men committed to democracy are under no moral obligation to obey "undemocratic" laws. Those who place a different weight on the shortcomings of the system may deplore their judgment in this regard, but if the shortcomings are serious and real they cannot in democracy's name be asked to give absolute obedience to a less-than-democratic (and to this degree undemocratic) system. Like the good churchgoers of Concord who were taken ill when Thoreau asked them also to read the Bible, protagonists of the system might well be discomfited and silenced when confronted, for instance, by a Negro suffering political and educational discrimination in one of our states, or an interned Nisei, who to justify an act of civil disobedience asks but a single question: "Is this the content of democracy?"

V

We come, finally, to those democrats who accept the system as essentially democratic and who are prepared, on the whole, to obey the laws. They understand that government by consent means consent not to each particular law but to the entire system of order itself, and ultimately to the idea of justice which that system represents. For the sake of the greater good secured by that system through its government and its laws, they accept specific enactments which they otherwise disapprove. They obey not necessarily because they think that the law is right, but because they think it right to obey the law.[24]

For this reason they reject the individualistic ethics of a Protagoras, who would justify disobedience to the law provided you can get away with it, or of a Harold Laski or of a Thoreau, who would demand of each law that it provide "moral adequacy,"[25] or of other legal and political theorists who would measure the obligation of a citizen to the law in terms of the degree to which it serves some other end. If a man's loyalty is to the system, then obedience cannot be determined solely by immediate approbation. He cannot attempt to evaluate the law simply in terms of its expressed content;[26] nor can he separate laws from their cumulative total effect on the assumption that disobedience to a particular law leaves unaffected the system of law. Very few laws are accepted unanimously, and if the considerable number of citizens who dislike a law are literally free to disobey it, the state and the social order can hardly be expected

73

to survive. A plea for total disobedience, or for the right of total disobedience, logically entails not a state at all but anarchy.

Does it follow that the citizen who admits his obligation to obey
the laws must obey *all* laws *always?* Is one who rejects the extreme
individualism of a Laski compelled to accept the extreme absolutism
of a Hegel,[27] or the near-absolutism of a Hobbes[28] or of a John Dickinson,
who join with Socrates of the *Crito* in entering an affirmative answer?
If a law is disobeyed, they tell us, the social order will collapse. In their
view, each law is an integral part of a coherent, corporate body of law,
which in turn sustains society. Consequently, disobedience to a law is
a challenge to sovereignty itself. As Dickinson put it: "It is not a question of a bare conflict between the individual and the sovereign; the
conflict must be regarded as rather between the individual and all that
the sovereign stands for." In disobeying the sovereign we bring "domi-
nantly into the foreground the large issue of the desirability of preserving
public authority and civil society itself." In disobeying the sovereign we
strike at just this essential method of civil society.[29]

This is a plausible argument. It avoids the individualistic fallacy by
emphasizing the need for order and the role of law in maintaining that
order. But it is not without fallacies of its own. What holds society
together, for example, is not simply law (and perhaps not even law) but
the customs and moral codes, the sentiments, of the people. The classic
formulation of T. H. Green still applies: it is not the state that produces
cohesive will; it is will that creates and sustains the state.[30] Political
loyalties and political obligations do not exclude other loyalties and other
obligations, and it is the meaning of democracy that it does not seek to
command a monopoly of man's allegiances. Democracy seeks to root
its fundamental unity not in the power of the state but in the sense of
common interest that sustains but does not obliterate the vital differences
among men.[31] So long as these differences are admitted, with respect
not simply to things that do not matter much but to things that touch
the very heart of the existing order as well,[32] the democratic state can
find its essential solidarity not in the structure of law but in the minds
of men.

Nor does the absolutist position rest on solid ground when it assumes
that all laws form a coherent unity, so that disobedience to a particular
law necessarily involves the destruction of the entire system of law.
Evasion of the law is a normal concomitant of all legal systems, and it
is doubtful that the existence of jails constitutes sufficient proof of the
breakdown of the system. We are all familiar with the propensity of
people not in jails to disobey laws that inconvenience them — e.g., traffic
regulations, income tax laws, and prohibitions on gambling and on the

74

traffic in liquor and women. Police and other political officials do not enforce all laws equally and at times they conspire with people who seek to disobey them. Governments too evade or disobey the law — witness the oft-cited examples of Southern states that have largely ignored the Fourteenth and Fifteenth Amendments to the American Constitution; of the many Congresses that have failed to apply the constitutional provision (Sec. 2, Amend. XIV) requiring that the representation of such states in the House of Representatives be reduced; and of the refusal of the Congress in 1920 to carry out the required reapportionment of the House of Representatives. Despite these and other acts of disobedience, the system of law has not, I think, disappeared. Clearly, *some* laws are not essential to the maintenance of the social order.

If, therefore, the state is not equivalent to the whole of the social order, and if all laws are not integrated into a single coherent unity, disobedience to a particular law need not imply an attempt to overthrow the political system or the social order itself. To Dickinson's charge that the conflict is between the individual and all that the sovereign stands for, we must reply: the conflict is also between the sovereign and all that the individual stands for. It may even, in fact, be between the actual sovereign and all that the ideal sovereign stands for. In these two points, I believe, we can find a sufficient justification for *some* acts of civil disobedience.

Consider, first, what is involved when the state demands that an individual obey not his conscience but the law. In a general sense, it appears to ask only that he recognize the necessity of compromise if men are to live together. But when the issue is joined so that men question the justice of the terms on which they are asked to live together, the state requires far more: it demands nothing less than that he submit to a civil theology.[33] For if action contrary to conscience is immoral, the state by insisting that the individual follow not his conscience but a command of the state contrary to his conscience thereby insists that he act immorally. Since the state will not admit that its command is immoral, it must — if it is to vindicate its claim to obedience — argue that the judgment of the individual conscience is wrong, and that by acting instead according to the state's judgment of what is right the individual will realize his true morality, his true freedom. There are many who still take seriously this teaching of Rousseau, Hegel, and Bosanquet. Nevertheless, the notion that the state embodies our real will, our true morality, our true freedom, as against our actual will, which is said to represent a false morality, is incompatible with the democratic principle. For democracy, if I understand it correctly, stands above all else for a method whereby men can resolve peacefully which of competing moralities shall

75

temporarily prevail. It cannot — if it is to remain a democracy — maintain that it has discovered the true morality which shall henceforth bind all men. Yet when the government of a democratic state demands of a citizen that he surrender his conscience to the state — as it demanded of Jehovah's Witnesses that they (or their children) salute the flag — it in effect demands that he submit to the true morality. From this point of view, imprisonment for civil disobedience becomes, paradoxically, a prolonged appeal to the prisoner's conscience, detention being but a means of permitting his conscience time in which to adjust,[34] after the state has by putting him in prison already denied the validity of his conscience.

To escape this dilemma democracy must deny the theological sanction. It cannot assume what Eric Voegelin suggests the Oxford political philosophers have assumed: namely, that by the mystery of incarnation the principles of right political order have become historical flesh more perfectly in their country than anywhere else at any time.[35] It must recognize that the political order is not perfect and that the laws are not always just. It must affirm no more than that a law is law not because it is absolutely good or right but because a legal majority has decreed it. Democracy would, of course, insist that it is right for the majority to have this power, and that men should respect this right of the majority as a necessary condition of democracy. But if it is true that the majority may act wrongly — i.e., affront on intrinsic or instrumental grounds the notion of justice held by a dissenting individual or minority — such insistence leads to the paradoxical principle that while the system and the laws that institutionalize that system are just, particular laws emanating from the system may be wrong and therefore unjust. A just system may produce unjust laws.

Now the Aristotelian question — whether a good man can always be a good citizen — has traditionally formed the basis for the problem of political obligation. But if there is validity to the conception of citizenship that I have argued here, the mark of the good citizen — at least in a democracy — is not loyalty to the laws but loyalty to the system, to the principle of democracy itself. The good citizen is obligated not to the sovereign but to all that the sovereign stands for.[36] Consequently, law can command his allegiance not because it is law but because it serves something that is good, because it respects the system of democracy and the purposes for which the democratic state exists.[37] If he obeys simply because it is law, he worships means, not ends; and this is surely a perversion of purpose.

When, therefore, a government holding office and trust under that system so acts — whether directly through its laws or indirectly through non-legal sanctions and the cultivation of a climate of opinion characterized by suspicion and fear — as to deny or to threaten the integrity of the system itself, it creates a situation in which men loyal to democracy may be compelled to defend it against the laws.

It has been urged, not perhaps without reason, that such defense should look first to the democratic processes of persuasion and election.[38] But where it is precisely these processes that the laws attack, where the incursions of government are upon freedom of opinion and the elements of democratic procedure, this may well prove a vain hope. Men are not without warrant in saying today what men have all too often had to say before: the times are "out of joint." Once again, this is a moment when the ordinary rules of decency are to some men in power apparently unknown, when some men cloaked in the sanctity of the law seek to exorcise the spirit of free inquiry.[39] Under such circumstances, it may well be that obedience to democracy can best, and perhaps only, be served by disobedience to the laws. It may well be that men of moral sensitivity and courage will have to say, with Thoreau: "They are the lovers of law and order who observe the law when the government breaks it."[40]

VI

Whether laws prescribing affirmations of loyalty, or sustaining legislative inquiries into one's past or present beliefs and associations, or proscribing the expression of revolutionary ideas, are of this variety, each man must judge for himself. If he dislikes such laws but does not regard them to be a crucial violation of or threat to democracy, he will obey them. If, however, he views such measures as destructive of the very principles that constitute the system to which he has given his allegiance and which he is pledged to uphold, he may see no moral alternative to disobedience.[41] In the judgment of others, his conscience may be wrong; but if he is to retain his dignity as a man he must act upon it. He may fail by such action to impress the value of his idea on others, but in no other way can he hope to correct the tragic lesson of history which "shows that good causes are more often defeated by negligence in the pursuit of the right than by positive forces of evil."[42]

So long as a man comes to this decision honestly, in accord with moral principles to which he is firmly committed, and so long as his act of disobedience is calculated — taking the whole situation into view — to achieve a greater good than is likely to be achieved by his acquiescence, I cannot believe that he can be said to have denied his fundamental obligation either as a good man or as a good citizen.[43]

Chapter 8

Power, Law, and Freedom of Inquiry

I

Freedom of inquiry is not a guarantor of truth but a precondition to the discovery of truth. Hence, for some who think they know the truth it is useless; for others who fear the truth it is obnoxious. Since most men both "know" and fear some truth, freedom of inquiry dwells always in double jeopardy.

Even those who plead most eloquently for freedom of inquiry do not themselves always believe in it. Plato's *Republic* defends the very principle of censorship that his *Apology* condemns. The author of the *Areopagitica* would have looked askance at the aged and disillusioned Milton who lent his support to the Puritan reaction against the free spirit. The leaders of Protestant sects in Catholic countries, and of Catholics in Protestant countries, claimed the freedom to proclaim truth but were often intolerant of the freedom to enunciate error when their respective power roles were reversed. And, in like manner, there are men today who recite with pride and professions of allegiance the First and Fourteenth Amendments to the American Constitution, yet find no apparent difficulty in restraining free utterance on matters of sex, sin, or political inclination.

The logic of a principle is not, to be sure, to be confused with the misinterpretations of its confounders; but what emerges from this familiar record is a limited rather than an absolute tradition of freedom. Historically, men have generally meant by freedom those specific freedoms that secure and further their interests and moral values, and have sought power in order to institutionalize their particular conceptions. This power need not be political; control of economic, military, or cultural organizations is often an alternative or complementary way of achieving the same goal. But political power remains crucial and overriding, for control of the state alone carries with it control over all individuals and associations within the state. And while power in any field of social action enables its possessors to remove certain obstacles from the paths they wish to pursue and to impose obstacles in the paths of others, political power enables them to maximize these controls by identifying their private notions with the common good and by investing their personal prejudices with the sanction and sanctity of law. It thus makes it possible to interpret and legally to define one's own speech and activities as "freedom," and to condemn and even exclude disliked doctrines and behavior as "license."

Thus power, and especially political power, is the means whereby men can secure or delimit freedom, can seek to establish through law — perhaps the most powerful instrument of social control — the good life or their own particular version of the good life.[1] But since freedom is itself an ethical category rather than an objectively given criterion for moral judgments of political or legislative policy, what is ethically significant in freedom (and law) must be derived from prior ethical norms.[2] A power analysis would quickly make clear that in considerable measure those norms reflect the interests (and corresponding sense of justice) of the dominant power groups. Hence the hierarchy of freedoms — and the survival value of freedom of inquiry in particular — is determined less by abstract propositions of justice than by the maneuverings of power groups striving for mastery over the law.[3]

This dependence of freedom on the locus of power and the source of law has given rise to curiously antithetical views. In the absolutist tradition of Thomas Hobbes, freedom exists in the interstices or silence of the law; hence men are free largely as those in power ignore them. Law and freedom thus become inverse magnitudes. Since Hobbes was primarily concerned with the maintenance of order, he recognized almost no limitations on the right of the ruler to curtail freedom.[4] In the anarchist view, on the other hand, freedom, not power, is the absolute good; consequently the anarchist repudiates all attempts at organized coercion and holds, not that "that government is best which governs least," but that "that government is best which governs not at all." Both Hobbes and the anarchist have, each in his own way, a valid insight: men are not free when they are restrained by law. But Hobbes all too often forgets that restraints can be imposed by men other than those in control of the state, in which case law may be used to neutralize a restraint. And the anarchist, in repudiating all forms of organized coercion, not only assumes a natural harmony of interests to be secured through voluntary cooperation; he also forgets that even voluntary cooperation is itself a form of organized power, that men have dividing as well as common interests, and that to protect and promote those common interests recalcitrant members of society may, as Kropotkin for example admitted, have to be expelled. "Society" is still government, even if by another name. Thus both Hobbes and the anarchist overlook a central role of law in assuring some freedoms through the imposition of some restraints.

It therefore remains true that law, like power, is both a condition of and an interference with freedom. It neither frees nor enslaves all men, nor does it provide or deny all freedoms. The basic political and moral questions therefore remain : Who does, who should, enjoy the freedoms that power and law provide ? Which freedoms should law assure, and which should it limit or destroy ? My comments will deal only with freedom of inquiry as it is affected by the answers to these questions.

II

If we adopt Machiavelli's precept and look at what men do rather than at what they ought to do, we note at the outset the identification of freedom of inquiry with certain special causes. Men in power rarely urge the validity of free inquiry as an absolute principle. For them, considerations of power compel attention to the dangers as well as the uses of unrestricted speech and investigation. Primarily, these dangers concern possible challenges to the power groups themselves [5] — challenges which may seek, in their more moderate form, to alter the special status and privileges of the power groups without disturbing in any essential way the legal and economic foundations of the existing power system, or which, in more extreme form, may deny the very legitimacy of existing power. To protect their interests, and in times of stress perhaps the security of the state as well, men in power often seek to restrict freedom of inquiry to safe or "proper" areas of investigation, or to matters of technical detail rather than of principle. They are ever zealous to safeguard freedom of inquiry that leads to satisfying conclusions, which explains why there is seldom any penalty for the conservative. They are less willing to tolerate "license," which explains why radicals, and radical ideas, are always suspect and viewed as "legitimate" objects of persecution. Yet it has generally been the case that attempts at suppression have succeeded both in degrading the suppressor and in strengthening the suppressed by focusing greater attention on the latter's doctrines.[6]

For the opposite reason, men out of power but seeking it generally profess to seek freedom of inquiry for all. They need it, clearly, for themselves : to discover the nature and impact of existing evils and the proper remedies; to explore the depths and implications of their own program; to find avenues and methods whereby their own interests and values may be advanced. It is often true that such men, when in power, assume or insensibly acquire the qualities of their predecessors and attempt to curb those freedoms they deem distasteful. This situation would, and in systems of oligarchy does, tempt power groups to deny to men not in power a basic freedom — the freedom to oust them from office. But in democracy the capacity to resist such temptation is reinforced by law, which imposes a restraining influence over rulers who might otherwise agree, with Oscar Wilde, that man can resist everything but temptation.

It appears, then, that law is not merely the instrument of groups in power, the means whereby they can maintain, enlarge, or suppress the areas of freedom. It is also the means whereby groups out of power can in some measure restrain the holders of power. For law in the minds of men is more than the expression of power; it is sanctioned or legitimate power. It carries the imputation that the power thus exercised is acceptable and morally right. Even those who would challenge this identification of law and right — and I am one of them — must recognize the symbolic value of law, a value that exacts devotion and obedience for no reason other than that it is *law*. And it is this symbolic value that helps to restrain men when in power from acting contrary to the patterns set by preexisting law. Men who come to power can rarely mold a new state, and never from out of a vacuum. Always they find themselves part of a going concern, with laws and procedures strongly entrenched and difficult to change. They become in some measure prisoners of the legal system they are called upon to enforce, and, to the degree that this is the case, men out of power find themselves protected from the ambitions and encroachments of their rulers.

This role of law (impossible, to be sure, without the underlying and sustaining force of opinion or custom) emerges then out of the power conflicts of men. Both groups — those in and those out of power — would, all too often, willingly suppress the freedoms of the other; and it is the special attribute of oligarchy that it permits them to do so within the framework of that system. But if men are to live in a democracy, then certain freedoms must be respected by all, or nearly all, power groups in the community. In a democracy the groups out of power are constitutionally guaranteed a chance to achieve power. This involves the protection of certain freedoms. Primary among them is the freedom to organize in opposition to the government and to the policies pursued by that government, which requires in turn freedom of inquiry and expression. Power groups agree to abide by these freedoms not because they like them but because these freedoms are necessary if power groups, when in the minority, are to avoid extermination. This arrangement is in one sense nothing more than a pragmatic alternative to revolution by violence; it is, indeed, a legal device that institutionalizes revolution by continuing consent.

In terms of the politics or sociology of power, therefore, we are brought to this: *Men seek power to secure the freedoms that promote their interests.* When in power they use law to obtain and maximize those freedoms and to deny or minimize freedoms that would permit other men to interfere with their pursuits. When out of power they seek it for much the same reasons, but not being in power they also plead for law to protect the freedoms that would enable them to get into power. Thus all groups, through the recognition perhaps that none of them alone or in concert can permanently command a majority and thus control the state, agree on a method that will permit them to win power for limited periods without recourse to violence. Crucial to this method, which we call democracy, is the freedom of inquiry and expression.

III

But practice does not always join hands with demonstrable standards of valid conduct. And unless we are prepared to accept the conventional view of morality — that what is law is just — we are still bedeviled by the question of why men *ought* to establish and maintain freedom of inquiry.

A legal approach to this problem cannot carry us very far. True, it would reveal the long and venerable list of great documents, such as the Magna Carta and the American Bill of Rights, that constitute a vital and noble tradition of freedom. But it would also reveal important documents that comprise an opposing and no less forceful tradition. Most patently, however, the legal approach fails to carry conviction because it is irrational: it argues in a circular vein that the justification of law which protects freedom of inquiry is previous law, but it does not justify the previous law.

The immense vitality of the natural-rights approach suggests that there is an element of truth in the insistence on the inherent dignity of man. But save for the views of a nihilist philosopher like Sergei Netschaiev, man's dignity has never been taken to mean that he is possessed of absolute freedom, that he is subject to no social controls. And if his natural rights are to be limited, we must search further for a criterion sufficient to justify a particular scheme of freedoms and restraints. Natural law is not such a criterion. Its precepts do not, somehow, teach the same things to all men. For those who affirm that rights are social rather than natural, the appeal to natural law carries even less conviction.

Some men have been led to entertain doctrines in which certain values and concomitant freedoms are held to be absolutely "right" or "good"; consequently, those laws are just which effectuate those right values and freedoms. These doctrines are variously "known" to be true: by divine instruction, as in the communications of God to Luther and Calvin; by intuition, as in the perceptions of a Kant or a Bishop Butler; by rational demonstration within a framework of accepted premises, as in the contemporary writings of a Jacques Maritain; and the like.

But if one remains unpersuaded of such truths, laws which seek to embody them still require vindication.

Another approach attempts to vindicate freedom of inquiry in terms of its practical consequences. From a psychological standpoint, for example, the denial of free inquiry cuts out the roots of individual initiative and prevents men from verbalizing and thereby in some measure alleviating their resentments. Economically and militarily, persecution deprives a state of useful citizens who, as John Locke might have remarked with amazing prescience of refugees in our own time, bring to the states which grant them refuge their knowledge, skills, and loyalty. In terms of the merits of the case, if we assume — with Milton and a long line of distinguished thinkers — that truth will prevail over falsehood when all positions are subject to free examination, then censorship is wasteful at best and harmful at worst. Wasteful because a censorship that silences error does what would in any case eventually be done; harmful because, since it is not based on unhampered inquiry, it may silence truth itself and prevent fruitful speculation that might otherwise take place. On moral grounds, if the purpose of the state is the promotion of the good life, which involves in large degree the satisfaction of men's wants, the denial of free inquiry becomes by its very nature the denial of a central need. It also prevents a government from knowing what men want and thus conduces to their misery rather than to their happiness.

Politically viewed, orthodoxy is dangerous. Persecution neither disproves the validity of anathematized ideas nor prevents men from communicating them; it succeeds only in driving them underground and in fostering conspiracy and rebellion. Men who have no peaceful channel through which to explore and express "dangerous" ideas tend to abandon moderation both in thought and in deed. From the standpoint of a civilized world, finally, the suppression of free inquiry is evil because it seeks to produce a uniformity that is not only unattainable but undesirable; for it is the differences rather than the similarities among men that give zest and interest to life. Friction is still the first condition of change; diversity is still the first hope of progress. For these reasons and others, an approach which concerns itself with practical consequences would justify and seek legal protection of the principle of free inquiry.[7]

There are, however, despite its truths, important deficiencies in a standard that looks exclusively to practical consequences. In the first place, not all men are agreed on the meaning of particular consequences even when they are agreed on the consequences themselves. It is, for example, no sufficient defense of free inquiry to say that its denial results in the loss of serious criticism unless we are agreed on the further proposition that the loss of such criticism is bad. In the second place, if we reflect on, rather than customarily repeat, the claim that suppression neither destroys radical thought (whether true or false) nor produces conservative convictions, we note that it is valid only if certain qualifications — even apart from the Orwell thesis — are entered. One such qualification concerns the difference in its applicability with respect to short-term as against long-time objectives. Governments that are concerned only with immediate success may find intolerance expedient and even effective. Another is that governments that suppress freedom of inquiry and expression are generally interested less in what men think than in what they say. Coercion may not make a man believe a certain doctrine is right, but it can prevent him from speaking against it; and if enough voices are suppressed there is a greater chance for orthodox spokesmen to win. This suggests that a "pragmatic" case might be made for the denial of free inquiry.

Each of the foregoing attempts at a resolution of our problem suffers from a common weakness : it assumes that certain values are good or right and argues therefrom that laws which institutionalize that "good" are just. But if we take the view that men do not know, or at least are not agreed upon, a particular scheme of values and related freedoms as "absolutely" good, then we must seek to establish not a particular claim but a rational method of resolving conflicts between competing claims, a method that may at different times enable different values and freedoms to prevail. Such a solution would be constant in method, tentative or experimental in ends. It would affirm that the process is right, but it would assert nothing concerning the rightness or wrongness, goodness or badness, of the ends of the group which emerged out of that process to power. But this emphasis on method or process — which is of course the very essence of the democratic principle, and which in turn compels acceptance of the principle of free inquiry — itself requires vindication, both on intrinsic and on instrumental grounds. For a method is not only a means to a certain end; it is always a partial realization of that end itself, what John Dewey would call an end-in-view. It is, so to say, both a value and a means to the attainment of other values.

Now if we accept democracy as the framework of our discussion, there are certain values of the democratic tradition in terms of which the values of free inquiry can be vindicated.[8] Thus, to say of freedom of inquiry that it is intrinsically good is to affirm that as a method it is better than any other method, that it is indeed the only right or just method, and that other methods — such as the appeal to force or the invocation of authority or the gratification of desire — are less valuable and even unjust. Corollary to and inherent in such affirmations are certain positive values : the dignity and importance of the individual; the recognition that each man's experience provides an important contribution to the common search for the good life; the appeal to reason, to the Socratic method, as the embodiment of that individual dignity and social importance; the conviction that men become better men through participation in this process of shared experiences and shared values. That these values are denied by systems which repudiate the principle of free inquiry can readily be demonstrated. The burning of Servetus at the stake for believing, contrary to Calvin, that Jesus was the "Son of the eternal God" rather than the "eternal Son of God," is, perhaps, a sufficient instance in point. From this standpoint, indeed, it can be argued that since men are not likely to agree on ultimate values, they might at least learn not to slaughter one another in advocacy or defense of their respective values. This end is what democracy, ideally speaking, seeks to achieve.

To defend within the democratic framework the method of free inquiry on instrumental grounds is to argue that a just system is one which seeks and assures diversity rather than uniformity of ends, that since no one system of values receives universal assent as being absolutely good or right it ought not to be given the power to impose itself permanently on all men, that men should therefore be left free to discover and pursue those goals or values which seem to them worthwhile. This is not to deny the right of the dominant power groups in democracy to write into law their own scheme of values and to seek thereby to establish those values as the prevailing pattern. That, after all, is one of the objectives of power; and it is proper that when a majority has consented to the policies of a particular group or coalition of groups the government representing these groups shall attempt to demonstrate to the community that those values and policies are right by requiring the community to live under them for a limited time. But if men are to be free to disagree with values and policies and to seek to persuade other men to alter them, the freedom to examine and critically to discuss policies must be perpetually guaranteed. Without that freedom, alternative values and policies cannot be intelligently constructed or organized oppositions formed. In this sense, freedom of inquiry is simply a species of a larger genus of civil rights crucial to a democratic system. As such, its denial in any sphere would be as destructive to democracy as would be the denial of freedom of expression or assembly.

The instrumental value of the principle of free inquiry, therefore, emerges from its necessary place in the structure and processes of democracy. It permits the discovery and expression of opposing value systems; it provides a permanent or constant method that enables a particular value system temporarily to prevail; it provides a way of correcting errors in the constructs of that value system as these are revealed in operation; and it leaves men free to believe and peacefully to disseminate their own versions of the right, the good, and the just. In this way, the democratic state binds rather than alienates the loyalty of free men; for that loyalty is to the process, not the result; to the value of the means, not the value of the legislative policies that constitute a tentative or experimental end.

IV

All that has been said to this point is applicable with equal validity to educational or academic freedom, by which I mean the freedom of the educator *and the student* to learn as well as the freedom of the educator to teach. This statement implies that schools are or ought to be centers of independent thought, even of intellectual leadership, and not servants of the power system. The problem of academic freedom emerges from the attempts by men in power to reverse this primary principle and to use the schools to indoctrinate students with the belief that the values and behavior patterns of the dominant group are alone right and just. On the negative side, they expect the schools to denounce as wrong and to exclude as immoral doctrines and practices they regard as loathsome and perhaps "subversive."

Now if the schools are to be servants of the power system, the function of law is plain: it is to make certain that the schools teach what those in power want them to teach. This restriction implies control by the power groups of all elements in the realm of ideas — of faculty, curriculum, books, speakers, and the like. It implies that the power group's view of truth and right becomes, if the power group remains dominant long enough, the conventional and therefore "just" view. But it also implies the denial of democracy; for democracy means nothing if not a system in which the free play of conflicting opinions is constitutionally guaranteed. The incompatibility of such controls with democracy becomes apparent as soon as we reflect on the results of the replacement of one power group by another; for when a power group is ousted, the new power group has an equal legal right to see that its version of truth and morality is taught in the schools. This reversal could mean, curiously, that each generation of students would be inculcated with different "official" versions of right and wrong, good and bad; more absurdly, since power groups in democracy generally circulate more quickly, the same generation of students would be told that what was once taught as right is now wrong, only to be right again when the first group returns to power.[9]

This process, whatever else it may be called, is not education. It substitutes the imposition of dogma for learning. It forecloses the avenues and processes of investigation and transforms both teachers and students into parrots. It denies not only the idea of the school as a center of free inquiry but the very idea of education itself, which is to help men learn to think for themselves.[10]

The proper role of law with respect to the schools is, therefore, the protection of intellectual freedom. Such freedom does not necessarily mean the emergence of ideas antagonistic to the values and interests of the power groups; the strange truth is that teachers, whether at the university or elementary-school level, are, all too often, timid and conservative. But it does mean that ideas shall be exposed to examination, that the validity of prevailing doctrines and institutions shall be subjected to the test of reason. Admittedly, this is dangerous procedure; for while there is no assurance that men, freely pursuing their diverse ways to knowledge, will decide that what is, is wrong, there is equally no assurance that they will proclaim it right. And the fear of inconvenient judgments has always motivated men whose cause is weak to attempt suppression.

It is often urged that power groups are justified in using law to restrain academic freedom at school levels below the college or university. At this stage, it is held, immature and impressionable students are easily persuaded of the validity of false and evil doctrine. This, clearly, is the path power groups have almost always taken; and it explains not only the careful scrutiny of textbooks but the great success of power systems in producing students with correct or "right" ideas. Since the overwhelming number of students never reach the college level, their "education" rarely leads them to question the values — economic, political, religious, etc. — of the dominant power groups.

One may, of course, concede the immaturity of children without concluding that the power group is alone competent to protect them from untruths. After all, educators have long known that a central task of the school is to free the minds of children from the shibboleths and falsehoods implanted there by others. But in America, I sadly submit, free inquiry at the elementary and high-school levels is in many essentials lost. State legislatures and non-faculty boards of education have employed their power legally to constrain the free expression and exploration of ideas.

Thus far the colleges and universities have not all completely succumbed. Since universities have until recent times attracted only a minute proportion of the population — many of whom came not to be educated but to fulfill necessary requirements for admission to professional schools, or to acquire a vocational skill, or to obtain a degree which would ensure added status or prestige — the consequences of free inquiry, though often disturbing, have not been so irritating as to cause power groups to insist on maximum controls. But in this age of anxiety, when men in power see their values and the very assumptions of their power system questioned, they look ever more suspiciously at the principle of

87

free inquiry. They tend to be less tolerant of educators who persist in examining sacred doctrine. They seek through non-disloyalty disclaimers and other means to constrain the processes of thought.[11] But they forget that if free inquiry is a way of discovering truth it is also a way of discovering error, and that to curb free inquiry is to proclaim heretical not error but a method of discovering error.

The educator to be true to his responsibility must be free to inquire. He may be compelled in the pursuit of his work to ask inconvenient and perhaps embarrassing questions. He may have to read and to ask his students to read radical and even "subversive" literature. For his responsibility as an educator is not to the men in power but to the great heritage of learning which constitutes culture, and which it is his professional obligation to preserve and to enrich. This indeed is the essence of his calling, and the educator who surrenders his responsibility in order to serve the interests of men in power has forfeited his only claim to be an educator.

Law, therefore, in its pursuit of the good life should protect the freedom that responsible educators must have. But it is a tragic fact that law is increasingly used by men in power to deny that freedom and to render difficult and sometimes impossible the fulfillment of that responsibility. This may, if unchecked, lead us into a dark age of intellectual sterility, where power and partisanship will replace freedom and morality as the criteria of justice and the good life.

Chapter 9

The Politics of Segregation

Politics, as everyone knows, is the art of drawing distinctions. It involves, to be sure, the pursuit and use — as well as the misuse — of power; but we seek that power for the potential good, not the evil, that its possession affords. We do not, therefore, legislate on all things. Nor do we seek always to control the same things, irrespective of place and circumstance. Nor, again, do we endeavor to act blindly even in pursuit of the "right" things at the right time. As rational men, we try to employ our power wisely; we distinguish, we *discriminate*, between its beneficent and baneful applications.

So much can be said for any sensible theory of just or limited political power; and it is often said impressively. But the articulation of such general principles is the beginning, not the end, of political wisdom. For in this form, the principles are no more than guides to action; they tell us little or nothing of the substantive merits of any particular issue. It is the virtue of Hannah Arendt's reflections on segregation that they seek both to enunciate "right" general principles and to apply those principles in a "right" resolution of the most pressing and important domestic issue of our time. In these respects her argument moves on a level of discourse that raises significant theoretical as well as factual issues. Unfortunately, however, her notion of what constitutes a valid political principle, along with her recommended course of action, testifies more to her sense of misguided courage than it does to her power of insight.

I

Consider, first, what I understand to be her central principle: that a meaningful distinction must be drawn and maintained between the political, the social, and the private life; and that it is not the business of political power to invade the non-political — i.e., the social and the private — realms of being. This, of course, is closely akin to the argument of John Stuart Mill in his celebrated essay, *On Liberty*. There Mill sought to defend the claims of individual liberty by drawing a line between self-regarding and other-regarding acts, between those things, that is to say, which affect only the individual and those things which affect society. With respect to self-regarding acts, Mill argued, society is properly unconcerned; neither the state nor voluntary associations have a right to intervene in what are purely private affairs.

But this distinction, so plausible and appealing on its face, collapses as soon as we attempt to specify those acts which affect *only* the individual. Clearly there are none. Even education and marriage, which Miss Arendt offers as illustrations of such self-regarding acts, prove on the most cursory examination to be issues of social concern.. Societies have always established rules and imposed sanctions to govern sexual conduct and the promulgation and dissolution of marriages; and it would be curious, indeed, were Miss Arendt to argue (as I believe the logic of her position would require her to argue) that incest and the sexual relationship described in Vladimir Nabokov's *Lolita,* for example, are purely private matters. No doubt she could show that incest, at least, was not denied to the immediate descendants of Adam and Eve, or to Lot and his daughters; but I doubt that such an appeal to Scripture would carry much conviction. So, too, for education. Surely Miss Arendt cannot deny that education is the most social, as it is the most socializing, of human activities. And if she admits that the community has a legitimate stake in the intellectual development of its citizens, on what ground can she maintain that the give-and-take among students, the exchange of ideas and attitudes and interests that is central to such associations, is not relevant to this concern ? Even Mill, who would not have the state assume the primary or exclusive obligation to *provide* a good education for its children, insisted that it is the obligation of the state to *require* that a good education be provided for every child.

It is clearly impossible to build a fence that can rationally divide human behavior into two compartments — one labeled social, the other individual. For human acts are not separable on such terms; always they belong to, because they directly or indirectly affect, *both* the individual and society It is, in fact, not the action but the situation in which the action takes place that gives an act its true meaning. A man who is drunk at home presents an altogether different problem from a man who is drunk while driving an automobile or while (as Mill suggests) on sentry duty. Not the act of drunkenness, then, but the situation in which that drunkenness occurs, is crucial. If this is so, liberty cannot be taken by itself and defended on the naïve ground that certain parts of a man's life do not affect, and are therefore properly outside the control of, society. We can argue for liberty only on the ground that certain liberties are essential to the well-being of society. Liberty is always social; and often, too, a particular liberty (e.g., my liberty to join a labor union) is in conflict with another (e.g., my employer's liberty to dismiss me from my job for having exercised that freedom). The problem of freedom, then, requires at the outset a reduction of liberty to a system of specific liberties and restraints, the latter entering to restrict those liberties which might otherwise impair the existence or free functioning of the liberties that are prized. Things are left free not because they don't affect society, but because society deems it socially advantageous for men in certain circumstances to be unrestrained.

Miss Arendt's attempt to proliferate Mill's artificial and false division by providing for three spheres of action seems to me only to compound Mill's difficulty. It is relatively easy, to be sure, to distinguish the state as a political association from voluntary groups that are non-governmental in character. It is also easy to derive as a corollary from this distinction certain liberties which the state must respect if such voluntary associations are to survive — e.g., the liberties of speech and of political association requisite to the existence of political parties, or the liberty of religious worship necessary to the life of churches and synagogues. But all such associations, and all such liberties, are social. There is no such thing as society constituting a "somewhat hybrid realm between the political and the private." The political and the private are not distinct and separate entities; nor do they exist apart from society; they are intrinsically and inextricably a part of society. Society is the web of all human relationships; the political and the private are at most distinguishable, but not separable, strands within the greater fabric.

Unless, then, we are to appeal to a standard external to society itself — to God or to nature, for example (and Miss Arendt makes it clear that she does not mean to make such an appeal; despite her repeated references to "human rights," her appeal is to the Constitution, which is a socially established standard) — the applications of political power can only be socially determined. And what, in such terms, a democratic society giveth, such a society can (so long as it respects its own democratic principles) take away.

II

Scarcely less crucial to Miss Arendt's argument is her quite superficial notion of federalism, from which she derives her peculiar defense of states' rights. Miss Arendt contends, in terms that would gladden the heart of a John C. Calhoun, that federalism is a principle designed to divide rather than to unite peoples. This, of course, is partly true; for the genius of a federal system is that it brings together people who seek also in some respects to retain their differences. But federalism is also a principle that strives to unite people; it creates before everything else a state that is *national* rather than parochial in character, that represents the common rather than the dividing interests of its citizens; and what is common to them all, what constitutes their bond of unity, is the complex of values that is spelled out in the Constitution. It is these values that articulate the *meaning* of the federation; and among these values, in the American scheme of things, is the principle of equality no less than that of liberty. What is at issue, then, is not whether there shall be a federal or a unitary state — not whether an allegedly covetous (even imperialistic) nationalism shall destroy the virginal independence of our suddenly prim and scrupulous states — but whether we can resolve peacefully and rapidly a conflict of values within the idea of American federalism itself. We must choose between equality, a key value of the federation, and liberty, specifically the liberty to deny some citizens equality of educational opportunity.

Miss Arendt's reverent invocation of the South's ever-convenient communal ghost, states' rights, is in these terms an evasion of the issue. Her argument might, perhaps, have some relevance if she could show that our federal system rests on a fairly clear-cut division between two sets of geographical interests — one embodied in the national community and its government, the other represented by the constituent state or states and their respective communities. Then a conflict between them would pit two homogeneous groups against each other, with the triumph of the larger group quite possibly constituting that tyranny of the majority which the framers of the Constitution, and later Calhoun, so greatly feared and sought to forestall. But in the present situation the lines of division are altogether different. Both groups — national and state — are internally divided, and peculiarly so. For the majority within the national community is, on the issue of desegregation at least, united with minorities within the constituent communities; while the majority within the constituent states finds adherents only among a national minority. Thus, the conflict is not properly represented as one of nation versus states, and the issue is not that of preventing a tyranny of the majority. The conflict is rather one between national majority and national minority, *and* between local majority and local minority, but in that odd concatenation of forces which unites the majority in one place with the minority in another. In such circumstances, for the national majority to abstain from coercing the national minority is to permit the latter, in the form of a local majority, to coerce a local minority. For the national majority to coerce the national minority is to prevent a local majority from coercing a local minority. In both cases the rule of a majority is involved; it is only a question of which majority is to prevail. In both cases the tyranny of the majority is seemingly involved; but whether the dominant majority is actually tyrannical or not turns on whether it acts in accord with the principles of the Constitution or contrary to them. And on this question, whether we recognize the binding force of judicial interpretation or look to the logic of the democratic principle itself, the national majority is clearly in the right.

If we are not, then, to sacrifice a real social and constitutional interest to a fictional geographic interest, we must ignore the nonsense that is generally written and spoken in defense of states' rights. (It is interesting to note, parenthetically, that those who are most ardent in defense of states' rights rarely exhibit a similar tenderness toward local and individual rights; for while the leaders of the Southern states do not want the national government to interfere in their activities, they do not themselves hesitate to interfere in the activities of local communities. It was, after all, not the community of Little Rock but the state government, primarily in the person of Governor Faubus, which sought, initially at least, to oppose desegregation in the public schools. And it is primarily the leaders of the state governments — e.g., Governor Almond and Senator Byrd of Virginia, Governor Griffin and Senator Russell of Georgia — who are most vociferous in opposing such desegregation, even where their view on this matter runs counter to the wishes of a significant, if not a major, portion of the white citizens of localities within their states.)

III

We return, accordingly, to the real issue in the struggle before us: the choice between two constitutional values — liberty and equality. And here, once again, we are plagued at the outset by Miss Arendt's perverse use of both these terms. When she talks of equality, she talks primarily of equality of condition, and hardly at all of equality of educational opportunity. But these are clearly different; and by reversing the order of things, indeed, by dragging in the idea of equality of condition at all, Miss Arendt distorts and obfuscates the issue. No one, after all, seriously contends that what is pursued is absolute equality in all things — in talent, in wealth, in status, in power. In all societies differences, and hence inequalities, of some kind must always exist. What is sought is a rational basis for such differences. What is sought is that measure of equality of opportunity that will allow men, by starting the race on equal terms, to discover and to display their true worth. In the democratic tradition, men are afforded an equal opportunity in order that they may show in what respects they are truly unequal. Anything less than this is an argument for artificial, and therefore false, inequality. To invoke Tocqueville and other gods in support of her diatribe against absolute equality (i.e., equality of condition) is to misrepresent the issue at stake.

Miss Arendt also misrepresents what is involved in the immediate situation. No one argues that the democratic state (national or constituent) should compel its white citizens to treat its Negro citizens equally in all relationships at all times — to dine and dance and intermarry with them, for example — any more than it should compel any group of white citizens to treat other groups of white citizens in that way. The argument is that *the state should not itself treat white and Negro citizens unequally;* and, it must be added, that the state should not use its coercive powers to punish those of its white citizens who voluntarily wish to treat their Negro fellow-citizens equally. The argument is for the state, insofar as it distributes its own services, to be a neutral rather than a partisan power, to treat both sides fairly — i.e., equally — and not itself to be a discriminatory agent. The argument, further, is that where access to *public* facilities is concerned, the state should not abet that part of its citizenry which seeks to limit or to deny such access to others. The argument, finally, is that the state should not penalize those of its citizens who prefer — in what Miss Arendt would call the private and social realms — to deal with other citizens in a non-discriminatory way.

From this standpoint, desegregation in the public schools and in other public facilities does no more than remove the state as a discriminatory power. It does not compel parents (white or Negro) to send their children to schools where they will be required to associate with children they (or their parents) do not like. It does not, as Miss Arendt thinks, enforce integration. Parents are still free to send their children to private schools, whether denominational or military or otherwise. Parents are still free to discriminate as well in other ways. What desegregation requires is that *the state* shall not discriminate; that the state shall not prevent white and Negro students from associating with one another; that the state shall not compel white and Negro parents to send their children only to segregated schools. The Fourteenth Amendment to the Constitution provides that no state shall "deny to any person within its jurisdiction the equal protection of the laws." Is this provision observed when a state makes it a crime for Negroes and whites to sit together in public conveyances, or to play together in public playgrounds, or to attend even private schools together, *when those Negroes and whites themselves want to do so?* Is it observed when a state makes it a crime for local school boards, in line with community sentiment, to operate their schools on a desegregated basis ? Is the law neutral when it thus forestalls local or private action that seeks *not* to discriminate? (It is surely an odd notion of freedom, not to speak of human values, that Miss Arendt entertains when she argues in effect that the freedom to discriminate is more important than the freedom not to discriminate.) Is the law neutral when it places a double burden on those who seek desegregation, in that it forces such people both to win community support and to bring about a change in the law itself, whereas those who argue for continued segregation can pose as

94

patriotic supporters of the law and have law both as physical coercion and as moral sanction on their side ?

To answer these questions in the only way that democratic theory and constitutional principle permit, is to make clear that what desegregation requires is not the abolition of social discrimination but the abolition of legal enforcement of social discrimination, of discrimination by law. And this, I venture to suggest, is to ask no more than what Miss Arendt herself demands —the application rather than the abrogation of the Constitution. Surely Miss Arendt does not mean to plead for the continued punishment in the South of those Negroes who ask not that the Constitution be overthrown but that it should be enforced.

A word must be added on Miss Arendt's specious idea of freedom. In the literal or Hobbesian — and I would add proper — sense, liberty is the absence of chains, the absence of restraints on those things that a man wants, is able and has the means at hand, to do. But liberty so conceived is precisely what no society can tolerate; for it is the very meaning of social order that liberties shall be constrained in the service of other values — whether these be particular liberties that might otherwise be suppressed or the maintenance of order itself. No society permits its citizens the freedoms to steal, to maim, or to destroy other men through slander or physical violence. Hence, no man or group can claim an absolute freedom to do whatever he or it wants to do. And in the present situation, no democratic society can give legal sanction to those liberties which, if unrestrained, would enable some men (our white Southern citizens) effectively to suppress the constitutional liberties and rights of other (Negro) citizens.

Liberty, that is to say, is not to be regarded as a given and permanent whole out of which, with each utterance, the law extracts a vital piece. Liberty is a complex and ever-changing system of liberties and restraints, in which law by restraining some men who would restrain others, guarantees to those others the enjoyment of certain prized freedoms. Law is often, in one sense perhaps always, a restraint. But it is a shallow view of law which neglects to add that law is often a restraint on a restraint. And it is on this latter function of the law that the issue of desegregation turns, complicated, alas, by the fact that two sets of laws are here involved. In the silence of the national law, the constituent state is free to enact laws that restrain Negroes from enjoying their constitutional rights and liberties, and that restrain even private citizens from *not* discriminating against them. And where this is actually done, as it is done in our Southern states today, national laws are required if some among our citizens are not to be thus arbitrarily and unconstitutionally deprived of their democratic rights and liberties.

Miss Arendt's contempt for something she calls "the mob," her solicitude for "natural inequality," her concern for the values of diversity, lead her (incredibly) to advance an argument that sanctions the liberty to deny constitutional liberties, the liberty of whites to deny constitutional liberties to Negroes. But it is a strange conception of the mob that identifies it in the North with the protection of democratic rights, and in the South with the suppression of those rights. It is a strange plea for natural inequality that ignores the realities of human existence in the South, realities that make it impossible to judge whether the inequalities that actually exist are the result of natural differences or of artificial privileges. Indeed, the fact that artificial privileges are so grimly maintained lends force to the suspicion that those who maintain them do so out of fear; for to remove those artificial barriers might well demonstrate that men who are now at the top are there because of those artificial barriers and not for reasons of intrinsic superiority. And it is a most strange concern for diversity that leads, in effect, to a position that defends the continuation of a near caste-like system, one that institutionalizes differences between races but precludes or renders extraordinarily difficult the possibility of differences across races.

What Miss Arendt seems to miss here is that equality of opportunity, far from assuring equality of condition, is the indispensable principle for eliciting true inequality of condition. It may be true, as she contends, that the greater the degree of equality, the greater the resentment of difference. But if this is true at all (which I doubt), it can only be so in that non-existent world where democratic equality is defined as absolute equality of condition. However, this is precisely the sense in which Americans (and democrats generally) have always refused to define it. Where equality is properly viewed as equality of citizenship and of opportunity, and where the liberties necessary to such equalities — e.g., liberties of speech and of political association — are assured, difference is respected rather than denied. Miss Arendt might well consider in this connection the somewhat ridiculous spectacle of a Frank Lloyd Wright who berates "the mob" for its alleged innate inability to recognize and respect distinction at the very moment that it honors him and his achievements.

IV

Of Miss Arendt's other points, two — her insistence that racial problems are not restricted to the states of the American South and her indictment of Southern parents who force their children onto a battleground created and maintained but not always manned by the adults — are too obvious, and obviously correct, to require more than repetition here. But a third point merits some attention. This is her view that Southern laws against miscegenation and not laws denying equal access to schools and other public facilities are the first order of business.

I would agree without cavil that laws prohibiting the intermarriage of peoples of different racial stocks are evil, and outrageously so. I do not know by what standard one can say that such laws constitute a greater or a lesser evil than many other laws which humiliate and debase people on the pretense that they are intrinsically inferior beings. But suppose we grant, for the sake of her argument, that in the hierarchy of human values anti-miscegenation laws are of primary, and segregation laws are of secondary, importance. What is the *political* relevance of this ranking of issues ?

I believe the answer is, none. For one thing, it is no vindication of an evil to say that it is not as great as another. For another, in the political as distinct from the philosophical arena, it is the wiser act of statesmanship to address oneself to the realm of the possible. And surely what is today possible, and what is today sought *first* by those who are oppressed, is not the right to be accepted as a brother-in-law but as a brother.

Miss Arendt dismisses this desire by cavalierly observing that "oppressed minorities were never the best judges on the order of priorities in such matters." She insists that "the order of priorities in the question of rights is to be determined by the Constitution, and not by public opinion or by majorities." Now, as one who has had occasionally to read the Constitution, I am not aware of any provision in that document concerning marriage, and certainly none that proclaims as a paramount right the freedom to marry whom one pleases. If, then, there is an order of priority in rights, it must come from a source other than the Constitution, in this case from Miss Arendt herself. Then if we concern ourselves, as I think we must, with the order of *political* priorities, the issue is between the judgment of public opinion or of majorities (in this case of the Negro people) and that of Miss Arendt.

Now, I think it is not unfair to say that Miss Arendt is convinced that she knows better than the Negro people what is good for them. In this as in her other writings, Miss Arendt has always sought to dissociate herself from the masses of the people. She is an aristocrat, not a democrat, at heart. She is also, as she admits, an outsider, in the sense that as a European she finds herself unable even *to understand* "the common prejudices of Americans in this area." Nevertheless, she does not question the superiority of her own practical judgment to the judgment of those who are themselves involved. Nor does she pause to reflect that her acknowledged inability to understand may have the effect of misleading her terribly here.

For politics, once again, is the art of drawing distinctions. And in the attempt to resolve political (including racial) conflicts, we must carefully distinguish what it is possible to obtain *now,* and what sources of public support we can marshal. To fight *now,* as a matter of first principle, for the repeal of anti-miscegenation laws is, I believe, to give strength to the very contention that is most frequently, and by all accounts most tellingly, employed by those who resist the repeal of segregation laws — namely, the contention that this is but a device to promote sexual intercourse among the races. White men even in the North who agree to work together with Negroes in factories and in offices still resist attempts by the latter to move into white residential neighborhoods; and if we are to bring Southern white citizens to accept what they regard as a more far-reaching personal association growing out of desegregation in the public schools, it will be, in part, because they accept the argument that intimate sexual relations between the races are no necessary consequence of this. There is, consequently, no surer way to prevent acceptance of the principle of equal educational opportunity for the Negro in the South than to push the issue of miscegenation into the forefront at this time.

The Negroes, if not Miss Arendt, know this. Quite properly, therefore, they concentrate on those ends that are politically attainable. And since, for the vast bulk of the Negro people, intermarriage with whites (intrinsically important though this as a right may be) is just about the last of their pressing concerns, the achievement of an immediate important gain is preferable by far to the loss even of that possibility in the vain pursuit of Miss Arendt's Holy Grail.

V

In her preliminary remarks, Miss Arendt avows her sympathy for the Negro and her abhorrence of racial discrimination. In all that I have said, I do not mean to be taken as implying any skepticism of this claim. I criticize her basic position, her arguments, and the consequences to which these lead; I do not for a moment question her motives or intention.

In one respect, too, I would add my voice to Miss Arendt's plea. There are dangers in excessive governmental control. There is the possibility that through rash action we may disrupt the bonds of community, the grounds of consensus, that make possible the perpetuation of the Union. Hence, some caution, some moderation, must be employed in the resolution of this, as of every, great issue.

But there are dangers, too, in not doing enough. There is the possibility that while we delay, private groups and state governments will continue so to subvert those same bonds of community as to destroy the Union from within. I think it is time for us to recognize that a good portion of the American South has in fact seceded from the Union; indeed, by choosing to close some of their public schools to all students rather than admit students of another race, they have made clear their intention to secede not merely from the country but from civilization itself. Despite the 100 years since the waging of the Civil War, many of the articulate spokesmen of the South have not progressed very far in their political thinking and their social attitudes; they have not advanced in their humanity. They seek to remain primitives, and if they are given their way they may well drown the country in that torrent of barbarism which is a continuing affront to democracy and to mankind. In this respect the South is America's greatest and most dangerous liability. It is also a liability to the world. If we are to overcome this liability, we will require not merely the good will of gentle people but an unrelenting pursuit in all the realms of man's being — political, economic, intellectual — for the implementation of constitutional rights for all our citizens. We must move, no doubt, as the Supreme Court urged, with all deliberate speed. But what is frightening, in the years since *Brown v. Board of Education,* let alone the century since the Civil War, is that in seeking to be deliberate we have made very little speed.

More than 125 years ago, Alexis de Tocqueville concluded the first volume of his *Democracy in America* by predicting that the great problem of the American future would be the reconciliation of the races. It does no honor to the American to reflect that were a Tocqueville to write this book today, he would have to conclude with a near-identical observation. Miss Arendt is wise to remind us of the gravity and complexity of the problem. But her understanding of that problem, and her suggested course of action, seem neither relevant nor opportune.

Chapter 10

Milton's *Areopagitica:* Testament for Our Time

I

Those who believe that the truth will make men free do not universally agree that men should be free to seek the truth. For the search for truth may involve the discovery of error, and error when disclosed may have sinful charms. Truth when known and enforced, on the other hand, is calculated to ensure right conduct and to preclude the possibility of evil deeds. Thus "true" freedom, in the minds of many men, implies not freedom of thought but freedom of *certain* thoughts. It is the freedom to entertain "right" ideas rather than the freedom to assert or to examine loathsome and erroneous ideas.

Freedom so conceived is the principle embraced by the dominant authoritarian movements of our time. Recently, and within the span of a single week, both the Roman Catholic Church and the Chinese branch of the Communist Party were revealed to have "curbed" once again the teaching or dissemination of "false" ideas. On May 25, 1952 it was reported from Hong Kong that three prominent Chinese educators, each of whom had accepted and at an earlier stage had praised Mao Tse-tung's New Democracy, were now deemed ideologically incorrect and hence unfit to continue in their university positions. In accordance with Communist policy as previously enunciated and practiced in the Soviet Union and other countries, and in line with the proclaimed mission of Chinese teachers as defined by the Shanghai Ta Kung Pao on March 31 of the same year, which is to help youth "establish correct thought," the educators were purged.

On the basis of a like principle, the Sacred Congregation of the Holy Office, by a decree dated May 20 and published May 26, 1952, placed on the Catholic Index of Forbidden Books all the works of Alberto Moravia, the Italian novelist. The Sacred Congregation deplored "the enormous damage that is done to souls both by the unbridled license to publish and divulge books, pamphlets and magazines that deliberately narrate, describe or teach lascivious or obscene things and by the wicked desire to read all this indiscriminately." They also considered it their duty to admonish:

> All faithful that they should remember their very grave obligation to abstain completely from the reading and circulating of such books and periodicals.

All those who are engaged in the education of youth that, conscious of their very grave duty, they should keep young people entirely away from such writings as from a subtle poison.

Lastly, all civil authorities who are responsible for public morality, that they should not tolerate the printing and circulation of such books which subvert the very principles of natural honesty.

In this way, Catholics and Communists believe, men shall be stayed from error and directed to truth.

This principle is not, of course, the exclusive possession of the two groups mentioned above. It is common to all fanaticisms, to all orthodoxies. It is the basis of all varieties of fascist thought. It is the principle that underlies the current, if still largely informal, censorship of ideas that now threatens America — a censorship which certain individuals and groups, having themselves or through their ancestors found truth, now seek to have formally and permanently secured.

But apart from the difficulties of defining truth and compelling unbelievers to act in accordance with its precepts, there remains a contrary view of freedom. This is the principle that freedom can only be true to itself, not to a value outside of it. We can, under certain circumstances, force men to do good. We can even, perhaps, force them to do evil. But we cannot, without distorting the very meaning of our terms, force men to be free. On the contrary, by such efforts we restrain and coerce them in a cause other than freedom's own. For freedom strictly defined is still but the absence of chains. It is not the quality of being "true" or "false" but simply the quality of being free.

This truth was perceived and eloquently affirmed by the poet John Milton some three centuries ago. Faced in his day with a threat of conformity not unlike that which attends us today, he set forth in the *Areopagitica* a testament for intellectual freedom that is more than relevant to the problem of liberty in our own time. Normally, it is true, one does not look to a dour Puritan for a philosophy and defense of freedom; and Milton can be quoted in detail against anyone who seeks to make an exception in his case. He called, for example, for the suppression of "popery and open superstition" and "that also which is impious or evil absolutely, either against faith or manners." He argued that government does not exist to secure liberty but to assure "that good men enjoy the freedom which they merit, and the bad the curb which they need." He admitted, even in the *Areopagitica,* that a church or commonwealth ought "to have a vigilant eye how books demean themselves as well as men; and thereafter to confine, imprison, and do sharpest justice on them as malefactors." And he exempted "blasphemous and atheistical, or libellous" books from his plea for unrestrained freedom of publication.[1]

Nevertheless, Milton's argument for the freedom of unlicensed printing — a freedom opposed by Communists, Catholics, and all who distrust man's capacity to be guided by his own reason — remains a noble and enduring statement of the free spirit. It assures him a permanent place in the history of liberal thought.

II

The occasion and purpose of the *Areopagitica* can be briefly stated. In 1643 Cromwell's Parliament renewed an old order forbidding unlicensed printing. This was not a period of religious toleration, and the fact that this order had originally been issued by royal decree and had been exercised through the odious Court of Star Chamber did not prevent its enactment. Milton's marital difficulties led him to publish, without license, several pamphlets on divorce. One of these was attacked before Parliament as "a wicked book," and Milton was named in another action as a violator of the licensing law. The *Areopagitica,* in the form of a speech to the Parliament of England, was his reply.

In it Milton was concerned to demonstrate four things. He sought, first, to prove that the Puritan attempt to control the publishing of books derived in its essentials from the Catholic Inquisition, with its resulting "catalogues and expurging indexes that rake through the entrails of many an old good author with a violation worse than any could be offered to his tomb" and that lead in turn to the controls of the Imprimatur. He attempted, secondly, to demonstrate that while the reading of books is dangerous, the suppression or censorship of books is catastrophic, more devastating in a way than the taking of a human life. For he "who kills a man," wrote Milton, "kills a reasonable creature . . . ; but he who destroys a good book, kills reason itself, . . . slays an immortality rather than a life." He argued, thirdly, that an edict of censorship will not succeed in suppressing scandalous, seditious, and libellous thoughts. He concluded that the primary effect of such an order will be the discouragement of all learning, indeed the suppression of truth itself.

The argument is familiar but merits recapitulation: both to release it from Milton's stiff and involved style — though, as Macaulay said, there is "gorgeous embroidery" in it — and infrequent errors, and to commend it anew to a nation so overcome by hysteria that while it continues to praise Milton it ignores the meaning of his contribution.

III

Concerning the first of Milton's arguments, little need be said. The origin of a censorship or of any other policy has nothing to do with its validity. It may make for effective polemics, but it does not address itself directly to the merits of the case. Moreover, Milton's allegation that licensing will lead to the controls of the Imprimatur overlooks his own admission that books which ill demean themselves ought to be confined.

Now if books are to be imprisoned, there must be judges and acceptable grounds for imprisonment, in which case the principle of a free press is abandoned and the only meaningful questions concern the selection and control of the judges, and the determination of the rules according to which the judges shall be presumed to adjudicate. The mere threat of censure is no less an infringement of a free press than the act of censure itself. Men who know that failure to conform will result in punishment are unlikely to invite it. If they do, the suppression of their books removes what they have to say from the marketplace of ideas.

It is one thing to recognize that books are dangerous — that they have a life and activity of their own, that their potency might even be such as to drive men to arms. It is quite another to conclude from this that vigilance over them may require their banishment. Milton's references to, and defense of, "good books" at this stage of his argument is an evasion of the issue that yields a point to the case for censorship.

We arrive at the real meaning of his message, however, in his defense of freedom of publication. He is scornful of the argument that evil books will corrupt innocent minds, holding,, with the Apostle, that "to the pure all things are pure." Knowledge, Milton asserts, whether of good or of evil, cannot defile, unless the will and conscience are already defiled. Among books, some are of good and some of evil substance; but the choice must remain a matter of individual discretion. For while "best books to a naughty mind are not unappliable to occasions of evil," bad books "to a discreet and judicious reader serve in many respects to discover, to confute, to forewarn, and to illustrate."

How, for that matter, asks Milton, are men to know good and truth and virtue unless they know also what is evil and false ? Good and evil emerge and grow up together almost inseparably, as polar opposites. They are twins cleaving together, the knowledge of one so involved and interwoven with the knowledge of the other as to make it an incessant labor to distinguish them. Without such labor, there is neither wisdom nor virtue in forbearing vice. "I cannot praise a fugitive and cloistered virtue," remarks Milton,

> . . . that never sallies out and seeks her adversary, but slinks out of the race, where that immortal garland is to be run for, not without dust and heat. . . . That which purifies us is trial, and trial is by what is contrary. That virtue therefore which is but a youngling in

the contemplation of evil, and knows not the utmost that vice promises to her followers, and rejects it, is but a blank virtue, not a pure; her whiteness is but an excremental whiteness.

Since, therefore, to know truth men must know error, and to be virtuous men must know vice, Milton concludes that of all ways to scout into the regions of sin and falsity the least dangerous is the reading of books and exposure to all manner of reason.

To the common objection that this course entails certain harm, notably the spread of infectious ideas, Milton replies that the alternative is to remove all human learning and controversy, even and particularly the Bible, which often relates carnal and blasphemous things. Moreover, it is not the book but the interpreter that corrupts; and

> if it be true that a wise man like a good refiner can gather gold out of the drossiest volume, and that a fool will be a fool with the best book, yea, or without book, there is no reason that we should deprive a wise man of any advantage to his wisdom, while we seek to restrain from a fool that which being restrained will be no hindrance to his folly.

IV

Censorship, if effective, would thus destroy the virtue of reading even evil or dangerous books. But censorship, whether exercised through this or any other licensing order, cannot achieve the end for which the licensing order is framed. There are, Milton contends, two reasons for this. One is the difficulty of administering such laws fairly and intelligently; this Milton examines both as to complexity of detail and the quality of the licensers. The other, and more important, difficulty is that heresy is spread by other means.

Concerning the first of these factors, Milton is content to show that, if the licensing order is really to work, it must immediately catalogue and proscribe all scandalous and unlicensed books already published, and prohibit the importation of foreign books until they have been examined and approved. It must also expurgate those books which are partly useful and excellent, and partly pernicious. These arduous tasks require licensers of unusual quality — and many of them to boot.

But by the very nature of the task, Milton argues, licensers are likely to be "illiterate and illiberal individuals" who will refuse their sanction to any work which contains "views or sentiments" at all above the level of "the vulgar superstition." Men of worth would refuse such an assignment as tedious and unpleasant, and as an immense forfeiture of time and of their own studies. To assume that "ignorant, imperious, and . . . basely pecuniary" licensers would be graced with infallibility and uncorruptibleness, is to close one's eyes to reality.

Even if these difficulties were overcome, the licensing order would still be fruitless. Condemned books always manage surreptitiously to reappear and to circulate, often to an audience enlarged and attracted by the very act of condemnation. Moreover, it is simply not true that the suppression of books ensures the suppression of heresy. The Christian faith began and flourished as a schismatic sect before any Gospel or Epistle was seen in writing. To close the gates against corruption requires that *all* the gates be closed.

> No music must be heard, no song be set or sung, but what is grave and Doric. There must be licensing dancers, that no gesture, motion, or deportment be taught our youth, but what by their allowance shall be thought honest. . . . It will ask more than the work of twenty licensers to examine all the lutes, the violins, and the guitars in every house; they must not be suffered to prattle as they do, but must be licensed what they may say. And who shall silence all the airs and madrigals that whisper softness in chambers? The windows also, and the balconies, must be thought on; there are shrewd books, with dangerous frontispieces, set to sale: who shall prohibit them, shall twenty licensers? The villages also must have their visitors, to inquire what lectures the bagpipe and the rebec reads, even to the balladry and the gamut of every municipal fiddler. . . .
>
> Next, what more national corruption . . . than household gluttony? Who shall be the rectors of our daily rioting? And what shall be done to inhibit the multitudes that frequent those houses where drunkenness is sold and harbored? Our garments also should be referred to the licensing of some more sober workmasters, to see them cut into a less-wanton garb. Who shall regulate all the mixed conversation of our youth, male and female together, as is the fashion of this country? Who shall still appoint what shall be discoursed, what presumed, and no further? Lastly, who shall forbid and separate all idle resort, all evil company? These things will be, and must be; but how they shall be least hurtful, how least enticing, herein consists the grave and governing wisdom of a state.

Such wisdom, Milton is convinced, would eschew a mass of wearying and ridiculous licensing. It would acknowledge boldly that God, in giving men reason, gave him freedom to choose.

> Wherefore did he create passions within us, pleasures round about us, but that these rightly tempered are the very ingredients of virtue? They are not skilful considerers of human things, who imagine to remove sin by removing the matter of sin. . . . Though ye take from a covetous man all his treasure, he has yet one jewel left: ye cannot bereave him of his covetousness. Banish all objects of lust, shut up all youth into the severest discipline that can be exercised in any hermitage, ye cannot make them chaste that came not thither so.

For goodness is personal and must be derived from right choices. To choose rightly, one must be free to choose — between good and evil, virtue and vice, truth and falsehood. To delegate such choice to others — whether state, church, or licensers — is to abandon goodness itself. It is to forsake individual reason and individual decision that alone constitute what we mean by man.

Goodness or morality, in fine, is not a matter to be legislated. Laws which eliminate or restrict freedom of choice all too often prevent rather than promote virtue and thus defeat the very purpose they ostensibly seek to secure.

V

It is to the undesirability rather than the ineffectiveness of licensing that Milton addresses the bulk and core of his argument. He believes not only that licensing can do no good, but that it causes manifest harm. It is "the greatest discouragement and affront that can be offered to learning and to learned men." It hinders the discovery of new truth and makes existing truth heretical. It enslaves not only the citizens but the enslavers themselves. And in seeking political unity through uniformity rather than diversity of thought, it destroys the very hallmark of a free society.

Now it is understandable that a temperament as sensitive as Milton's should be shocked and humiliated by a law which stipulates, in effect, that "debtors and delinquents may walk abroad without a keeper, but unoffensive books must not stir forth without a visible jailer in their title." His excursus on this theme contains some of his most passionate and enduring prose, as in the celebrated passage that reads:

> When a man writes to the world, he summons up all his reason and deliberation to assist him; he searches, meditates, is industrious, and likely consults and confers with his judicious friends; after all which done he takes himself to be informed in what he writes as well as any that writ before him; if in this, the most consummate act of his fidelity and ripeness, no years, no industry, no former proof of his abilities, can bring him to that state of maturity as not to be still mistrusted and suspected, unless he carry all his considerate diligence, all his midnight watchings, and expense of Palladian oil, to the hasty view of an unleisured licenser, perhaps much his younger, perhaps far his inferior in judgment, perhaps one who never knew the labor of book-writing; and if he be not repulsed, or slighted, must appear in print like a puny with his guardian, and his censor's hand on the back of his title to be his bail and surety that he is no idiot or seducer, it cannot be but a dishonor and derogation to the author, to the book, to the privilege and dignity of learning.

But men in power are generally prone to indulge their own sensibilities rather than the feeling of learned men. If Milton's defense of intellectual freedom is to persuade a Parliament, it must rest on other grounds. These cannot be such trivia as the inconveniences and delays that are likely to attend an author anxious to correct and recorrect galley and page proofs before his manuscript is finally published, or the resort by timid and parochial ministers to stock or ready-made sermons with ideas that are unlikely to disturb the serenity of their parishioners' minds. Consequences such as these are not unique to lands where licensing orders prevail; nor are they vital to the argument.

In one other respect Milton renders his case vulnerable. His devotion to truth leads him to overestimate its powers. Thus he writes:

> ... though all the winds of doctrine were let loose to play upon the earth, so Truth be in the field, we do injuriously by licensing and prohibiting to misdoubt her strength. Let her and Falsehood grapple; who ever knew Truth put to the worse in a free and open encounter?

And again:

> ... who knows not that Truth is strong next to the Almighty? She needs no policies, nor stratagems, nor licensings to make her victorious; those are the shifts and the defences that error uses against her power: give her but room, and do not bind her when she sleeps.

It is to be noted that Milton does not say that truth will always prevail. He argues only that it will prevail if the encounter is "free and open," if truth is not bound. But even with this qualification, the doctrine is not altogether convincing.

In the first place, error or falsehood may rule where men are in no mood to accept a truth that injures their interests or affronts their prejudices. Thus the technique of the big lie, the vile but highly developed art of character assassination, the disproportionate publicity given to sensational or scandalous falsehood as against the later and sobering truth, and the like — all these have in our own day made it very clear that truth seldom or only after an excessive delay catches up with falsehood. By that time a man's reputation may have been destroyed, a nation may have abandoned democracy for dictatorship, a judgment of men and events may have been formed that may never be completely erased. In the second place, not all men can recognize the truth when it is paraded before them. Whether for lack of knowledge or intelligence or ability in pleading, men on the side of truth do not always carry it to victory. Finally, a commitment to reason and the scientific method is a commitment to uncertainty; it compels us to view truth as a tentative rather than an absolute and final hypothesis. Truth so conceived is always open to examination and possible correction, and correction implies that the earlier truth was in error or was at best only a partial truth (and therefore perhaps a partial error). All that we have a right to say is that, under conditions of "free and open encounter," truth has its maximum if not its only chance to prevail.

These objections do not impair Milton's broader argument against censorship. In fact, they make his case all the more convincing; for if truth is not final, we must give range to the continuing search for real truth. Thus Milton's argument for freedom of the press remains eminently sound. It is difficult to see how learning can flourish in the absence of provocative ideas; and since licensers are likely to be men of no special merit or attainment, they will expunge such ideas from even the more famous books of deceased authors. New generations of students and writers, unacquainted with and unstimulated by those thoughts, can thus build not on the best of what has gone before but on that portion of past thinking which is staid, proper, and convenient to the minds of the licensers. Indeed, they will themselves restrict their own writings to things that flatter and do not rise above those narrow and traditional bounds, lest they sever the ever-present Damocletian sword. Out of such ignorance and fear will emerge nothing less than a new "tyranny over learning."

Truth, Milton believes, if it comes at all, comes from exercise, not from conformity to tradition. A man who believes only because he is told to believe and knows no other reason for doing so, is essentially "a heretic in the truth"; even "though his belief be true, yet the very truth he holds becomes his heresy." Consider, says Milton, the man who finds religion so great a burden of mysteries that, though he wants to be deemed religious, he refuses to tax his mind any further.

> What does he therefore but resolves to give over toiling, and to find himself out some [agent], to whose care and credit he may commit the whole managing of his religious affairs, some divine of note and estimation that must be. To him he adheres, resigns the whole warehouse of his religion, with all the locks and keys, into his custody; and indeed makes the very person of that man his religion; esteems his associating with him a sufficient evidence and commendatory of his own piety. So that a man may say his religion is now no more within himself, but . . . goes and comes near him according as that good man frequents the house. He entertains him, gives him gifts, feasts him, lodges him; his religion comes home at night, prays, is liberally supped, and sumptuously laid to sleep; rises, is saluted, and after the malmsey, or some well-spiced brewage, . . . his religion walks abroad at eight and leaves his kind entertainer in the shop trading all day without his religion.

The licensing order, by delegating thought, establishes and dignifies this sort of nonsense; and by making truth heretical it renders the discovery of new truth difficult. For unless we assume that some men know the truth, and possess it whole — an impossible assumption for those who, like Milton, believe that perfect truth is known only to God — we must continue to seek it. But how are we to seek truth when the licensing order "enjoins us to know nothing by statute"? What is generally forgotten,

Milton adds, is "that if it comes to prohibiting, there is aught more likely to be prohibited than truth itself : whose first appearance to our eyes, bleared and dimmed with prejudice and custom, is more unsightly and unplausible than many errors."

As a result, liberty and the unity of the state are destroyed. It is not true, Milton argues, that uniformity binds and glorifies a state. On the contrary, licensers who prevent men from discovering and putting together fragments of the truth are themselves the destroyers of unity. They forget that perfection in a state, as in a building, consists in a symmetry of many varieties, that a rigid external formality is likely to produce a gross conforming stupidity, and that if all cannot — as all should not — think alike, it is more wholesome that they be tolerated than compelled to simulate conformity.

For if they are compelled, society suffers. Errors are made by even a good government, but if ideas are silenced magistrates are likely to be kept ignorant of proper remedies. Their continued misinformation, in fact, will commit them to continuing error. It is true, Milton admits, that wrong ideas might otherwise reach them, but in the absence of new and right doctrines they are already the victims of wrong ideas. The true answer to erroneous views is in any case "gentle meetings and gentle dismissions," in liberal and frequent debate. For if men want liberty, they must be prepared to live with the expression of grievances. Indeed, the very purpose of civil liberty is to assure that "complaints are freely heard, deeply considered, and speedily reformed." The suppression of complaints does not eliminate the grievances; but the enslavement of citizens enslaves the enslavers.

> Ye cannot make us now less capable, less knowing, less eagerly pursuing of the truth [Milton tells the Parliament], unless ye first make yourselves, that made us so, less the lovers, less the founders of our true liberty. We can grow ignorant again, brutish, formal, and slavish, as ye found us; but you then must first become that which ye cannot be, oppressive, arbitrary, and tyrannous, as they were from whom ye have freed us.

For these reasons and others, Milton demands above all other freedoms "the liberty to know, to utter, and to argue freely according to conscience."

VI

Milton as a spokesman for intellectual freedom is not, perhaps, to be praised too much. His tolerance was not always in evidence, and even in the *Areopagitica* it was essentially limited to those who were agreed on the fundamentals of the social order. He failed, as generations of his critics have never tired of pointing out, to distinguish the dangers of absolute or unbounded liberty and the dangers of circumscribing it. Moreover, while Milton was not himself prosecuted for publishing without license, and the licensing order became, in effect, a near-dead letter, his appeal of reason to authority did not produce an immediate and avowed reversal of policy. Indeed, more than half a century was to pass before licensing was to disappear from English legislation; while in other parts of the world, as in the totalitarian states of our own day, and in the authoritarian attitudes of certain religious and political orthodoxies, the principle of censorship has been retained, institutionalized, and even extended. Everywhere, of course, the censors, or those who seek to establish them, are "good" men — men who "know" what is right and who seek only to cleanse others of error and sin. But as is so often the case, he who applies the disinfectant may be himself possessed of the greater poison.

To avoid the evil that such "good" men do is, perhaps, an endeavor beyond human control. But to minimize that evil, to place obstacles in its desolating (and, because it plays God, desecrating) path, men can, at the very least, reaffirm their faith in reason and in the virtues of difference. For without reason and the freedom of choice that reason entails, the individual cannot hope to realize his stature as man. And without diversity — in thought, in manners, in human values — a society cannot be unified, free, or flourishing.

These considerations, so ably articulated in the *Areopagitica,* are today often obscured. We have few Miltons and many would-be or actual censors, and the voices of reason are small if not yet stilled. But those who are emancipated from the worship of authority and find no intolerable discomfort in uncertainty, will recognize in those small voices, as in Milton's *Areopagitica,* a wellspring of the liberal faith.

Chapter 11

Labor and Liberty:
The Discourses of Harold J. Laski

Despite an uncommon brilliance and felicitous pen, Harold Laski has never been an easy writer to analyze. The variations in doctrine from one book or group of books to another have regularly taxed the ingenuity of the reader who sought an inner consistency among his shifting patterns of thought. Of late, moreover, Mr. Laski has begun to intrude his several diversities into each book, arguing, for example, both the extreme individualistic principles of liberty and the Marxist dogma of economic collectivism. It is not entirely clear that these are compatible doctrines. Mr. Laski, after all these years, is still tormented by what Morris Cohen once called his "unavowed craving for absolute distinctions," and because of this he affirms contrary propositions with equal eloquence and, doubtless, sincerity. But the inclusion of opposites may produce not a synthesis but intellectual schizophrenia. Mr. Laski's two books, *Liberty in the Modern State* and *Trade Unions in the New Society,* illustrate the difficulty.

This is not to say that Mr. Laski's volumes are lacking in acuteness of insight or cogency of analysis. On the contrary, the qualities that have long set Mr. Laski apart from the mediocre are here displayed in rich and telling form. Mill and Milton apart, I know of no more incisive argument for freedom of the mind, and no more devastating exposition of the evils of suppression. There are passages in *Liberty in the Modern State* on the relation of administrative activities to civil liberties, on the necessity of constitutional guarantees and the separation of the judiciary from the executive, on inattentive power and the conditions that make for rebellion, that are pregnant with meaning for those of us who cherish freedom. Mr. Laski is firmly convinced that reason and the demonstrated incapacity of aristocracies dictate democracy. I share that conviction; hence I applaud his argument and welcome the republication of his book.

However, it is important to realize that while Mr. Laski is on the side of the angels, his central ideas as to the nature and implications of liberty are by no means free of ambiguity or confusion. Despite the opportunity afforded him by a new edition to revise injudicious pronouncements, Mr. Laski still means by liberty two disparate things. On the one hand, he agrees with Hobbes that liberty is simply the absence of restraint. On the other hand, he defines it as the absence of restraint on the necessary conditions of individual happiness. These are not merely dissimilar; they involve Mr. Laski in a basic contradiction that does much to vitiate his entire thesis.

If liberty is the absence of restraint, then all law is an invasion of liberty and men are free only in the absence of, or to the extent that they successfully disobey, the law. But restraints are also imposed by men and organizations other than the political government, as when a bully prevents a man from crossing the street, in which case restraint of the bully becomes a necessary condition of that man's liberty. Thus law enters as a restraint on a restraint; it is a restriction of some kinds of liberty in order to realize other kinds of liberty. Law (as a restraint) and liberty are not antithetic but complementary, for complete liberty is a meaningless and impossible thing. There are many kinds and degrees of liberty, and all cannot be realized at the same time by an individual or a society. To regard law as a deprivation of liberty is to look upon liberty as an absolute concept. It is more sensible to conceive of law as a necessary restriction of some liberties in order to guarantee others. The problem then becomes one of a choice of liberties, *and of restraints.*

Mr. Laski appears to recognize this truth when he argues that men "are free whenever the rules under which they live leave them without a sense of frustration in realms they deem significant." But under this conception, the slave who is satisfied with slavery is free; which is an absurdity. Nor does it help to relate liberty, as Mr. Laski does, to other conditions, for example, economic security, equality, knowledge. Obviously some men are free and perhaps happy though economically insecure. They may be free even though ignorant. And any system of equalities necessitates a system of restraints. Such restraints may further certain liberties, but in no sense do they provide *complete* freedom.

Basic to Mr. Laski's difficulties, I think, are two misconceptions. One is his desire to equate liberty with an ideological goal such as happiness. But man is not necessarily happier if restraints are absent. He may treasure certain liberties which are made possible only by the imposition of certain restraints. The nature of liberty, moreover, is confused rather than clarified by identifying it with some other notion of the good; for if liberty means anything it is the right to choose between notions of the good, in which case my liberty may lead me to unheavenly pastures.

The other and more fundamental error underlying Mr. Laski's treatment of liberty is his persistent refusal to abandon absolute alternatives and his regard for liberty as a totality. For Mr. Laski, the choice is between good and evil, freedom and slavery, and there is rarely a middle ground. Yet it is overwhelmingly clear that liberty conceived as a totality can have no relevance to the world in which we live. Hobbes's difficulty was not in his definition but in the implications he drew from that definition. Liberty is the absence of restraint, but *liberties,* paradoxically, can only be assured by the intrusion of *restraints.* Liberty, to have meaning, must be seen not as a totality but as a system of liberties and restraints. Mr. Laski's failure to realize this simple truth leads him into an uncomfortable dilemma: he wants the individual to be free yet he wants the state to deny the individual his right, say, to possess private property, at least in the means of production. Now this latter desire may be wise or foolish, but it cannot be justified in the name of liberty. It has meaning only in a system of liberties, in which restraints enter to limit some kinds of liberty so as to assure the existence of other kinds of liberty.

I had hoped that Mr. Laski's more recent book, *Trade Unions in the New Society,* in treating the relationship of the union to the individual, the employer, and the government, might clarify some of these aspects of the problem of liberty. Unfortunately, much of this problem is overlooked. Mr. Laski believes that government in what he calls a capitalist democracy will always enter a labor dispute on the side of the employer. This is in accord with his conviction that those who control economic power necessarily control political power. Consequently he is anxious that workers combine into unions — indeed he would provide no legal protection for the worker unwilling to join a union — and that the unions form the economic base of a political party which will capture control of the state.

This conception raises a number of important questions. Mr. Laski is undeniably right when he argues that "the worker who is freed from his trade union is thereby left in servitude to his employer," but is it not equally true that the worker who is forced into a union is thereby denied his freedom to choose and may be subjected to restraints he may deem intolerable? Such an infringement of the anti-union workers' liberties might be defended on the ground that where we have democratic unions with no membership restrictions such workers would in all likelihood be a very small minority, and that the infringement of their freedoms would be counterbalanced by the guarantee of conditions making for fuller liberties for the multitude of other workers. In taking this position, Mr. Laski in effect admits the idea of liberty as a system of liberties and restraints and selects that equilibrium of freedoms and controls that will give him the liberties he prizes most.

Throughout, Mr. Laski rightly insists upon democracy within the trade union. However, it might have helped considerably if he had gone on to examine in greater detail the conditions under which democracy can be established and maintained in the trade union, as Robert Michels in his *Political Parties* examined the conditions under which labor oligarchies arise and tend to prevail. Tyranny may exist within a labor union no less

113

than in a political government, and Mr. Laski demonstrates his awareness of this when he attacks the benevolent despot in trade unionism. However, one might well question the consistency that allows him to condemn Mr. Lewis and Mr. Petrillo as undemocratic while lauding Sidney Hillman as one of the greatest American labor leaders; for if internal democracy is lacking in the miners' and musicians' unions, it can hardly be said to have a firm home in the Amalgamated Clothing Workers.

No less important is the problem of freedom for the worker when his union is the core of a political party in control of the government. Despite an excessive affection for certain features of Soviet structure and practice — such as "the democratization of culture" — Mr. Laski is not eager to establish in his new society the kind of trade union that is completely subservient to the monolithic state. His model is, broadly, socialist England, not totalitarian Russia. But the English experience has made clear that when trade union leaders take government positions they cease to be labor leaders and give their primary allegiance to the state. Thus, in the event of a clash of interests between labor and the government, the unions from which these leaders emerged are faced with the embarrassing and difficult choice of repudiating their former leaders or surrendering claims.

This is not to deny the long range identity of interest between a labor party and the trade unions that are central to its being. However, not only are there likely to be clashes on immediate policies or tactics, there is at least one perennial problem of major significance. This is the relation of the union to management in a nationalized industry. Mr. Laski seeks to resolve this problem by setting up a series of rules designed to integrate such unions into management's line of communication. Notable by its absence, however, is any rule which would preserve the union as the agency to press for the redress of members' grievances. Does Mr. Laski thereby imply that once an industry is nationalized, its union will cease to fight for labor's objectives when these are in conflict with the goals of management? This conception of unionism, which I hope Mr. Laski does not accept, comes dangerously close to the pattern of trade unionism in the USSR. Clearly it obliterates the freedom of the worker for whom the union is presumed to speak.

In a world in flux liberty cannot remain a static thing. It must shift with the times and constantly adjust to changing circumstances. It is well, therefore, to have a reappraisal of the problems of liberty, and of the relations of trade unions to free society, in our own day. That Mr. Laski has failed to resolve all the questions that seem to us most pressing, may, in the long run, be less important than the fact that he has raised vital issues and has demonstrated a devotion to the cause of freedom that all men may well emulate.

Chapter 12

The Nature and Limits of Freedom

I

In logic, as in common sense, we understand that a thing cannot both be and not be at the same time. No man can meet himself coming around a corner; nor can he serve, much as it might amuse him to do so, as a pallbearer at his own funeral. The law of contradiction imposes an unavoidable, if regrettable, limitation on human life. But in language, especially the language of politics, words often seem to defy this simple law.

In language, words are used not merely to communicate but to veil or distort meanings. They are used to make things seem other than what they actually are. Thus the term "freedom" is employed to mean both the absence of restraint (e.g., Hobbes) and submission to restraint (e.g., Rousseau); to describe actions taken in the silence of, or even in defiance of, the law (e.g., Bentham and Thoreau) as well as actions taken in obedience to law (e.g., Montesquieu and Hegel); to account for a way of life (e.g., President Eisenhower, who in his first Inaugural Address declared that the conflict between the U.S. and the U.S.S.R. is one in which "Freedom is pitted against slavery; light against dark") and to condemn the denial of certain political rights (e.g., Patrick Henry, who though he had the freedom to proclaim his alleged unfreedom, nevertheless demanded "liberty or death"). "Freedom" is the rallying cry both of anarchists who oppose all government action and of conservatives like Herbert Hoover and Senator Barry Goldwater, who oppose only that government action they deem offensive. Theologians like Jacques Maritain and Bishop Fulton J. Sheen apply freedom only to acts that constitute "right" choices, i.e., acts that conform to the good, or the truth, or God's will (all of which, in this conception, amount to the same thing); while democratic theorists like John Stuart Mill and R. M. MacIver apply the term without regard to the ethical quality of the action chosen. To compound this confusion, psychoanalysts like Erich Fromm tell us that positive freedom, as distinct from negative freedom, "consists in the spontaneous activity of the total integrated personality," thereby excluding from the term, we must presume, actions taken as a consequence of considered judgment or by neurotic or maladjusted men; while Soviet apologists, in defense of Socialist Realism, insist that writers in the Communist world are free to say whatever they think, provided only that they first think the right things, i.e., the things approved by the momentary masters of the Kremlin.

Clearly, most of these (and many other) definitions of freedom are incompatible with each other. As a result, we can no longer know what a man means when he speaks of freedom; for a plea for freedom made by X may in fact be nothing less than a call for the exercise of coercion over Y, as Dostoevsky's Grand Inquisitor made plain when he observed that men "will only become free when they renounce their freedom to us and submit to us." This is what led George Orwell to compose a grammar of doubletalk called "Newspeak" and to coin as a slogan of the new totalitarianism, the motto: "Freedom is Slavery."

It would take us too far afield to enter into the reasons for this curious diversity of meanings with respect to the term "freedom." History and tradition would undoubtedly contribute a portion of the explanation; deliberate distortion so as to enlist people's sympathies in a cause they might otherwise reject would also be included in such an account; and always, of course, we would have to consider the honest but misguided efforts of those who seek to identify the things they believe to be good with words that are commonly accepted as good, on the principle that noble causes merit honorific names.

It is the virtue of the books to be considered here [1] that the term "freedom" (or "liberty") is unambiguously employed. Both writers know what they mean when they use the word, and they say what they mean — without cant or humbug or recourse to that esoteric terminology that leads men to mistake a political cliché for a philosophical insight. Their essays are thus, at the outset, adventures in common (or must we now say "uncommon"?) sense. It would be excessive, and in one case misleading, to say that they are also both original and significant adventures in the resolution of the problems and paradoxes of freedom; but since few works, contemporary or otherwise, can make such a claim, we must be grateful for what we have: a pair of serious and thoughtful explorations into the nature and limits of freedom.

II

Two Concepts of Liberty is Isaiah Berlin's inaugural lecture as Chichele Professor of Social and Political Theory at the University of Oxford, a chair previously occupied by G. D. H. Cole. To follow so distinguished a predecessor cannot be easy for any man, and Berlin must (or should) have pondered long and arduously over the choice and execution of his topic. It is surprising, therefore, that he selected the subject he did; for his central thesis had already been set forth and admirably argued by Dorothy Fosdick some twenty years before in her book *What Is Liberty?* Berlin, I am bound to report, adds nothing of consequence that is new; and much of what he does add raises as many problems as it resolves. But Berlin is a superb craftsman: he is in command of the issues, at home in the language, and very much aware that he is writing in the shadow of Mill's celebrated essay *On Liberty,* published just a century ago. Consequently, though he covers familiar ground, he does not always do so in familiar ways.

By negative freedom — the first of his two concepts of liberty — Berlin means, at the outset, no more than the absence of human restraint. "I am normally said to be free to the degree to which no human being interferes with my activity. Political liberty in this sense is simply the area within which a man can do what he wants." Coercion then is not one's incapacity to attain his goal but "the deliberate interference of other human beings within the area in which I wish to act" (p. 7). From this it follows that the wider the area of non-interference, the wider the area of my freedom. Carried to its logical limits, this proposition implies one or both of two things: (a) that the free man is one who lives alone, for when he lives in society he inevitably collides with and thus interferes with other men; or (b) that the free man is one who can interfere as much as he might like with other men, for the principle of non-interference would prohibit the imposition of any restraints even upon one who would hinder the activities of another. In this latter case only the strong of course can hope to be free, and then only until the emergence of a stronger; which is hardly a desirable situation.

To avert the ensuing chaos or rule of the strongest, it is necessary therefore that some liberties be curtailed — either in the service of other goals (e.g., security or happiness or varying degrees of equality) or in the cause of certain freedoms deemed to be more valuable than others. To be free to do some things, restraints — whether legal or social — must be imposed on those who would otherwise prevent others from doing the things men ought to be free to do. Thus we have the first and greatest paradox of freedom: *restraints restrict freedom, but without restraints there can be little or no effective freedom, at least not for most men.* The problem then is to determine which combination of liberties and restraints best assures the attainment and preservation of the good life. From the standpoint of the negative idea of liberty, we need to define at least the minimum area of personal freedom which must on no account be violated. We must draw a line between the area of private life and that of public authority, for only in this way can we give scope to man's quest for self-realization.

But the quest for self-realization, it is often argued, is not the same thing as its achievement. For this one needs not simply freedom of choice but the wisdom to choose "rightly." Man needs knowledge both of his "self" and of the means appropriate to its realization. He needs, too, the will to act in accordance with this knowledge. But such knowledge and will, it is contended, are possessed by only a few men, not by the masses of mankind, who are too blind to see and too weak to do what is "right." If these latter are to realize their "true" selves, they must consequently be guided by those better than themselves. If necessary, they must be "forced to be free." But such coercion, since it compels them to do only what they would themselves choose to do if they were more enlightened than they are, is not "really" coercion but freedom; for it alone makes possible the achievement of their "true" selves, their "true" desires. In this sense "real" or positive freedom, far from being opposed to authority, is submission to authority. It is obedience to the right precepts, to law.

Now this argument, as Berlin properly points out, confuses two things: the proposition that I may be coerced for my own good which I am allegedly too blind to see; and the proposition that if it is my good, I am not being coerced, for I have willed it, whether I know this or not. Because of this confusion, or manipulation of terms, it is possible for the philosophers of positive freedom to argue that a man is free even while his poor earthly body and foolish mind bitterly reject the act of coercion, and struggle desperately against those who seek to impose it. It is possible to treat men as objects without wills of their own, "to use them as means for my, not their own, independently conceived ends," and by thus treating them as sub-human creatures to degrade them, to deny them their human essence. It is possible, utimately, to assert even the barbarous doctrine that despotism, or slavery, is freedom (pp. 18, 22).

But despotism, even if paternalistic, is still despotism. In fact, paternalistic depotism, as Mill and Kant rightly argued, is more oppressive than naked tyranny; for by ignoring the reason that resides in even the ordinary man, and by denying his conception of himself as a human being, as a man seeking to make his own life in accordance with his own purposes, whether these are rational or "right" or otherwise, it treats him as less than a fully independent human being. It regards him only as an instrument to another's purpose, not as an end in himself.

Because he values and would respect each man's humanity, Berlin rejects this idea of positive freedom and returns to the notion of negative freedom as an area within which no man can impose his will on another. "If I wish to preserve my liberty," he writes, "I must establish a society in which there must be some frontiers of freedom which nobody should ever be permitted to cross" (p. 50). "There are frontiers," he believes, "not artificially drawn, within which men should be inviolable"; and he defines these frontiers in terms similar to those set forth in Erich Kahler's *The Tower and the Abyss* and Erich Fromm's *The Sane Society:* as "rules so long and widely accepted that their observance has entered into the very conception of what it is to be a normal human being, and, therefore, also of what it is to act inhumanly or insanely." Unlike the advocates of positive freedom, who would place authority in their own hands, Berlin argues for negative freedom, for the curbing of authority as such. He insists on the recognition of "the moral validity — irrespective of the laws — of some absolute barriers to the imposition of one man's will on another." And he asserts that "the freedom of a society, or a class or a group, in this sense of freedom, is measured by the strength of these barriers, and the number and importance of the paths which they keep open for their members — if not for all, for at any rate a great number of them" (p. 51).

In thus opting for a pluralism of goals, Berlin repudiates the belief in a single final solution. He holds that human values and human ideals are not all compatible, nor do they even entail one another. Consequently, the fulfilment of some of our ideals may well make impossible the fulfilment of others. "The world that we encounter in ordinary experience is one in which we are faced with choices between ends equally ultimate, the realization of some of which must inevitably involve the sacrifice of others" (p. 53). This is why such immense value is properly placed on the freedom to choose, why negative liberty is "a truer and more humane ideal" than the authoritarian structure of positive freedom. It is truer, Berlin argues, because it builds on the fact that human goals are many and in perpetual rivalry with one another, and since often incommensurable they cannot be graded according to some mathematical scale. It is more humane because it does not deprive men of what is indispensable to their lives as human beings. To respect the fundamental needs of men, we must learn, with Kant, "the truth that out of the crooked timber of humanity no straight thing was ever made" (p. 56). To ignore this truth is but to manifest one's moral and political immaturity.

No one can gainsay the sincerity, even nobility, of Berlin's plea for individual freedom. With Mill, he seeks to establish the permissible limits of social and political coercion over a person or group of persons. But unlike Mill, he seeks to draw the line not at the point where the activities of one man directly or significantly hinder or affect the activities of another; for he concedes that everything that one does may have results which will harm other human beings. He draws the line, instead, at that point where the denial of privacy, or of personal rights, is calculated to prevent the individual from living as a man, as an autonomous human being.

This is persuasive doctrine, and much can be said in its defense. But it is not altogether convincing, for Berlin concedes, too, that no man can be completely autonomous, and that "no society literally suppresses all the liberties of its members" (p. 46). If this is so, the issue is not properly posed as a conflict between the negative and positive concepts of liberty, between an area of freedom and an area of constraint. Human life and human activities are not divisible in such compartmentalized terms. It must rather be stated as the determination of which complex of particular liberties and concomitant restraints is most likely to promote those values that, in Berlin's theory, are distinctively human. But since men differ as much in their conception of what constitutes human nature as Berlin admits they differ in their conception of human goals, it requires too a determination of the nature of man that transcends what he calls "long and widely accepted" rules. Moreover, to say that there are frontiers of freedom "not artificially drawn" is but another way of saying that there are "natural" limits to social and political regulation. But it is precisely these "natural" limits that need to be demonstrated. In fact, by eschewing the doctrine of natural right and arguing instead for the relative as against the absolute validity of his convictions, Berlin must ultimately fall back on a concept of humanism and on a defense of freedom essentially akin to Mill's. This is not, of course, a bad place on which to rest one's argument, but it is considerably short of Berlin's pretensions. It leaves open, too, the crucial questions: who is to determine the proper limits of the exercise of public authority — the individual himself or society or a dominant group (be it majority or minority) within that society? And if such limits are not to be determined by the individual, what is he to do when in his (or Berlin's) judgment the legitimate frontiers of his freedom are violated?

III

To the first of these questions Professor David Fellman of the University of Wisconsin addresses himself in his brief but sensible book, *The Limits of Freedom*. Fellman is concerned not with philosophic speculation about the many and diverse ideas of freedom, for he recognizes at the outset that liberties in society necessarily jostle each other and thus require choices to be made. He deals, more narrowly but not less importantly, with political principles and legal practices in the American democracy, which is constitutionally committed to the preservation of at least *some* freedoms. Among these are three which he makes the focus of his discussion: religious freedom, the freedom to communicate, and the freedom to talk politics. In each case Fellman carefully shows that despite the constitutional wording surrounding these freedoms, wording which would seem to throw a blanket protection against legislative infringement on any of them, the realities of political life have compelled a more or less rather than an either/or approach to their practical implementation. This, he holds, is not only inevitable; it is also desirable, "for the only freedom we can possibly live with is one in which an equilibrium is found between competing interests, all of which carry great validity taken singly" (foreword). But once it is recognized that no freedoms are absolute, that even those freedoms essential to democracy can and indeed must be limited to some degree, we require a standard in terms of which that determination is properly to be made. The quest for this standard, Fellman shows, carries us away from the Constitution to that body which, in the American system of government, has the decisive say as to what the Constitution means — the Supreme Court. Thus his study of the limits of freedom, and of the principles appropriate to their determination, is a study of democratic theory and judicial practice, and of their inter-relatedness.

With respect to democratic theory, Fellman says little that is new; but the few pages devoted to this subject (pp. 87-97; also 52-53) constitute as admirable a statement of the meaning and free speech implications of democracy as can be found in the literature. He correctly reminds us that "democracy is not so much concerned with correct answers as it is with a methodology for reaching essentially tentative decisions in a workaday world." He dwells appropriately on the importance to this method of the freedom to differ — in thought, in speech, and in political activity. And he emphasizes above all the often neglected fact that a free society is inescapably a noisy and disorderly one, and hence psychically disquieting to those "to whom relaxation is man's supreme achievement." But if the right to be disagreeable, to bicker, and to be contentious is one of the hallmarks of a democratic state, by what standard may this right be limited? Here Fellman reverts to the work of the Court, for it is the business of the judiciary to reduce general principles to concrete situations. And what is most striking is the fact that the standard of the Court is not a precise formula, nor the words employed to translate the Court's judgment into an opinion, but what Fellman calls "the judicial feel for a situation' and the "necessarily vague" rule of reason (pp. 107, 113-115). What governs the judges, he believes, is their reaction to the concrete facts of each particular situation, their "feeling" that Congress has or has not acted unreasonably, or that there is or is not a clear and present danger to the safety of the state sufficiently acute and urgent to justify a restriction on speech. But the rationale supporting their decision, he thinks, is both a product of and an appeal to reason. Moreover, the judges are deeply conditioned by membership in an institution bound by traditions and committed to constitutional principles. Hence, he concludes, the standard of reasonableness, which in any case cannot be defined in the abstract with any precision, is not as arbitrary as it might otherwise seem.

It is unfair, perhaps, to demand of an author that he deal with issues he has not himself posed in his book; yet, without a consideration of certain relevant and pressing questions, Fellman's study is of limited value. It remains but an exposition of contemporary American constitutional law and not what the perceptiveness of the author might lead us to expect: an exposition as preliminary to serious theoretical inquiry. It is clear, for example, that Fellman values democratic principles and wants the law to adhere to them. But he does not confront the question whether the law as it has been and now is, does in fact conform to those principles. If it does, no change is signified or called for. But if it does not, we need to know what changes are required and how these are likely to be achieved.

It is clear, too, that while Fellman recognizes the fallibility of the judges, he values the role of the Court in our political system. But in his account of the evolution of our constitutional law he does not ask why the Court has acted as it variously, and not always consistently, did. He does not inquire into the economic and political interests represented, or at least reflected, by individual judges. Has it made no difference to the content of liberty, for example, that the vast bulk of our Supreme Court justices between the Civil War and the New Deal came from the ranks of corporation lawyers? Nor, again, does Fellman face up to the old but still decisive query: is the American practice of judicial review consistent with the principle of democracy? Does the Court not in fact constitute an aristocracy of the robe, performing a legislative function, yet without responsibility to the people? And if this is so, why should the Court have the final say as to what is reasonable or not? It is one thing to argue that this is the way things are, and that they are not likely to be altered soon. But if it is truly the function of the citizen to keep the government from falling into or perpetuating error, and not the reverse, we ought never to ignore, or cease to protect against, so important an institutional obstacle to the performance of this democratic function.

IV

A final word may perhaps be permitted me on the general debate over the nature and limits of freedom. As one surveys the literature, the most striking single fact that emerges is that men mean by freedom a variety of things. Hence the conflict between them is often, though not of course always, more verbal than real. They talk past each other rather than to each other. They exchange soliloquies rather than ideas. If men are to debate the problems of freedom seriously, they need therefore to agree first on a common meaning of the term. But despite the regularity with which such a plea is made, they persist in a refusal to do so. For most commonly, they want not merely a definition of freedom but a definition that will identify freedom with other things, things they conceive to be good — e.g., reason or duty or power. They thereby confuse the actual issue, which in the real world always arises from the fact that different men want not freedom as such but different and sometimes conflicting freedoms.

Where it is possible for men to pursue or to practice different things or beliefs in such a way that the practice of one does not militate against the practice of another, we have, in general, a prima facie case for allowing them to do so. But since this is not always possible, especially for example in the economic sphere, the issue of freedom becomes the reconciliation or accommodation of these different claims to particular freedoms. Moreover, not all freedoms are equally desired, and some men desire some things even more than they desire freedom. We need, therefore, in addition to a meaningful definition of freedom, a standard or value in terms of which we can order and adjust these conflicting claims. But there is no more agreement on such a standard than there is on the meaning of freedom itself. For Berlin, this standard is the idea of a common human identity. For Fellman, it is the principle of democracy. For others it is God's will, or nature, or tradition, or some other subjective or allegedly objective criterion. We are thus driven back from the issue of freedom to the question of *how* we are to decide the issue of freedom. And here again we find a division, most broadly between those who look to democracy as the proper mechanism for the negotiation and resolution of this conflict and those who prefer some aristocratic or authoritarian alternative.

From all this it follows that the idea of freedom will continue to evoke, and to provoke, disagreement. This is why freedom is disturbing to some men and appealing to others. What distinguishes the essays we have examined here is their recognition of this vital fact and their willingness, despite their own clear commitments, to tolerate, even to encourage, the free competition of ideas, including the idea of freedom itself. In this respect they are truer to the concept of freedom than those who, fearing to place their own ideas in jeopardy, would pervert freedom by curtailing it in freedom's name.

Part Three

THE CONSERVATIVE MALAISE

Chapter 13

The Jungle of Conservative Thought

The central issue between conservatives and liberals may be put simply: can society be governed by the light of immutable "right principles," as conservatives insist, or is the search for "right principles" chimerical, as liberals argue?

Not that liberals contest the need to ground social policy on well thought-out principles of some kind. What they deny, however, is that such principles have the character of absolute and infallible truth. And since, in any case, the quest for such infallible truth is vain, in a world of uncertainties and mere probabilities, they argue, societies cannot pin their hopes on some alleged immutable first principles. Societies must look, instead, to an experimental method — such as democracy — by which conflicting views as to what are the "right principles" may be peacefully resolved. Otherwise, liberals fear, men may well resort — as they have in the past — to mutual slaughter and the imposition of authoritarian regimes in the name of what they conceive to be *their* first principles.

From the conservative standpoint, the trouble with the liberal position is that through this democratic process the "wrong" principles may win the approbation of a popular majority and thus prevail. This explains why conservatives find themselves driven to a distrust of democracy and majority rule and a partiality for aristocracy, provided of course that the "right" aristocrats rule. All that is needed, therefore, to complete the conservative case is a demonstration that their particular principles are both workable and "right"; from which it would follow that only those committed to such principles should govern.

What is disconcerting to the liberal, however, is that conservatives are in no sense agreed as to what those "right" principles are, or why they are warranted. Hence they cannot tell us what things are worth preserving, and by what sanction. Where some few among them are agreed on a particular principle, it is usually at so broad a level of generality as to defy application. To take an obvious example: it may readily be conceded — who indeed would argue to the contrary? — that men should do good and avoid evil. But from this worthy precept it is impossible to derive any specific guide to action in a concrete case. To salvage this and similar principles, as conservatives seek to do, by urging that in such instances prudence and circumstance must decide, is to invoke but a question-begging device; for if not all judgments are equally prudent, how are we to know which is the truly conservative judgment? Whose reading of circumstance is "right"? Who, really, is the authentic conservative?

To these questions, alas, conservatives offer no coherent or consistent answers, and for two reasons primarily. One is that conservatives are preeminently men governed by sentiment, not by reason. The other is that conservatism as a body of doctrine is not a montage but a pastiche — an *omnium gatherum* of diverse and not always consistent appeals to authority.

Thus, in his reverential work *Conservatism in America,* Professor Clinton Rossiter tells us that "It is the Conservative who weeps at Gettysburg or Dunkirk, the Conservative who gets goose flesh when the band plays the national anthem, the Conservative who joins societies for the preservation of old ways, names, and houses." It is the Conservative who "is not afraid to acknowledge a feeling of sheer sentiment for the mystery and majesty of his nation's past." It is not surprising, therefore, that in Rossiter's judgment, as in that of other writers, conservatives need not be concerned with such intellectual niceties as consistency. With refreshing candor, Professor Rossiter assures us that what is common to all conservatives is "a healthy distrust of pure reason" and an "indifference to charges of inconsistency." [1]

Even more to the point is the simple but disquieting fact that conservatives share no common standard. I say disquieting both from the standpoint of a liberal who believes in the necessity of a vital opposition and of a teacher of political theory who searches diligently for the principles the neo-conservatives talk about so much and profess to stand for. It is never enough merely to oppose; one must offer a meaningful and viable alternative as well. But there is no alternative, there are no principles that all conservatives themselves accept as a literal statement of their creed. Each conservative splinter group has a different credo, usually inconsistent within itself, and the only thing they have in common is a dislike of the way the world is moving, plus a nostalgia for the past. They agree, to be sure, that there is — or must be, or ought to be — such a body of principles. But their articulation of those principles makes it clear that what is involved here is but the pursuit of an intellectual Holy Grail, yielding as it does no more than the customary importunities to return to God (or, in some constructions, to his teachings as these are mediated by and through his One True Church, whichever it may be), or to tradition, or to the alleged natural order of things, or even to intuition. [2]

It is curious that these old shibboleths should now be presented in the guise of a "new" conservatism, when conservatism is nothing if not a doctrine that disparages things new.[3] But it is bewildering that conservatives should persist in disregarding the specious and illogical character of their hostility to change.[4] Those who argue against change — as do Peter Viereck and Russell Kirk, for example — on the ground that what is, or (better) what once was, is good and should therefore be preserved, always maintain that the mere fact that a thing changes is no demonstration that the change is "good." But they always forget the necessary corollary — that the mere fact that a thing persists, or has long persisted, is also no conclusive demonstration that it is "good." Prostitution and war are obvious cases in point. But in this, as in other things, conservatives do not look to logical consistency.

It would be much too depressing, and possibly a violation of the constitutional prohibition against cruel and unusual punishment, to subject a reader to all the varied and numerous manifestations of the present conservative revival. It should be more than enough to limit our examination here to the doctrines expressed by two of its more striking and effective proponents: Senator Barry Goldwater, a leading Republican politician and by general consent the new saint of a certain wing of the conservative movement, and Professor Willmoore Kendall, perhaps the ablest and certainly the most sophisticated mind on the conservative weekly, the *National Review*. These, taken together, will (I suggest) reveal (a) that those who call themselves, or who are imputed to be, conservatives are literally lost in a jungle of mystical and inconsistent doctrines; and (b) that it is only by an extreme act of faith, by a fantastic, indeed fanatic, will to believe, that such men can cling to the illusory hope that political salvation is to be found in conservatism.

Barry Goldwater : The Quest for a Conservative Conscience

Consider, first, the remarkable Mr. Goldwater. Here is a man who, by his own admission, is not a philosopher but a salesman of ideas; yet he is now the author of a book, *The Conscience of a Conservative,* that in some quarters is taken to be a classic expression of conservative doctrine. Since this book (and his speeches) discourses of what Goldwater affirms is "a proven philosophy," whose principles are beyond debate — for they are "derived from the nature of man and from the truths that God has revealed about His creation" — it seems reasonable to ask whether the ideas that emerge conform, in the first place, to conventional conservative teaching; whether, secondly, they constitute a consistent body of thought; and whether, beyond this, they provide

129

clear-cut directives to relevant political action. For as Goldwater himself observes, the task of the conservative is not to demonstrate the *validity* of those principles but only "to *apply* [those] established truths to the problems of the contemporary world."[5]

Take, first, as an example of Goldwater's adherence to conventional conservatism, his flat assertion that "One of the foremost precepts of the natural law is man's right to the possession and the use of his property" (p. 61). Now both Aristotle and Aquinas, who might be supposed to have known something about natural law, specifically denied that this is the case. For these men, private property is not dictated but only *permitted* by the natural law, and then only when it serves the common good. It is thus a social, not a natural right. It is not easy for Goldwater to rationalize this departure from principle by appealing to the American tradition or the American Constitution, as he repeatedly does. For should he, on the one hand, invoke the authority of our Declaration of Independence, he would find that it deliberately and explicitly substituted Jefferson's trinity of life, liberty, and the pursuit of happiness for Locke's natural right trinity of life, liberty, and property. Should he, on the other hand, look to our Constitution, he would face the equally unhappy fact that it nowhere incorporates the notion that property is a natural right; it stipulates instead only that the deprivation of property must accord with due process of law. On what, then, does Goldwater's fundamental premise — the inviolability of property rights — rest but on his own arbitrary preference ?

Take, further, and as an example of his inconsistency as well, Goldwater's dismissal of liberalism and socialism as materialistic doctrines, concerned only with the economic well being of man. In contrast, he says, conservatism alone takes account of the *whole* man and by that concern manifests its superior claim (p.10). (Had Goldwater read and not simply accepted a popular misconception of the teachings of Karl Marx, he would have known what every competent student of Marxism well knows — that a concern for the whole man is precisely what lies at the core of Marx's writings. In his early *Economic and Philosophic Manuscripts,* for example, Marx argued — as so many another liberal and socialist writer has argued — that modern industrial society, especially in its capitalist form, is to be condemned above all else for its disregard of those factors that constitute the integrity and wholeness of man.

In these terms, it is curious if not startling that Goldwater should attack John Dewey (whose educational theories, I regret to say, Goldwater gives no evidence of having read and which in any case he seems thoroughly to misunderstand) for urging that education should concern itself with the whole child rather than — as Goldwater, now abandoning his concern for wholeness, would have it — with the intellect alone.[6] But it approaches the dimensions of tragedy when Goldwater so far repudiates this principle as to propose (in strict accord with aristocratic theory) that we construct our social order on the basis of the things that divide, not (as democratic theory would have it) on the basis of the things that unite or are common to men. "We are all equal in the eyes of God," Goldwater writes, "but we are equal *in no other respect.*" Consequently "artificial devices for enforcing equality among unequal men must be rejected" (p. 64). Above all, he insists, we must abandon democracy and the principle of majority rule, for when "the people" rule freedom is lost. What is required instead is a Republic — by which of course he means an aristocracy of Goldwater conservatives.

I cannot presume to challenge Goldwater's special knowledge of God's vision or God's will, though at moments like this I am reminded of that old cynic (and staunch conservative) Thomas Hobbes, who observed that when a man tells you God spoke to him in a dream, he is really saying he dreamed God spoke to him. But surely Goldwater cannot be unaware that in the American tradition — at least since the abolition of slavery — men are equal not only in the eyes of God but in the eyes of the law; and surely he must know that equality of opportunity is the necessary and proper condition for the discovery of whatever inherent inequalities may exist among men. It is not the mark of a responsible thinker to impute to liberals the absurd idea that all inequalities — of intelligence, of talent, of status and power and the like — must be removed. What liberals urge instead is the removal of *artificial* inequalities that make it impossible to say whether a man at the top is there because he deserves to be there or because his influential parent or relative, or those artificial inequalities, put him there.

Similarly, Goldwater's strictures against democracy and majority rule become meaningful only when it is realized that what Goldwater fears is not the conformist pressures of public opinion that worried Alexis de Tocqueville and John Stuart Mill, but the fact that ordinary people, through their popularly elected Congress and President, can control private concentrations of economic power. No man, says Goldwater, can be economically free if he is politically enslaved; nor can he be politically free if he is economically dependent — but here Goldwater inserts not a period but a qualification — on the state (p. 12). He says nothing of the consequences for human freedom of economic dependence on business and corporate power, though he has much to say of the adverse consequences of economic dependence on the power of labor unions.

Now clearly, just as political power may be required to curb what Goldwater conceives to be the excessive power of labor leaders, so political power is required to curb the excessive power of the business-man and the giant corporation. But in Goldwater's thinking, only the first is good; the second is bad. Why? Because more than anything else we need *"to preserve and extend freedom."* And since, in Goldwater's view, "every man ... is responsible for his *own* development" — a proposition which would logically seem to imply, though Goldwater illogically does not say so, the total elimination of (say) public educa-tion — he can assume this responsibility only when no other man "is able to deny him the exercise of his freedom" (pp. 12-14). It follows, then, in Goldwater's view, that governmental action to restrain labor is good, because it prevents labor leaders from depriving wage earners of their freedom to work when and where and at what wages and hours they please; but that governmental action to restrain business is bad, because — to employ another of Goldwater's phrases — "The conscience of the Conservative is pricked by *anyone* who would debase the dignity of the individual human being" (p. 13). And it is perfectly clear, to Goldwater at least, that for government to regulate business so as to aid the indi-vidual, which is "welfarism," is to transform the individual "from a dignified, industrious, self-reliant *spiritual* being into a dependent animal creature" (p. 75). One could only wish that Goldwater would, among other things, apply this principle to subsidies and tax and tariff aids to business, or walk through some of the depressed areas of Penn-sylvania and West Virginia, or follow our one million migrant workers (whose average earnings of $800 per year give them the poorest educa-tion, the poorest health, and the shortest life expectancy of any American) into the cotton and fruit fields and miserable rest camps that disgrace the American landscape and degrade the American dream.

Take, finally, as additional examples of Goldwater's policy recom-mendations and their relevance to his own conservative principles, certain of his economic proposals. He urges, as a major reform, that we abandon the graduated income tax and substitute instead a tax policy based on an equal percentage of each man's wealth. Thus a man earning $400,000 a year would be required to pay the same percentage — say forty per cent — as a man earning $4,000 a year, without regard, let it be added, even to such a consideration as the number of his dependents. Anything other than this, Goldwater says, "is repugnant to my notions of justice" (p. 63).

What is also repugnant to Goldwater's unique sense of justice is federal aid to education, foreign economic aid, the United Nations, recognition of the Soviet Union, the suspension of nuclear testing, and a concern for indigent if illegitimate children. "I don't like to see my taxes paid for children born out of wedlock," he announced in July, 1961.

Typically, he sees no inconsistency between his proposal (in a speech to the National Association of Manufacturers in December, 1960) to abandon all foreign economic aid and his Christian obligation to be his brother's keeper. Nor does he consider that by thus driving impoverished nations into the Communist orbit he is combating his own proclaimed purpose to defeat Communism.

Nor does Goldwater see any inconsistency between his alleged commitment to high principle, which presumably includes truth, and such utterances as that made in a news conference preceding his address to the National Interfraternity Conference in November, 1960, when he reportedly said that "where fraternities are not allowed, Communism flourishes,"[7] and went on to single out Harvard University as a nonfraternity institution where (he claimed) communist and socialist philosophies breed a faithless generation. And as Goldwater added: "Young men who are inexperienced but have faith are more useful than older, experienced men without faith." Goldwater conveniently forgot, of course, to tell us which faith is the right faith; all gods, if not all men, are apparently equal. Nor did he add what it is hard to believe he did not know: that there is no statistical evidence whatever to show that Harvard boasts a smaller proportion of conservative or a larger proportion of communist and socialist students than does (say) any of our large midwestern state universities. (I note, parenthetically, that in these latter institutions fraternities and sororities sometimes play so large a role in campus life as to make one wonder if the school really is a university or a social club with a few colleges attached.)

In all these examples, and they can readily be multiplied, Goldwater falls considerably short of what scholars at least would hold to be the minimum requirements of any philosophical position, "proven" or otherwise. He departs from the established principles of that philosophy; he affirms inconsistent beliefs; above all, he recommends policies and practices incompatible even with his own alleged principles. Whether these achievements demonstrate that Goldwater is an unusually astute man, adept at the rational exploitation of irrationality, or is himself simply irrational, I do not pretend to know. But that they reveal the customary confusions and inconsistencies of conservative thought, and thus offer no meaningful solution to the problems of our time, I find it impossible to doubt.

Willmoore Kendall: Conservatism as a Closed Society

It may be objected at this point that Goldwater is a politician, not an intellectual, and thus not properly representative of the conservative

133

position. This may be granted. What is crucial, however, is not that Goldwater is not an intellectual, which is indeed true, but that there is in fact no conservative position; hence no one man or group of men can properly be styled its spokesmen. In this latter respect at least, I find myself fully supported by Willmoore Kendall, sometime Rhodes scholar and teacher of political science at Yale and other universities, a former high-ranking official in our State Department, author of an important and provocative book on *John Locke and the Doctrine of Majority-Rule,* among other works, and now a leading and regular contributor to the *National Review.* In a striking article in that journal,[8] Professor Kendall categorically denied (a) that there is any one moment in the past when conservatives may be said to have shown their true colors and to have handed down principles it is now our duty to preserve, or (b) that we can construct a *dramatis personae* of "real" conservatives — that is, men who are consistent and thoroughgoing conservatives as distinct from those who, like former Senators Bricker or Knowland or McCarran or McCarthy, happen to adopt a particular conservative position at a particular time. To be sure, we have many books that purport to describe *"The" Conservative Mind* — witness the volume of that title by Russell Kirk — but the most impressive feature of such books is the multiplicity of doctrines that are to be found among the many disparate thinkers included therein; and this is equally true of many of those books which seek, even in scholarly fashion, to attack the so-called conservative position — for example, M. M. Auerbach's *The Conservative Illusion* and W. J. Newman's *The Futilitarian Society.*

I find both persuasive and unexceptionable, too, Kendall's denial (c) that conservatism is to be equated with sheer opposition to change, without regard to the character and direction of that change or to the obvious fact that conservatives are often in the forefront of those who most insistently demand change, even drastic change, provided that change is for the restoration of "the good." All that is required of Kendall, therefore, is that he clearly articulate those principles that constitute and define "the good"; for without knowing *beforehand* what those principles are, we have no way of knowing who (by Kendall's standards) the conservatives are and what changes are to be supported or opposed.

That Kendall's recognition of these elementary truths should distinguish him from the bulk of present-day American conservatives would be in itself the most revealing of all commentaries, were it not for the more interesting fact that when he turns to the articulation of those principles he offers not a positive set of doctrines but a rejection of what he conceives to be liberal doctrines. In this respect Kendall would seem to be less daring (though not, as will shortly appear, actually so) than many of his conservative colleagues and some of the more aggressive of the few juvenile conservatives in college halls.

Notable among these last — if I may be permitted a slight digression — is a group known as the Young Americans for Freedom. In September, 1960 the YAFF adopted "A Conservative Credo" in which they affirmed "certain eternal truths." These truths do not, of course, include the proposition that all men are created equal, or that they are endowed with certain unalienable rights, or that among such rights are life and the pursuit of happiness. What those alleged truths do include, however, is the individual's "God-given free will," from which, they assert, derives his right to "indivisible" liberty. Despite this stated fact that liberty is indivisible, the Credo recognizes at least two liberties, political and economic, which seemingly can be divided, though it is the obligation of government "to protect these freedoms." How? Apparently by recognizing these simple further "facts": first, that by the mystery of incarnation the principles of right political order have become historical flesh more perfectly in the American Constitution than in any other form, or time and place; second, that states' rights is the essential key to the genius of this right political order; and third, and most crucially, that the market economy is the economic embodiment of this political incarnation. Regrettably, the Credo does not specify whether this incarnation extends to the constitutional amendments, including for example Articles XIV and XVI. But having thus united God, the Founding Fathers ("properly" interpreted), and Adam Smith in a new trinity, it is no difficult task for these young conservatives to conclude, with Goldwater, "that when government interferes with the work of the market economy, it tends to reduce the moral and physical strength of the nation; that when it takes from one man to bestow on another, it diminishes the incentive of the first, the integrity of the second, and the moral autonomy of both."

By abstaining from this quest for a positive set of conservative principles — because, as he puts it, "there is no line to go down, no corpus of Conservative doctrine to be faithful to" — Kendall avoids many of these confusions and inconsistencies. But he does not, alas, escape other difficulties of his own making. For in spelling out those liberal doctrines the conservative rejects, or should reject, Kendall is in fact but asserting those doctrines to which the conservative is, or ought to be, intrinsically committed.

What are these liberal doctrines? Briefly and basically, says Kendall, they are three: first, the belief in an "open" society; second, the acceptance of majority rule as the hallmark of a right political system; and third, the commitment to "the principle of equality in its crudest form."

By an "open" society Kendall means the idealized world of John Stuart Mill, a world in which (as Kendall interprets it[9]) one may think and say whatever he pleases, and even publicly defend an opinion repugnant to morality. Accordingly, says Kendall, the American liberal views the First Amendment to the Constitution as a sanction for the expression of all ideas, including the most loathsome, and cites this Amendment to support his claim that he is nonetheless a good or acceptable citizen. In contrast, argues Kendall, the conservative "knows" that the First Amendment does not in fact recognize any such right to think and say whatever one pleases; nor does it stipulate "a duty on the part of American citizens to tolerate and live with and interminably discuss any and every opinion that their neighbors may take into their heads." If it did recognize such a right and duty, then "the moment is coming when the First Amendment will have to be brought into line with Conservative principles regarding the character of the good society."

Those who are familiar with Mill's essay *On Liberty* may find it difficult to identify this statement of his teaching, for Mill clearly admits, among other things, that legal restraints may properly be imposed against libel, slander, and those utterances which in a given situation constitute a clear and present danger that criminal acts might ensue. But let this go. For what is more to the point is Kendall's notion of the good society. This, says Kendall, involves at the outset an orthodoxy, a set of fundamental beliefs that "cannot and should not and, in any case, will not submit to the vicissitudes of the market place." Why? Because they are the beliefs of a society rooted in religion and aware of the fact that as a good society it is "moving through History . . . under God . . . for a purpose that lies outside History." Hence debate over the character and direction of such a society is inevitably an impediment to God's will.

So, too, Kendall argues, the conservative views with horror the liberal idea that the American political system should rest on the principle of majority rule. For the conservative "knows" that the American people and the American tradition do not want and have in fact repudiated this principle. This is why, Kendall asserts, we have the filibuster in the United States Senate, the seniority system in our congressional committees, non-programmatic or ideological political parties, and a multiplicity of other checks that make it difficult to mobilize the people for political purposes. And it is the conservative's mission, he continues, to resist "to the last" all liberal attempts to alter these arrangements.

Finally, says Kendall, the liberal notion that because *we* are rich and *they* are poor, it is our obligation to aid other countries; or because some have privileges and others lack them, it is our duty to end segregation; or because we have a Bill of Rights and men elsewhere in the world do not, we must promote (say) a United Nations Bill of Rights; all this he denounces as crude egalitarianism "whose predictable result would be world-wide uniformity." It is a truth happily perceived by conservatives, however, that rights and privileges are not to be indiscriminately enjoyed but are to be given only to those who perform their duties and to be withheld from those who do not perform them. But if the liberal should ask, what are men's duties and who is to define and allocate them? he need not pause for an answer; for this, alas, is not forthcoming.

Kendall's vision of a closed, minority-governed, and duty-conscious society is clearly in line with the main stream of conservative thinking. What is not so plain is its alleged consistency with American ideals. It reflects, to be sure, the aristocratic yearnings of the Puritan theocracy of Massachusetts Bay; and it has much in common with the aspirations of such otherwise diverse statesmen as Hamilton, Calhoun, and now Barry Goldwater. But it is hardly in keeping with the ideas of Jefferson or Lincoln (both claimed, on occasion, by the conservatives), or with the main thrust of the American experience, which has increasingly sought to extend and to implement the egalitarian promises of the democratic creed. The expansion of the suffrage and the extension of civil rights to previously disesteemed groups are but two of many cases in point.

In these terms Kendall is surely warranted in expressing a preference for stability and tradition rather than change, for order rather than freedom, for hierarchy rather than equality, for God-given truth rather than skepticism and intellectual inquiry. But apart from the convenient vagueness of these terms — does "order," for example, imply the order of an oligarchical or of a democratic society ? — he has no warrant for seriously maintaining that these conservative values are in fact *the* American values rather than a particular selection of them. America has always been a land of multiple traditions, of conflicting conceptions of order, of competing gods, of clashing ideas concerning the nature and limits of freedom. If it can be said to have a distinctive creed, it is surely not some variant of the principle of orthodoxy but rather the principle of dissent; for, paradoxically, the many and diverse claims to orthodoxy have been politically possible only because dissent has prevailed. Orthodoxy seeks to preclude dissent, especially the dissent of other orthodoxies; but dissent not only tolerates, it fosters all varieties of orthodox and non-orthodox thought.[10] This is why Kendall is free in an open or liberal society to attack what he conceives to be a liberal regime and hold out the promise of a presumably superior alternative, but why liberals — or at least certain liberal doctrines — might well be silenced should Kendall and his idea of a closed society come to prevail.

Conservatism : Its Uses and Its Consequences

But when all is said and done, it may well be that the conservatives know exactly what they are about. Doctrines, after all, can serve a purpose, however lacking they may be in empirical truth or logical cogency. And the primary purpose those doctrines presently serve is resistance to social and political change.

Conservatives generally tell us, for example, that Man — can they mean men other than themselves ? — is a sinful and irrational creature. He is also stupid and uninformed. Action by such men to "improve" the existing order of things is bound, therefore, to result only in catastrophe. The duty of the conservative, accordingly, is to oppose and prevent such action. This explains why a Congress controlled by conservatives is likely to be a "do-nothing" Congress. It also explains Goldwater's observation (in a television appearance in March, 1961)) that "I've always felt that the things we don't do in Congress are more important than the things we do."

Failure to act, however, entails curious consequences of its own. For one thing, it aids the economically privileged groups in society by obstructing legislation which, in the modern democratic state, is often and perhaps increasingly egalitarian in character. Those who stand on the lower rungs of the economic ladder constitute, by their numbers alone, an always potential and sometimes actual political majority. Thus it is frequently possible for them to satisfy their desires through political rather than through economic means. Moreover, those who stand on the higher rungs of that ladder must contribute (through taxation) a good share of the cost of satisfying those desires. Hence a policy of resistance to change is in effect nothing less than a device to protect their interests. That such a policy gains strength from the fact that it also appeals to the apathetic and the timid, to all who prefer what is familiar and fear what is untried or unknown, is but an added reason for employing it.

But in political as in personal life, few things can be gained without a compensating loss. And for the conservatives, there is another and less desirable set of consequences that follow upon a successful policy of obstruction to change. This is that the conservatives thereby succeed only in perpetuating the world as it is rather than in converting that world to what (in their view) it had once been and ought now to be. They but preserve a state of affairs that in important respects they themselves disapprove. For this reason the more philosophically-minded of the conservatives find themselves in the anomalous position of serving merely as defenders rather than as critics of the status quo. But critics of some sort, if they are to be true to their "principles," they must be.

Here lies one of the prime sources of their ever-present dilemma; for the conservatives, all too often, try nonetheless to have it both ways. They want to preserve the status quo; they want also to alter it. But the psychological attitudes and political doctrines appropriate to the one are generally incompatible with the attitudes and doctrines required by the other. Thus Goldwater, while he takes pride in the things that Congress does not do, is one of the more vociferous in urging the Congress *to do* certain things — for example, to repeal the graduated income tax and to legislate further and more severe restraints on labor unions.

Of all the consequences that follow from the conservative's drive to reduce state control over the economic and social order, the most formidable is yet to be mentioned. This is that with the diminution of political controls, a society may move, if not toward anarchy, at least toward that type of individualism which may well prove destructive of the American ideal of equality of opportunity. For in the absence of political controls, private power groups are free to deprive disesteemed minorities (and even, let it be added, ineffectual majorities) of their fundamental civil and human rights. This consequence is all the more striking when we consider that it rests upon a complete reversal of traditional conservative doctrine. Historically viewed, conservatives have always denounced liberals for their alleged propensity to view Man as intrinsically good and to believe therefore in something called "progress." Conservatives, and not least their greatest figure, Edmund Burke, have consequently urged the necessity of a strong government to curb the "evil" in man. What we find among the "new" conservatives of our own day, however, is quite the reverse position. Thus, in a recent syndicated column,[11] Raymond Moley, adviser to Goldwater and in ideological agreement with William F. Buckley, Jr., the messianic editor of the *National Review,* observed that what is at the heart of conservatism "is the concept of the individual as the center and root of authority." Now this is clearly an ancient liberal ideal. It is also one directly opposed to the traditional conservative doctrine that emphasizes, instead, the weak and sinful nature of man and the frailty of his judgments, and that builds therefore on the sense of community rather than on individual autonomy. How, then, can one maintain that he is a conservative if he presses for egoism as the central principle of life, rejecting even that collective action necessary to curb the excesses of an ultra-egoism or to make some contribution to the general welfare ? Perhaps it is just as well that Plato, Aquinas, and Burke are not at hand to peruse the

139

writings of their alleged conservative disciples.

But in these terms it becomes comprehensible why Goldwater (in that same television appearance) can call for a clear statement of principles in the Republican Party platform to which all Republicans can subscribe, and at the same time insist that each man must retain the right to interpret those principles in his own way. Little wonder then that even a Republican Senator, George Aiken of Vermont, should have wryly remarked: "I'd rather be right than conservative."

Chapter 14

Some Conservatives in Quest of a Theory

It has become fashionable in recent years to emphasize the qualities that unite rather than those that divide liberals and conservatives. The ideal conservative, it is argued, wants to conserve not everything but only the good; he is prepared to accept change that will remove the bad. The ideal liberal, on the other hand, while he seeks to obliterate evils, realizes too the value of conserving the good. Thus both stand astride the same fence, though they have approached it from different sides.

There is important truth in this reasoning, particularly when a common attachment to freedom sharply distinguishes conservatives and liberals from totalitarians. But there are differences so crucial that they ought not to be obscured. Liberals and conservatives rarely agree on a definition of the good; consequently their goals seldom coincide. No less important, men seldom act in accordance with the ideal. Conservatives, especially American conservatives, all too frequently seek to conserve for the sake of conserving; liberals tend at times uncritically to foster change. It is the task of those who would formulate a meaningful theory of conservatism — or, for that matter, of liberalism — to make clear the factors that separate conservatives and liberals, as well as the elements that provide a common ground. The group of conservative or neo-conservative theorists we shall examine here do not all address themselves directly to this problem, but all contribute in some way to the formulation or application of what they conceive to be true conservative principles.

Peter Viereck: The Poet as Aristocrat

Peter Viereck, poet and historian, is a conservative who would like to be a reluctant liberal. Throughout his many writings, in particular his *Conservatism Revisited*,[1] he reiterates his conviction that liberals and conservatives each own half of the truth as against the whole lies of the totalitarians. But on examination we find that Mr. Viereck's ideas of the conservative half of the truth are themselves only half-true, and that the things for which Mr. Viereck ultimately stands are in basic conflict with the liberal credo.

Mr. Viereck, for example, loves order, and insists on obedience to law. "You weaken the aura of all good laws every time you break a bad one." However, a careful reading of Mr. Viereck's argument shows that he applies this only to the laws — good or bad — established by *his* order. He would feel justified in breaking bad laws established by a popular majority of which he disapproves. Indeed, he goes so far as to say that, where a law violates a treasured right, "it is our moral and legal duty to resist the majority, though we die in the attempt."[2]

It is difficult to see how one can *legally* resist a bad though lawful law, but the more important fact is that Mr. Viereck is forced into his contradictory doctrine of obedience by a fundamental belief in aristocracy. He is not really interested in order, least of all a democratic order. He wants to conserve a particular kind of order, one that will ensure the values of a conservative minority. Mr. Viereck believes in law made by men of "standards," of quality — men who embody the aristocratic spirit. He has only contempt for the common man, whom he dismisses as the vulgar, "the commonest man." Consequently he derides the relativism of democratic rule and takes refuge in a "tradition of moral restraints," which he identifies as the "truth." Since these restraints are, and have been, determined by aristocratic men (whose abuses and perversities have made intolerable all nondemocratic systems of power), it is evident that Mr. Viereck's judgment of truth is a product of his poetic fancy rather than historical insight.

Frank Lloyd Wright: Genius and the Mobocracy

Unlike poetry, which has often been intimately associated with politics, architecture and politics seem to bear no necessary relation to each other. Yet it is a curious fact that architects, when they discourse politically, tend to form a community of aversion to "the mob." Just who or what this mob is, is rarely made clear; but that it exists, and that it is anathema to men of architectural distinction, are vigorously affirmed. Thus Ralph Adams Cram a generation ago denounced democracy for its reliance on the people, whom he held to be a Neolithic mass incapable of understanding genius and therefore antagonistic to it.[3] And now Frank Lloyd Wright, in a book celebrating the talents of his master, Louis H. Sullivan, restates the thesis that "genius is a sin against the mob."[4]

Mr. Wright, of course, has an axe of his own to grind. The man he most revered failed to receive that veneration from others. "The profession to which Sullivan belonged, unable to value him, neglected him";

and when he departed this earth it was in poverty and relative obscurity. For this shabby treatment of his idol, Mr. Wright is bitter. This book is his vengeance.

Now one may sympathize with Mr. Wright and deplore with him the lack of acclaim given to Sullivan in his own time. But if it was the profession that ignored Sullivan, why does Mr. Wright attack "the mob"? Why does he attribute to "the common herd" a high regard for insignificance? More important, is it true that genius eternally struggles against the mob, that "mobocracy" resents the achievements of superior beings and opposes progress? Both logic and history evidence a negative answer to this question.

The people do not resent genius; they seek and applaud it. The popular respect given a scientist like Einstein, a philosopher like John Dewey, a musician like Toscanini — not to speak of leaders in industry and the law, in the theatre and the arts — offers adequate testimony to this point. Mr. Wright himself can hardly complain at the immense popular esteem in which he is held.

Who, then, does oppose the genius? It is the near-genius, the man who lacks the spark of divine madness yet who is unwilling to surrender the position of preeminence into which fortune and absence of real genius have thrust him. It is the men with a vested interest in the perpetuation of the present, the self-proclaimed "elite," who battle the innovations of the genius for fear of change and the altered status which change will bring upon them. It was not the mob that denounced the genius of Galileo; it was a religious "elite" trembling under a presumed threat to its intellectual leadership. It was not the mob that put Socrates to death; it was the "elite" of Athens, which feared the consequences of free inquiry. It was not the mob that rejected the architect Roark in Ayn Rand's novel *The Fountainhead;* it was the leading architectural critic of the day and the profession of architects that stood alongside him. And so it was with Wright and his master, Sullivan.

The "elite," to be sure, uses "the mob" to carry out its will. Through control of the press, the church, and (where it can) the state, the "elite" propagates its lies and disguises the truth. The "elite" whips up mass hysteria and leads the people astray. At any one moment "the mob" may swing into action, but throughout it is the "elite" which instigates and directs the opposition to new ideas.

Mr. Wright is a distinguished architect but he has given us an ill-conceived and immature political tract. If it serves no other purpose, this book should help to remind us that eminence in architecture, as in any other ·non-political field, is no guide to political competence.

Wilhelm Röpke: Liberty in the Crisis of Our Time

If poetry and architecture may be said to represent intuitive, and hence analytically deficient, approaches to conservatism, the elements that constitute a valid conservative theory must be sought elsewhere — in the writings of economists, political scientists, and philosophers. Of such systematic tracts, few books have achieved the recognition accorded Wilhelm Röpke's *The Social Crisis of Our Time*.[5] Originally published in 1942 as *Die Gesellschaftskrisis der Gegenwart*, this work now comes to us highly recommended by Benedetto Croce, Frank Knight, Bertrand de Jouvenel, and others. It is written by a distinguished economist of the neo-liberal school of Mises, Hayek, and Lionel Robbins. It treats seriously real and persistent problems emerging from the relation of the state to the economic order, and evidences a degree of learning calculated to compel attention. Nevertheless, in all major respects it remains a naïve and unconvincing work.

Röpke's argument may be summarized briefly: We dwell today in a "spiritual interregnum," a vacuum of moral and intellectual disintegration resulting from the repudiation of traditional values. Democracy cannot fill this vacuum, for democracy is itself in crisis; indeed, "the limitations inherent in the democratic . . . principle" have led to the breakdown of the unity and authority of the state and produced totalitarianism. Nor can we look to the existing economic system for a solution, for through urbanization and proletarization the independent peasant and artisan have been replaced by servile and rootless mass man (as Ortega y Gasset described him). Socialism or a "planned economy" is as one with totalitarianism, and collectivist approaches are even less likely than a misdirected capitalism to achieve a balanced and creative society. What is needed, Röpke concludes, is a "revisionist" liberalism — call it "economic humanism" or the "Third Way — a program that will employ state intervention "compatible" with the basic laws of the market economy to re-establish the political and economic requisites for the spiritual life.

Three aspects of Röpke's book press for consideration: his methodology, his analysis of economic power, and his political theory.

Röpke belongs to one of several self-contained schools of economic thought, whose members read and quote from each other's books but disdain the work of outsiders. Thus Röpke makes ready reference to Hayek, Jewkes, and similar writers, but ignores the work of Veblen, Commons, and Pigou. Along with this isolationism in economic method there is a judicious selectivity of historical evidences: Switzerland and the Soviet Union are often cited, the former to illustrate Röpke's Valhalla, the latter to establish the vileness of "socialism." Sweden and other mixed economy systems, however, are virtually ignored, and the identification of Russia as a "socialist" state rests upon a most superficial reading of socialism. Finally, Röpke's methodology is an attempt to build on the Aristotelian mean, but Röpke (not unlike Aristotle) fails to demonstrate that his alleged extremes — e.g., fascism and communism, competition and collectivism — are truly opposites, or that his "mean" exhausts the possible alternatives within the huge middle ground.

If we accept, with Röpke, the postulates of neo-liberal theory, then economic power, strictly speaking, can originate only in the free competition of the market-place; it is determined from within the economic system, not imposed from without. Thus Marx (more traditional in his economic views than most Marxists care to admit) was led to the conclusion that concentrations of economic power were the inevitable consequence of the capitalist system; he erred in not seeing that economic power could originate from outside the economic system even after that system had been firmly established. Orthodox economists like Lionel Robbins, on the other hand, argue that economic restrictionism (monopoly) can arise only as a result of interferences from outside the economic system; he errs in not seeing that economic power can originate from within. Thus both Marx and Robbins are right in what they affirm of their own insight. But are wrong in denying the vision of the other.

Röpke does not make the mistake of falling completely into either camp. Throughout his book he points to the flaws inherent in the capitalist system and calls finally ((pp. 159 ff.) for "compatible state intervention." But if government is to interfere to protect the free market (interfere so as not to interfere), then the free market must be inherently incapable of maintaining or perpetuating itself, or of sustaining freedom. Similarly, if the state is primarily responsible for monopoly (p. 230), how can Röpke expect the state to combat it? These confusions have long attended the efforts of those who sought to legislate "free enterprise" only to discover that freedom and control are inseparable. When Röpke goes on (pp. 187 ff.) to urge, in the interests of "free enterprise," the nationalization of such utilities as electric power, radio, railroads, and the like, one can only wonder at his claim to "exact thinking, precise concepts, and clear-cut decisions" (p. 20).

To ensure the proper workings of this economic system, Röpke argues, the state must be in the hands of the right guardians. This precludes democracy. "Only those can be the guardians of freedom who really love it: the elite which, with instinctive authority, leads society and all genuine communities below, above and outside the state"; for "neither the state, with its natural tendency towards despotism, nor the masses as such can be expected to produce anything but a tyrannical government" (p. 97)). We must turn instead to the law courts; these, in Röpke's view, should be made the organs of national economic policy, for nowhere else are integrity and impartiality of so high a quality to be found (p. 193).

Now an epithet is not an argument, and to invoke so mystical a term as Ortega's "mass man" is not to refute the principle of democracy. Nor is it helpful to locate Röpke's "instinctive elite" (whatever this might mean) in the judiciary; for even were judges to embody his values of intellectual hierarchy and order, they are in no sense competent to decide matters of economic policy, which must be resolved more in terms of interest and justice than of integrity and impartiality.

Röpke is certain, however, that spiritual regeneration will eventually follow when the peoples have returned to the land and a peasant and artisan economy has been restored. Curiously, however, Röpke does not appear to realize that such a transition requires a vast bureaucracy to re-educate and move peoples, indeed to reverse history, *and keep it reversed.* Thus his remedy is worse than the evil he argues against; for it would not only aggravate the bureaucratic malevolences he attacks, but would foster the conditions that make for dictatorship.

This book is set forth by its author as "a desperate effort in spiritual orientation." If it can be said to achieve its purpose, it can only be in the ethical rather than the political-economic realm; and while I am disposed to quarrel with many of Röpke's values, it may be enough here to point out that his concept of humanism is not that of the Renaissance — of men like Montaigne, Colet, and Erasmus — but of an order rooted in faith and ultimate truth, institutionalized in man's inequality, deference, and subservience to certain selected traditions.

Russell Kirk: Christian Conservatism and the American Tradition

Along with Peter Viereck and Willmoore Kendall, Russell Kirk is generally put forward as one of the more searching intellectual spokesmen for modern conservatism. In a wide-ranging series of books he has pleaded eloquently — and for a portion of the public, effectively — for the recapture and reobservance of traditional conservative principles.[6] Now, in a work addressed specifically to Americans, and in particular to Americans in uniform, he seeks to root the American cause in the American tradition . . . and in God. In these sources, he believes, we can alone find our true faith, which is conservatism.

It is a curious fact, however, that when the first American Congress authorized the mint at Philadelphia to coin and issue a penny piece, it saw to it that the inscription bore an appropriate motto: Mind

Your Business. This motto — generally attributed to Benjamin Franklin — was also employed on the first American dollars. But the wisdom of our ancestors was understandably (if regrettably) disregarded in the turmoil of the Civil War, and one Reverend Watkins had little difficulty in persuading Secretary of the Treasury Salmon P. Chase to invoke the aid of the deity by inscribing on our coins the present motto: In God We Trust. This public reaffirmation of faith, as everyone knows, is now going on at an accelerated pace — witness President Eisenhower's incorporation of the religious motto into our traditionally secular pledge of allegiance.

I mention this odd bit of Americana to illustrate what I would have thought is a quite obvious point: namely, that those who appeal both to tradition and to God are sometimes engaged in a schizophrenic enterprise. But a reading of Russell Kirk's latest book, *The American Cause,*[7] reveals that there are still some who think that an appeal to the one is also an appeal to the other, and who invoke the guidance of our ancestors on a highly selective and arbitrary basis.

Kirk, however, is in fact much less of a traditionalist than he is a believer in God. He *uses* tradition but does not respect it. This is why, despite his seeming genuflections to the past, he ignores those elements in it that do not advance his argument. He quotes approvingly that crusty old aristocrat, John Adams; he does not mention Paine or Parker or Thoreau; and when he cites Jefferson it is primarily to explain him away — to argue, or at least to assert, that Jefferson did not mean what people have taken him to mean when he denied that the United States is a Christian nation and affirmed that all men are created equal. What Kirk really reveres is the "divine intelligence," though it is not althogether clear whether this intelligence is to be found in God or in Kirk's hero, Edmund Burke; and since, as Kirk believes, the United States *is* a Christian nation, he is concerned to spell out those beliefs "which are at the heart of the American Cause" — the fatherhood of God and the brotherhood and dignity of man.

Now Christians and some others can no doubt subscribe to these beliefs without agreeing as well to the particular moral, political and economic principles that Kirk derives from them. For these principles — once we get away, as Kirk cannot, from God the stern judge but loving Father and the sins of His tormented servants — show Kirk to be not merely a man divided but a man who is tragically uninformed.

It is unfair, I suppose, to compare *The American Cause* to Kirk's earlier books, for in these, as a true (i.e., Kirkean) conservative, he was a critic of America, a Jeremiah wailing at the wall; and now he is a defender of the American faith. But the man beneath the armor cannot always conceal his true identity, and what the defender affirms the conservative often denies. The result is a potpourri in which conservative doctrines and American beliefs and practices dwell discordantly together.

This contradiction apart, what are the principles that Kirk believes define the American cause—not, let it be emphasized, from the standpoint of a conservative ethic but as these principles are applied in American life?

Morally, Kirk begins, they are the trinity of natural laws, natural rights, and natural duties; though "precisely what these rights are," Kirk admits, "never have been entirely agreed upon, even among professed Christians." Further, they embrace toleration of, but not indifference to, religion, which means that as a Christian nation we properly restrain immoral (i.e., unchristian) conduct; and if we do not restrain *all* immoral acts it is simply because no political authority can possibly do so. We are, if anything, a prudent people.

Politically, our three great concepts are justice, by which Kirk means not equality but assuring to each man the things that are his own (whether inherited or aquired); order, by which he means a graded arrangement of classes ruled by a natural aristocracy; and freedom, by which he means not the absence of restraints, but "a disciplined, traditional, moderate, law-respecting freedom . . . obedience to the laws of God."

Finally, the American economic system is a free economy based on competition — "human beings are content only when they are struggling against obstacles" — tempered by charity. In fact, because we have "very widely and equitably distributed" our wealth, because we now have millions of "capitalists" and no depressed classes, it is possible, Kirk muses, that our real problem is to reward better than we do the upper classes.

I leave for the delectation of the reader two chapters that must be read to be believed. In one (chap. 6), the American political system is described in terms that put it beyond all recognition. In the other (chap. 9), the Communist claims are disposed of as the product of ignorance and sin, envy and the lust for power; and what attention is given to Communist doctrine is focused on as absurd a presentation of the canons of communism as this commentator has ever read (see pp. 138-139).

How shall we explain this book? Clearly, on the basis of some of his earlier writings, Kirk is too sensitive a person not to be aware of some at least of his flagrant distortions: repeatedly, for example, he resorts in *The American Cause* to a double standard of judgment, condemning the Communists whenever their practices depart from their verbal professions but justifying the Americans whenever they do the same on the ground that such inconsistencies are merely the normal differences between imperfect man and ideal society. What accounts for this performance, I suspect, is that Kirk is here trying to rally Americans, particularly the military — "it is a compliment to an American soldier to ask him to die for the ashes of his fathers and the temples of his God" — to the support of a cause in which he does not altogether believe.

For this reader, however, precisely because the American cause is in its commitment to democracy a noble cause, it merits a noble defense; and this can be achieved only by one who sees that cause for what it is, and who can condemn those who attack it both from within and from without.

E. Jordan: Order and an Aristocracy of Mind

It will not have escaped notice that none of the foregoing group of conservative writers can properly be called a philosopher. Where they verge on philosophical question, they do so as ideologists, not as philosophers. To introduce the name of Elijah Jordan at this point, therefore, may be somewhat misleading; for while Jordan is indeed a philosopher, a thinker distinguished by a subtle and sensitive intelligence, as a philosopher his work does not readily lend itself to inclusion within the rubric of conservatism, or of any other stereotyped political label. To the extent that Jordan is concerned with legal and political problems, they are problems of political philosophy, not questions to be dealt with at the level of partisan politics. Nevertheless, like Santayana, Jordan has been embraced by conservative thinkers and claimed by them as one of their own. This is because his teaching articulates certain doctrines congenial to conservative thought, both in morals (because of his wholesale assault on subjectivism, among other things) and in politics. This is not the place to discuss his important ethical treatise *The Good Life,* other than to note that its publication in 1949 met with such critical attention, and in certain philosophical quarters acclaim, as to lead his publishers to reissue, with a new preface, his major political work, *Theory of Legislation,*[8] originally published in 1930. And it is this book, characterized by a plea for a certain type of aristocracy, that has most endeared him to certain conservative spokesmen and that merits discussion here.

There is no doubt that *Theory of Legislation* is a major (if linguistically involved) effort at the formulation of a systematic legal and political theory. Whether it proves entirely persuasive, however, is dependent, among other things, on the avidity with which one is prepared to yield modern political democracy for a corporate order that institutionalizes certain proclaimed ultimates—in particular, the notion that not man but "order principled by law is the End" (pp. 183, 209).

149

Though one might suppose that every system of order is in fact principled by law, Jordan has in mind only "corporate organization as made concrete in the facts of will and as objectified in nature" (p. 273). By will he means the corporate will, which while identical in principle with the individual will differs from the latter in three respects: the corporate will is unimpersonate; it includes the human individual as a constituent factor; it "can *do*, but it cannot *see;* whereas the human individual can *see* but cannot *do*" (pp. 244,250). In these terms legislation as an act of the speculative intelligence is concerned not with statutes or the practical application of means, but with the definition of ends, the making of policy. "In its highest form legislation is the process of the organization of values" (p. 202).

Now for Jordan values, like principles, cannot be tentative. In so far as they are true, they express "the continuity of the real or the uniformity of nature" (p. 164). They require, for practical application, a system rationally conceived and properly institutionalized. In Jordan's view, democracy is not this system. It relies on a non-existent public opinion. It presupposes on the part of average citizens an intelligence and a right-mindedness which they do not and cannot possibly have. It looks to individual conscious effort, to subjective forces, rather than to permanent and continuous agencies of order in the maintenance of stability in human life. It forgets that "political activity is the prerogative of the corporate Individual" (pp. 192, 315-345, 417-422).

For Jordan, the only right basis of political order is an aristocracy of mind — "a corporate class of free intellects whose speculative imagination is allowed to wander at will in the construction of the schema of ideas; and whose hand is free and absolutely unhindered in the process of experimental verification of those ideas within the laboratory of social life until they can be reduced to law" (p. 345). This aristocracy of mind is not primarily a selection of individual men; it is rather the system of cultural institutions. But cultural institutions do not operate without men. Hence Jordan looks ultimately to "a specially organized body of men selected from the life-whole on the basis of extraordinary capacity" (p. 345).

It is not altogether clear how or by whom these extraordinary men are to be selected, or in fact what capacity is extraordinary. In his concluding paragraphs Jordan looks to "the judgment that wills the unity of the social order" (p. 481), which might seem to call for philosophic or at least practical wisdom. But he curiously locates this judgment in the special rationality of the judiciary, based, he says, on "the technical competence of its members" (p. 450). Now technical competence, as Jordan himself recognizes in other connections, is no sure guide to wisdom; and if one is to label the judicial act "the ultimate principle of unity in the world" (p. 478), it is necessary to establish the identity of technical competence in the law with right or corporate will. When Jordan in a lyrical moment compares the competent judicial mind to the poet, the prophet, and the savant, and says that of these "the judicial mind requires the highest degree of perceptive inerrancy combined with the most refined delicacy of affective penetration" (p. 456), he in effect abandons practical philosophy for what might be called a metaphysic of legislation.

It is not the least of Jordan's difficulties that this metaphysic leads him to reject not democracy but a misconception of democracy. More important, because it vitiates his central purpose — which is to construct not only a true but a *practical* theory of legislation — is his failure to provide an adequate transition from his metaphysical views to corrected practical philosophy. If legislation is to serve not interest but law (conceived as end), then a practical theory of legislation requires not only speculation as to policy (the legislative function)) and experimentation to establish maxims of action (the administrative function) and a process to test these principles of policy through deliberation (the judicial function); it demands, far more, real rather than fictitious men to operate the institutions designed to fulfil these functions. An aristocracy of mind, as Jordan conceives it, can have no relation to the forms of practical life. If it were so related, its necessary autonomy would have to be squared with the ancient truth that power divorced from responsibility produces tyranny. Thus Jordan, in his quest for justice in the practical life — and politics, he emphasizes, is the form of practical life — ends by giving us not a political but a metaphysical theory.

An Epilogue for Conservatives

I began by noting the contemporary propensity to emphasize the things that unite rather than the things that divide liberals and conservatives. It is well, in the face of the totalitarian challenges of our time, to stress such bonds of unity; for if a political community is to endure, the things that are common to men must be esteemed more highly than the things that divide them. Those who hold extreme views, whether of the far Right or of the far Left, emphasize the dividing interests; the Center emphasizes common interests. It is axiomatic, consequently, that only where the Center is sufficiently large and vital can a people maintain the fabric of their political order. Where the extremes are the major forces, victory by one alienates the other. This produces intense conflict, intolerance, suppression, even revolution. It is thus the function of the Center to compromise opposing interests and to serve as the balancing and integrating force.

Balance, however, does not imply movement; and it would be a dismal prospect indeed to rest the conception of a good life on a Center that precludes the possibility of change. It is the strength and viability of an intelligent Center that it does not require a static society; for while the Center binds, it is itself divided. Conservatives who battle alongside liberals and radicals to preserve political democracy — where, that is to say, conservatives do seek to preserve democracy — leap to the other side of the barricades when the ends to which that domocracy shall be directed are at issue. Consensus on the fundamentals of the political order does not compel agreement on day-to-day economic and social policies.

What distinguishes conservatives from liberals, however, is not merely the fact that conservatives live, all too commonly, in fear and trembling, in the brooding shadows of great myths and hoary traditions, in values rooted in some kind of class inequality, while liberals move, in general, in a changing and adventurous world, seeking not merely to preserve but *to make* tradition, and to make it for a free *and politically equal humanity*. What distinguishes conservatives, far more, is their distrust of democracy itself, and their longing for some form of aristocratic society. In these respects conservatism is not merely a static doctrine; it is a reactionary doctrine. And it is reactionary not simply in its opposition to particular economic and social policies, but in its opposition to the very structure of the democratic order.

Conservatives in quest of a theory, therefore, must decide first just what it is they most wish to conserve. If it is democracy, those who now call themselves — or who are generally regarded as — conservatives will be the first to divide. If it is not democracy but a set of external values or standards that might more readily be achieved by an oligarchical form of government, conservatives will find that they will have ruled themselves out of the very Center they otherwise avowedly esteem. What is confusing to one outside the conservative camp is the inability of conservative thinkers to agree on what conservatism means, and the consequent inclusion among conservatives of diverse and inconsistent political factions or groups. Until conservatives succeed in putting their house divided into some sort of coherent order, the amorphous doctrine known as conservatism will remain, not — as Peter Viereck believes — "ever fascinating," but, as he also says, "ever elusive."[9]

Chapter 15

Conservatism and the Medieval Mind

If some of the more extravagant reviews of Bertrand de Jouvenel's *Sovereignty*[1] are to be believed, this book is nothing less than a classic. The London *Times Literary Supplement* proclaimed it "a remarkable achievement . . . a great work in political philosophy, a work which with all the restraint proper to scholarly comparison must be firmly placed in the ranks of the masters." Willmoore Kendall endorsed this judgment in a concurring opinion in the *National Review*. And even Denis Brogan, who seemed unwilling to go quite this far, asserted in the New York *Times* that "every page of this brilliant and successful effort . . . is loaded with ore."

I do not believe that Jouvenel's book merits these accolades, but I can think of at least three reasons to account for them. The first is that the concept of sovereignty has for a good many years been relegated to the backwater of political theory. Not since the savage assault on sovereignty in the early books of Harold Laski has anyone working within the liberal tradition attempted to make constructive use of this concept. To have the concept explored anew, and by a man working within what he at least conceives to be the liberal or democratic tradition, is an almost startling event. Whether in point of fact Jouvenel contributes to our understanding of sovereignty, whether he advances his own political theory through its use, is a matter on which I will have something to say a little later.

A second reason for the reception given Jouvenel's book is that it is one of the few attempts at a systematic treatise in the conservative mood. Because conservatives wish to conserve not all things, but only those things that are good, they require above all else what they do not now have — a rational principle or standard by which to distinguish the good from the bad, the noble from the base, *and* by which they can come seriously to grips with concrete problems. It serves no real purpose, for example, to agree that we must do good and avoid evil; for however meritorious this moral stance may be, it offers no specific guides to right behavior in a particular situation. Jouvenel's book is important, therefore, as a sophisticated effort to provide such a principle.

Finally, Jouvenel's *Sovereignty* stands in that tradition of political philosophy which is concerned, as he puts it, with the uses rather than the sources of power. What is crucial, in his view, is not the way in which power is gained, nor the principle of consent as a legitimate source of power, but the ends for which power is employed, the idea of justice or the public good. Accordingly, he criticizes democratic theory for relying on the process through which power-holders are chosen rather than on the intrinsic qualities and purposes of the power-holders themselves. He indicts democratic theory for looking to public opinion — which in this tradition is identified with the inferior judgments of average, and therefore inferior, men — instead of trusting to the wisdom of superior men, of those who know what is good and how best to achieve it.

In these respects Jouvenel's book appeals to an important, though not controlling, portion of the intellectual community.

I

Let us start with the stated purpose of Jouvenel's book.[2] This, he tells us, is to inquire into the political good. But it is not really so; for to inquire into the political good presupposes at the outset that the political good is already known, else one cannot know what he seeks or recognize it when it appears. Then his quest is rather for the conditions that make possible the attainment and perpetuation of the political good. But such a quest is intelligible only if we assume that knowledge of such conditions can lead to the improvement of deficient societies; and this assumption Jouvenel cannot — for reasons I will discuss later — readily accept. In one place, in fact, he follows Burke rather than the classical political philosophers in arguing to the contrary that reason can enable us to *discover* but not to *bring about* the political good. "The forms making for stability," he writes (and stability, for Jouvenel, is the crux of the political good), "partake of necessity, not will" (p. 25). But Jouvenel does not really believe this either; for if men can only understand but not control their history, his own book — which is avowedly a manual for statesmen — becomes a senseless enterprise. And if there is anything that Jouvenel intends, it is to make prescription rather than description the object of political science. This implies that rulers can both know and act in accordance with the political good, and Jouvenel makes it abundantly clear that he wants them to do so, even, let it be emphasized, against the wishes of a majority of the people. Reason, then, can and should govern the behavior of states. But whose reason? And to what ends?

Here we come to the heart of Jouvenel's argument, and it would be pleasant to record that at this juncture Jouvenel is unmistakably coherent and clear. Unfortunately, this is not the case. For Jouvenel is rent between the realities of power and the mystique of justice, and his answers to these questions reflect his underlying uncertainties.

He begins, simply enough, by asserting the superior claim of stability. As a man who loves order and respects customary usages, he wants "an authority aimed at keeping things in place" (p. 46); he insists that the sovereign's duty is above all else to maintain the existing equilibrium. Only in this way, he believes, can the benefits of human cooperation be secured. But what if the existing equilibrium is unjust? What if it is a totalitarian order? Here Jouvenel offers conflicting answers. Because he loathes totalitarian government, he cannot and does not approve *any* equilibrium, *any* form of human cooperation. He argues instead for the equilibrium of an open society.

But an open society is a society in flux, an equilibrium (if it is an equilibrium) in constant process of adjustment; and change, it is clear, may lead a society in the wrong as well as in the right direction. Jouvenel needs, then, a true conception of the right social order if he is to argue on other than arbitrary grounds that conservation is the first obligation of public authorities. Such a conception, however, he tells us, is a utopian dream; "it is impossible to establish a just social order" (p. 164). Then any equilibrium, any form of human cooperation, including a totalitarian one, must be good in itself; and if so, all change is evil.

This, however, will not do; for Jouvenel believes that some novelty is good, and that to govern justly the sovereign must alter the existing equilibrium by adopting such changes as will promote the public good. But if the public good is equated with the maintenance of the existing equilibrium, then all novelty must be scorned. To admit some changes, Jouvenel requires a standard other than the equilibrium itself; he needs an external norm by which he can judge which of many proposed changes are desirable, which of alternative orders or equilibriums are valuable.

This standard, says Jouvenel, is the natural law. It is also, he adds, the established customs. But these are not always compatible standards; in a particular situation they may even stand in direct opposition to each other. For the first — natural law — is an appeal to principle, to an allegedly objective criterion independent of group or national practice. The second is an appeal to subjective experience, to what communities have done and believed. But what communities have done and believed is precisely what disturbs Jouvenel and has motivated him to write his book; for he is convinced that they have indulged, by and large, in the wrong things.

In particular, he is distressed by the trust that modern democratic states have put in public opinion, in the rule of the majority. This he regards as both unwarranted and as a perversion of democracy: unwarranted because the masses of the people are customarily driven by their private passions rather than by a concern for the good of the whole; a perversion because true democracy requires action exercised in accordance with the needs, not the desires, of the people. What Jouvenel proposes instead is a reliance on the sovereign Will, which both desires and knows the public good.

Now, to decry the rule of public opinion is an old if still fashionable preoccupation. From Plato through Madison and Tocqueville and John Stuart Mill to theorists of our own day, much emphasis has been placed, and properly so, on the dangers ensuing from the "tyranny of the majority" and the "passions" of the multitude. What democratic theorists in replying need contend, however, is not that these dangers do not exist but that they are universal. Majority rule, after all, is in one sense a necessary reply to the tyranny of the minority, a tyranny which has governed mankind far longer, and with more disastrous results, than any alleged tyranny of the majority. And who can read history without an awareness of the crimes and follies of passionate rulers, whether they be kings or self-styled aristocracies? What Jouvenel must do, if his argument is to have relevance, is to demonstrate empirically that majorities are more prone than are minorities to invidious acts, that majorities but not minorities — at least, not the "right" minorities — pursue their private interests rather than the common good. And this he does not show. He contents himself instead with assertions to the contrary. But assertions are not evidence; they are conclusions to be derived from the evidence. And here, I suggest, Jouvenel, who talks much of history, ignores history.

For men possessed of power, it is clear, tend to pursue their private good as they conceive it; and this, curiously, Jouvenel in one place concedes to be a natural rather than a monstrous phenomenon (p. 94). Does it follow, however, that such men are oblivious to the common or public good? Or that the pursuit of one's private good is evil? I do not think so. For, in the one case, there are many things — e.g., education, religion, the maintenance of a peaceful social order, etc. — which men can customarily enjoy only in common; here the pursuit of one's private good is of necessity a quest for the common good as well. And in the other case, unless men are to be thrust into a common mold, they must be free to pursue *some* different, even dividing, interests. If, moreover, it is "natural," as Jouvenel contends, for men to use their power for their particular ends, it is only on the basis of some "unnatural" or artificial standard that such natural action can be condemned. But Jouvenel's standard, as we have seen, is nature; from which it must follow that what is natural is right, not wrong. To argue otherwise, Jouvenel must appeal not to nature but to a standard outside of nature, say, to convention or God. But convention, as we have noted, is a subjective and shifting and therefore improper criterion; hence Jouvenel must turn to God. And this is what he ultimately does. He falls back on the precepts of the "natural law," as these (in his interpretation) derive from God.

It is the incorporation of these precepts in the edicts of the ruler that constitutes, for Jouvenel, the sovereign Will, and gives a ruler a legitimate claim to be called sovereign. A number of questions, however, quickly come to the fore. In the first place, who or what embodies this sovereign Will, and how do we recognize it? Secondly, how do we know that it both knows and desires the public good? Further, what assurance have we that it *will* act in conformity with this knowledge? Finally, *should* it act on the basis of such knowledge?

II

To all these questions Jouvenel offers contradictory or circular answers. The sovereign Will, he says, embodies these precepts because it is through the embodiment of these precepts that it becomes the sovereign Will. Whatever tends to destroy sovereignty is beyond the competence of the sovereign; he has no power to do evil; he cannot do what ill accords with his own end. Hence the sovereign, who is all-powerful, is paradoxically enjoined by his powerlessness from committing wrong. This is the meaning of Jouvenel's insistence that the sovereign can only will what is just and reasonable; for if he wills otherwise he must be deemed not to have willed it (pp. 204-205, 209-210). But who apart from him who is called sovereign is to say whether the sovereign has willed what he should not will? If it is someone other than the sovereign, this other is in fact the sovereign; while if it is the sovereign himself, there can be no appeal to a force outside of him. Then the argument is circular or tautologous, for it asserts only that the sovereign wills what he ought to will, for if he does not will what he ought to will he is not sovereign. I do not see that this furthers our understanding, or helps us locate the sovereign Will.

To the second question there are two sorts of answers. On the one hand, *we* cannot know that the sovereign Will both knows and desires the public good, for *we,* since we are outside the sovereign and thus of the mass, are incompetent precisely by our exclusion to know these things. If we could know them, we would be part of the sovereign Will; and since we are not of the sovereign Will, we cannot know them. This leads, then, to the obvious alternative: namely, that the sovereign Will knows and desires the public good precisely because it *is* the sovereign Will. But this, too, is a circular and therefore unconvincing argument.

The third and fourth questions must be taken together. Jouvenel seems to argue, in keeping with the Socratic tradition, that right knowledge compels right action, and that the sovereign Will, because it knows what is right, should and will do what is right. He even asserts, in Rousseau-like fashion, that such action, because it accords with the needs rather than with the desires of the people, is democratic. Now democracy is a word that historically is neither clear nor unambiguous, and if Jouvenel means to use it as he does he has literal license to do so. But what must be noted is that such a definition is alien to the ordinary use of the term in Western societies, a usage that may be epitomized by Mill's *Representative Government* and that is articulated in our own day in the writings of such men as A. D. Lindsay, Ernest Barker, and R. M. MacIver.

Moreover, if democracy is to be defined by the *results* of the acts of the public authorities, there is no way to distinguish democratic from oligarchic states; for even a dictatorship, it is clear, may on occasion serve the needs of its people. The real test, of course, turns on the question, who is to determine the needs as distinct from the desires of the people? If it is the ruler, then all states can claim to be democratic; and on this basis certain totalitarian dictatorships have ventured precisely this claim. But if it is the people themselves, then not the result but the *source* of political action is decisive; and this is what is meant by the rule of public opinion. Jouvenel, however, because he dislikes and distrusts public opinion yet professes to respect democracy, must somehow detach democracy from public opinion. And this he does by returning to Rousseau's notion of a real will, and of a ruler who knows, even against the judgment of a majority of his people, what the people "really" want. We are back, once again, to a disembodied, even mystical, sovereign Will. And there is no force (in Jouvenel's theory) outside this sovereign Will to tell us whether the sovereign Will has really acted in the real interests of the people, or to protect us from this sovereign Will if it has not in fact done so.

Since Jouvenel regards himself as a Christian, one can, I suppose, point to the inconvenient doctrine of sin, which would seem to suggest that no human power will always act rightly even if it always knows what is right. But a more interesting question arises when we ask Jouvenel whether he really means that the sovereign *should* act for the common good. It would appear from his teaching that the only possible answer is an affirmative one, for why should we seek a ruler who knows and desires the public good unless we mean him to act in its interest? Such an inference, however, would be disputed by none other than Jouvenel himself. For, while he follows Socrates in holding that justice consists in rendering to each man his due, he does not believe that the proper function of the sovereign Will is to render justice or, more grandly, to initiate policies designed to promote the common good. He holds instead that the sovereign — who in this connection he labels *rex* — should limit himself to maintaining the social framework, the rules of the game; he should uphold society's conventions; he should not himself seek to initiate right action. Such initiative should be left rather to private individuals — the *duces*. But what if the "right" initiative is not forthcoming? This, if I understand Jouvenel correctly, is of no great moment; for while the sovereign should encourage initiatives which make for change, his essential function is "to ensure the reliability of the individual's environment." He must repair the insecurities caused by initiatives. He must achieve stability in the face of change (p. 300).

III

Let us look more closely at the argument, for what Jouvenel now seems to be affirming is (a) that the sovereign should not initiate acts to advance the common good but should content himself with preserving the existing order of things, allowing, to be sure, a modicum of change, and (b) that the sovereign in maintaining the existing equilibrium *is* in fact promoting the common good. The second of these propositions implies, I take it, an appeal to custom rather than to natural law; and this Jouvenel explicitly accepts when he argues repeatedly for the imperative of equilibrium, for the primacy of stability. "So great a blessing is moral harmony," he writes, "that whatever tends to weaken it must be dangerous and bad" (p. 123). But to argue for social cohesion without regard to the principles on which that cohesion rests, is to vindicate even authoritarian government, which Jouvenel rejects. And if not all cooperation promotes the common good, we must look once again for a standard by which we can distinguish good from bad forms of cooperation.

Jouvenel tells us that this standard is to be found not in will but in justice; but he also says that the ruler is not free to apply the conclusions of his speculative reasoning. On the contrary, he must be guided and controlled by existing conventions; he must apply the socially accepted standards. Then justice is not to be found in the individual conscience, not in "reason" as the individual or the ruler may conceive it; it is rather to be sought in the agreements of a social order. It is thus reduced to submission to convention.

But diversity and change, Jouvenel argues, must be allowed. And it is here that he builds most directly on his distinction between sovereign (or *rex*) and innovator (or *dux*). For the sovereign, as Jouvenel conceives him, "is the natural enemy of widespread initiative" (p. 301). He seeks to stabilize, not to initiate. If he were to initiate, especially if he were to claim a monopoly of the power to initiate, he would impose an authoritarianism that would destroy liberty and stifle initiative. He would seek to

159

play God, but not being God he would rule imperfectly, and hence at times unjustly. It will not do, Jouvenel insists, to say that the ruler will act rationally; for in Jouvenel's view (as in Burke and in Michael Oakeshott) rationalism — i.e., the notion that planned action can produce the good — is nothing less than utopian. Not only is it impossible to judge future consequences, there is no such thing as a just social order; consequently the effort to improve society through rational thought is likely to produce the very tyranny it seeks to escape. Thus, Jouvenel concludes that the sovereign should be no more than a sort of umpire, adjudicating and adjusting the initiatives that stem from the innovators. The innovator alone must remain the driving force toward some positive goal. In this way, Jouvenel believes, the sovereign can secure both stability and change.

Now, there is a sense in which the public authority may be said to be inherently opposed to change, and this is clearly the case where that authority is the representative of a stable or traditional ruling class. But it is the mark of a democratic state — and Jouvenel professes not to oppose democracy — that classes or groups or parties are free to compete for the control of the public authority. Under such circumstances, the state may properly be regarded as the medium through which various innovators battle, so that a particular innovator may become sovereign. Then the sovereign is not the enemy but the instrument of initiative; the innovator in becoming sovereign is able to use the political apparatus not merely to preserve but to produce desired changes in the existing order of things. And since, in the modern state, significant changes are most commonly possible only, or most effectively, through state action, the dichotomy that Jouvenel postulates between innovator and sovereign breaks down. The sovereign is not someone distinct from the innovator; he is the innovator in power. What democracy does, then, from this standpoint, is to create the conditions under which the various innovators can most freely compete for the conquest of political power, to make it possible for a particular innovator or coalition of innovators to rule — to become the sovereign — and at the same time to protect the innovators out of power from being annihilated so that they in turn may someday move to the control of the public authority. And if all this is true, as I believe it is for a genuinely democratic state, then not only Jouvenel's distinction but also his prescribed policy becomes meaningless or irrelevant. For he would have the sovereign limit himself to the preservation of the existing equilibrium, and the innovator to its change; while democracy, as I understand it, assigns to the sovereign — who from this standpoint, I repeat, is the innovator in power — not merely the preservation but the promotion of the common good, as it gives to the innovator not merely an opportunity to improve the common good but an obligation to preserve the system which makes it possible for him both to survive and to seek in turn to become the sovereign. In both cases what is clearly required is the application of reason to human affairs — not only to comprehend irrational behavior but to channel, even if but in limited degree, the forces that constitute our history. If reason cannot do this much at least, it serves no useful purpose for men to reflect on the troubles of their world. They ought rather to resign themselves to the buffetings of a pointless fate.

IV

How are we to understand this book? I think we can do so only if we view it as the work of a man overcome by nostalgia. He reads the story of power as a retrogression from the rule of Christian monarchs, in which able men governed a natural community of unequals, to the rule of secular democracies, in which public opinion based on the artificial doctrine of equality governs despotically. He would restore Christian justice, but he knows too well that men in power are prone to define justice in ways counter to his own. Hence he would restrict men in power from effecting such alterations in the existing equilibrium as they might desire. Instead he would leave these initiatives to men out of power, hoping that those in power will adopt such initiatives as will permit improvement along with stability. But he provides no way of identifying and securing the adoption of the right changes, or of removing a sovereign who institutes the wrong changes, or indeed of establishing the "right" equilibrium to begin with.

What Jouvenel has written, then, is a medieval tract for medieval man, conscious of place and order and of the inspirations of a Christian god but unconscious both of his romantic image of medieval justice and of the grim experiences of our own time. What Marx and Freud and totalitarianism have taught us of the irrationality of man, of the role of economic forces in history, of mass political parties and the uses of terror — these and other things go unnoticed here. We move rather in devious ways to the ghostlike notion of a sovereign Will — a will divorced from all reality and even, in Jouvenel's terms, from all clear purpose. This, I am forced to say, is bad political theory and bad history. It is also, I fear, bad theology.

Whether conservatives will, on reflection, gain solace from this massive pastiche, I cannot say. Since conservatism is more a mood than a doctrine — since, that is to say, most conservatives do not seriously reflect on these things — it is probable that they will. But few students of political theory are likely to derive from this volume either a better understanding of sovereignty or a rational principle that will explain, let alone vindicate, the conservative idea.

Chapter 16

Freedom, Virtue, and the "New" Scholasticism:
The Supreme Court as Philosopher-Kings

I

Once again, as in the days of the New Deal, the Supreme Court is the center of a vigorous national debate. But the issues now are different from those which agitated the country two decades ago, and the participants have by and large reversed their roles. Then it was the liberals who led the attack against the Court, arguing that a tribunal vested with the power of judicial review was essentially undemocratic, for thus public opinion could be overridden by a body of men neither elected by nor responsible to it; that the Court was acting as a legislative as well as a judicial body, making as well as declaring law; and that it had generally used this legislative power in a reactionary way, to protect "property rights" rather than "human rights." Now, however, it is the conservatives who are primarily discomfited, because the controversial issues before the Court, as Alan Westin has shown,[1] no longer concern matters of property but civil liberties and civil rights.The conservatives now argue that the Court, allegedly in the control of liberal Justices, is so concerned to protect individual liberties and civil rights that it neglects important dangers to our national security, such as Communist subversion, and also that it has impaired states' rights in such areas as segregation.

But it is not only conservatives who are criticizing the Supreme Court today. Such a liberal as Professor Herbert Wechsler of Columbia Law School, for example, has been troubled by the theory which the Court evolved to justify its rulings in the desegregation cases. Other liberals feel that the Court stood on firmer ground in civil liberties cases when it avoided judging substantive questions and, instead, secured the release of defendants merely by insisting on the observance of the rules of fair procedure. Still other liberals — including Dean Erwin Griswold and Professor Paul Freund of Harvard Law School — declare that the Court's work in recent years has been marked by a very serious decline in judicial craftsmanship.

Taken together, these criticisms constitute a formidable indictment; and the Court may not escape unscathed from the attempts now being made in Congress and elsewhere to limit its powers and correct its "erroneous" decisions. Whatever the results of this battle, however, what seems least likely is an attempt to overcome what Professor Walter Berns of Cornell holds to be the Court's most serious dereliction of duty: its failure to promote "virtue."

In his book, *Freedom, Virtue, and the First Amendment,*[2] Berns argues that it is justice, rather than freedom, which is "the central political virtue." The Court's primary business is to mold men's characters, to educate the citizens, by interpreting the Constitution and the laws in such a manner as to make them conform to the canons of "natural justice." It is sheer foolishness, Berns maintains, to pretend that judges can secure justice by applying the standards of the Constitution or statutory law. They (and we) must first repudiate all modern, and especially liberal, notions about the nature of freedom; for such notions represent a defection from the great truths of classical political philosophy. The function of law is to direct the inner life of man so as to produce right conduct; and only if the Court's love of virtue surpasses its love of freedom, Berns says, can we hope to achieve a just society.

This conception of law, freedom, and the work of the Court has had little impact on the legal profession or on political practice. Nevertheless, Berns is significant — not as an interesting if isolated critic of American constitutional law, but rather as a representative of the neo-conservative and anti-liberal camp typified by such otherwise disparate figures as Leo Strauss and Walter Lippmann, Eric Voegelin and John Hallowell, Bertrand de Jouvenel and, in lesser degree, Hannah Arendt.

What unites these very different thinkers is a deep suspicion of most liberal assumptions. Berns is, strictly speaking, a member of Professor Strauss's particular school of natural-right philosophy; yet his attack on the Supreme Court, which he views as an instrument of liberal politics, becomes meaningful only in the context of the much broader assault on modern liberalism. Here, as it were, is a case study of the rather vague and unworldly neo-conservative philosophy being applied to a definite, limited area of public life, the "new" scholasticism employed to judge current political issues.

II

The neo-conservative indictment is essentially a repudiation of one of the major assumptions of liberal thought — namely, the belief that the ordinary man is sufficiently intelligent and informed to be an able judge of his own best interests. The truth is, however, that man is part of the natural order of things; he occupies a place appropriate to his nature and must perform those duties necessary to maintain that system of order. Liberalism's mistaken view of the nature of man in society, argue the neo-conservatives, leads to two major fallacies: freedom rather than virtue, rights rather than duties, becomes the ultimate political value; and the rule of wise men is subordinated to that of public sentiment. As a result, in a democracy philosophy becomes the slave of public opinion when it should be its master. Most of the disasters of recent decades — or indeed centuries — can be traced to this condition, the neo-conservatives argue.

Although neo-conservatives generally use the word "liberal" and "freedom" in a disdainful and pejorative sense, they do not reject these terms entirely but sometimes invest them with quite different meanings. Thus Leo Strauss, in an article in the *Review of Metaphysics,* distinguishes between classical or "true" liberalism, on the one hand, and modern or "perverted liberalism," on the other. "Originally, he writes, "a liberal was a man who behaves in a manner becoming a free man as distinguished from a slave." But how does a free man behave? He is respectful of and submissive "to authority which, in order to deserve respect, or to be truly authority, must be a reflection through a dimming medium of what is simply the highest."[3] He does not, therefore, like "perverted" liberals, forget "quality, excellence, or virtue."

Similarly, when Professor Hallowell praises freedom, he does not mean freedom as the absence of restraints, the freedom to do what one wants; rather he means "true freedom" or rational choice, which "requires both knowledge of the good and the will to choose the good when known."[4] Such knowledge, Hallowell emphasizes, derives not from man but from God. Freedom, therefore, is a choice which accords with God's will; for a secular theorist like Strauss, a choice which accords with the dictates of natural right. For neither writer does freedom involve a choice to act "wrongly." Thus, in somewhat Orwellian fashion, restraint becomes freedom; for freedom is now defined not as doing what you want to do (or *think* you want to do), but what you ought to do, what God (or nature) commands you to do, and what, indeed, you would do if you could apprehend the truth.

All this, of course, implies the existence of a body of absolute truth. And, indeed, the neo-conservatives, whether of a natural-law (religious) or a natural-right (secular) orientation, all appeal to moral principles which are external to any political or legal principle and which are deemed to possess a higher validity. By natural law or natural right, they have in mind a conception of rights and duties which are derived from and which express the principles of human nature itself. There is, they hold, a rational order in which all natural beings, including man, have a fixed and ascertainable end. This natural order exists only to be discovered, and when discovered to be obeyed. In Strauss's words: "All natural beings have a natural end, a natural destiny, which determines what kind of operation is good for them. In case of man, reason is required for discerning these operations: reason determines what is by nature right with ultimate regard to man's natural end."[5]

The contention that nature is indeed rational (rather than essentially chaotic) is not, however, a self-evident truth. If it is to be more than what Walter Lippmann, in *The Public Philosophy,* calls a "necessary assumption," the truth of nature's rationality must be established by the same objective standard, by the very principle of reason, to which natural-right philosophers otherwise appeal; in other words, the assumption that there is a rational order must itself be sustained by reason. But it is precisely on this point that theological and secular neo-conservatives divide. The former contend that it is impossible to prove any explanation of the universe without invoking an objective reality that is outside that system, i.e., God. The latter assert that the very principle which explains the universe, reason, constitutes the objective proof of its rationality. The theological argument is a direct appeal to faith. The argument of the secular natural-right philosophers is rather circular, but it also appeals, ultimately, to an alternative faith.

Lippmann, while he admits the need for the demonstration of the existence of the rational order, is likewise compelled to admit, with Strauss, that its principles cannot be verified empirically. He seeks instead "to repair the capacity to believe," and asserts with respect to these principles that "we have to believe in them."[6] Obviously, an appeal to man's will to believe is not a very convincing demonstration of the truth of what is believed.

Attempting to circumvent this difficulty, Lippmann and Strauss invoke the authority of the "rational" and "decent" man. Such men, Lippmann holds, can have no doubts about the validity of the principles of natural law. "They are the laws of a rational order of human society — in the sense that all men, *when they are sincerely and lucidly rational,* will regard them as self-evident. . . . They are the terms of the widest consensus *of rational men* in a plural society. They are the propositions to which all men concerned, *if they are sincerely and lucidly rational,* can be expected to converge. . . . The highest laws are those upon which *all rational men of good will, when fully informed,* will tend to agree."[7] This, unfortunately, tells us little about the content of these highest laws. It also begs the very point at issue, namely, what is the test of the rational and decent man? Apparently he is one who is able to perceive the principles of the rational order — another circular argument.

When neo-conservatives indict liberalism for its philosophical relativism, for holding value statements to be matters of preference rather than of scientific proof, so that it cannot say with any objective certainty whether anything is good or bad; or when they attack liberalism's failure to apprehend and build a political order on the "true" principle of aristocracy, hierarchy, and degree, they imply that their own judgments rest on established metaphysical truths. Yet how established are these "truths" when Strauss, for example, rejects God,[8] Voegelin and Hallowell embrace him (so long as he is the Christian God), and Lippmann tries to bring the two factions together under a common umbrella labeled the "traditions of civility" or the "public philosophy"?

When neo-conservatives assert that government should be entrusted to the superior group of "rational and decent men," they imply that there is a body of such men who can readily be recognized. Yet, theorists of aristocracy have always been at loggerheads over the question of who are, politically, the best men. Intellect, wealth, strength, race — these are but a few of the qualities that have been suggested as criteria for defining the best. But nobody has yet demonstrated the connection between any of these "virtues" and effective political leadership. And even if it were possible to decide who the best men are, there is still the question of how they shall be put in power, and how removed if they cease to be best. One can only sigh over the answer Salvador de Madariaga gives to such question:

> No one appoints, elects, or chooses the aristocrat. He knows himself to be one because he hears himself called to his high and arduous endeavor by an internal voice — his vocation. There is no voice with more commanding power; none which can obtain punctual and loyal obedience. Chief and soldier within one soul, under one will, within the same executive body, the aristocrat obeys his vocation without any possible excuse or evasion. He is his own slave. ... He is his own police, judge, and executioner.[9]

The difficulties here are all too patent. Who is to decide between the claims of competing "aristocrats"? What if the aristocrat does wrong (as aristocrats have been known to do), but refuses to arrest, imprison, or execute himself? We cannot look to another aristocrat for the remedy, because by the logic of this construction only the aristocrat can judge himself. Yet the most cursory reading of history reveals that responsibility only to oneself, when combined with power over others, is not a sufficient brake on man's capacity to act unjustly toward other men.

This is why liberals, as John Stuart Mill argued in his *Representative Government,* look primarily to public opinion to prevent misgovernment. The ordinary man may not be the best judge of particular legislative enactments, but he can tell whether those who govern treat him badly or well. In the democratic state, all that is desired is that the ordinary man express his broad preferences and dislikes, that he announce whether the political shoe pinches or fits. He does this by deciding who is to govern. Through his periodic answers to this question, he also decides the question: to what general ends?

In the democratic state, philosophers (and theologians) are free to persuade public opinion to accept their findings; but since there are competing philosophies and theologies, democracy refuses, very properly, to surrender political control to a single "true" philosophy or faith. Instead, it compels them all to compete, to expose their teachings to adverse criticism, and to become a part of the prevailing opinion if they can.

III

Professor Berns, as a disciple of Strauss, holds that this democratic or liberal idea is essentially barbarous. His book on the Supreme Court is an indictment of its alleged service to liberal conceptions of society. The proper role of a judiciary, he maintains, is to dispense justice, and this the present Supreme Court, with its concern for civil liberties, has not done.

Freedom, Berns argues, is not a right but a privilege. "No citizen," he asserts, "has a *right* to free speech, whatever the Court has said to the contrary in the past or will say in the future" (Berns's italics here and following).[10] The citizen has only the obligation to do what is right, for "the purpose of law is and must be to promote virtue, not to guarantee rights of *any* description." Freedom should be extended only "to those we can trust not to misuse the privilege," to "citizens of *good character.*"[11] It is a mischievous liberal idea that freedom means the freedom to do as one may please; this permits evil men to do evil deeds. Freedom is, rather, what John Winthrop proclaimed it to be: "a liberty to that only which is good, just, and honest."[12] In Berns's terms, it is the "freedom to do good and speak the truth." Hence the First Amendment must be reinterpreted to read: "Congress shall make no law abridging the freedom of *good* speech." Commitment to the democratic idea of civil liberty is not enough — indeed, "freedom is not enough" — for "civil liberties guarantee [only] peaceful change, not change for the better," and this is an ignoble ideal.[13]

Berns argues that the judge deciding cases involving freedom of speech requires, at the outset, a moral principle by which he can distinguish "good" speech from "bad." This moral principle cannot be freedom, for "freedom in itself has no intrinsic merit." It cannot be the liberal faith in full and free discussion, which is a "formalistic" and "empty process"; the liberal who exalts discussion is indifferent to the merits or truth of competing claims, and his faith in discussion is "unsupported by reason." Nor, finally, can the judge's moral standard be the principle of democracy, which in Berns's view rests on the passing whims of public opinion; "that the noxious doctrine might win over the democratic doctrine is a possibility . . . liberals do not entertain."[14]

The only legitimate moral principle, according to Berns, is virtue or justice; and justice, Socrates taught, consists in giving each man his due. The judge, therefore, "must not only know the right, he must also possess the rhetorical skill to explain, teach, and convince in order to do the right."[15] He must be a teacher and legislator, not an arbitrator or referee.[16] To achieve justice, the judge must recognize that "the formation of character is the principal duty of government." Law must concern itself with "the inner life of man" — not, as liberals would have it, with external behavior. This, of course, implies censorship, and Berns, though he admits that it is dangerous, insists that censorship is necessary. For, just as "civil society is impossible if every man retains an absolute freedom of opinion," so moral education is impossible without some censorship. "Only if the community is made up predominantly of citizens of *good character,* who trust one another, is freedom not only possible but desirable."[17]

In this manner, then, we come down from the new scholasticism to such mundane matters as the Communist Party and allegedly obscene novels and motion pictures. Berns's position on these matters is the predictably conservative one, however much it may differ from that of other conservatives in other respects. It is useful, therefore, in the light of rather widespread support for this position, to examine its theoretical underpinnings.

IV

Let us consider, first, Berns's notion that justice — giving each man his due — is the proper end of government. Although this teaching has persisted for some two thousand four hundred years of human history, it is deceptive political doctrine.

To begin with, to conceive of justice primarily in terms of specific right acts — rather than as a political arrangement or regime — is to focus one's quest for justice not on institutions or processes but on the rule of allegedly wise men; when morally right acts are the chief concern, only those who know what is right, and what should be done to achieve it, ought to rule. However, the quest for philosopher-kings, as Socrates well knew, is a utopian one. No actual "aristocracy" has in fact been based on the principle of merit. The real choice, instead, has always been between systems that tend to oligarchy and those that approximate some degree of democracy.

To secure justice, then, what matters most is a political regime that curbs, so far as humanly possible, the mistaken or oppressive acts of temporary rulers. In this sense, justice is inherent in the political arrangement of a people, rather than in the specific acts of officials. It is no sufficient indictment of a democratic or judicial system to point to "bad" policies or decisions; for no government or court is infallible, and the most democratic system may enact some unjust laws. What is necessary is that the system contain the machinery to correct these injustices.

By making justice the supreme, even the sole, end of government, Berns attempts to identify ethics and politics. Yet Socratic justice can be at best only one of the many virtues of social institutions; the law must look to order and system as well. Socratic justice apportions and divides; it seeks not to reconcile opposing claims but to give each its due. Yet a state must do more than this: it must establish rules of conduct which relate to the general convenience (and which may not themselves be based on ethical distinctions at all — e.g., traffic regulations) and the common good. It must create a political order that balances or harmonizes competing claims, lest some portion of the community be alienated and estranged. And because a democratic state in particular seeks always to strengthen the bonds of social cohesion, it must distinguish, rather than identify, ethical ideals and political rules. The state need not, and should not, be the arbiter of all moral issues.

As for giving each man his due, what is one's due? How is that due to be determined? One looks in vain in Berns's book, and in other works by neo-conservatives, for a meaningful definition. Like Lippmann and Strauss, Berns appeals to the knowledge of decent and reasonable men. They "know" what is one's due because they are decent and reasonable men, and they are decent and reasonable because they know it, etc., etc.

The liberal view of freedom, which Berns rejects, is that of an ordered system of liberties and restraints — not some absolute freedom or non-freedom, but rather a choice among particular liberties. We value the liberty of a pedestrian to cross the street in safety more than we do the liberty of an automobile driver to drive his vehicle without any limitations; hence, traffic lights and speed limits restrain the latter's freedom. In the liberal view, the problem of freedom in the real world is to decide which from among the many diverse liberties we most prize, and to impose appropriate restraints in order to secure those liberties.

Berns argues that the liberal conception of freedom exalts the individual man at the expense of the community. Yet even a nineteenth century liberal like Mill contended that the problem of freedom was twofold: freedom from the arbitrary controls of government, and also freedom from the arbitrary restraints of private powers. Liberals can, and do, support governmental restraints which curb the potential oppressive acts of private powers, for a governmental restraint on X, who would otherwise restrain Y, often conduces to the greater liberty of Y. The real question is to decide which restraints are to be imposed, by whom, and for what purposes — and that question is the very substance of politics in a democracy.

Berns terms it "positively un-American to speak of the American democracy as a mere process of reaching political decisions, or more specifically, as a regime based not on a moral principle but on full and free discussion."[18] Yet the essence of the American democracy is precisely this commitment to a process. Authoritarian states can have stated ends to which all are required to submit. Democratic states, because they recognize that men seek to pursue different ends, build instead on a method through which conflicts can be negotiated. The alternative to such a process, to the idea of peaceful change which Berns rightly ascribes to our conception of civil liberties, is the authoritarian suppression of change, or the acceptance of mutual slaughter as a technique of violent change. Thus, in a democratic state free speech must be regarded not as a privilege but as a right — not a "natural right" in Berns's sense, to be sure, but a right essential to the very nature of democracy. Only if men are free to speak, to persuade others to join with them in pursuit of other freedoms, can we hope to achieve a just resolution of conflicts as to which freedoms are to be secured. Freedom of speech, that is to say, is the necessary means of determining our other freedoms, if we are not to surrender this determination to a group of allegedly superior men.

It is preposterous to insist, as Berns does, that liberalism must argue for the unfortunate statement of Justice Holmes that the test of truth is its ability to win acceptance in the competition of the market place. Popularity is not a guarantee of truth; all that liberalism stands for is the principle that in the absence of final truth, freedom of expression is essential—lest our opinions harden into that rigidity which authoritarians mistake for truth. Freedom of speech is necessary not because it assures truth but because it makes possible the correction of error.

Similarly, it is preposterous to hold, with Berns, that liberals close their eyes to the possibility that the "noxious doctrine" may win out in the free competition of ideas. The more important liberal thinkers — men like Morris Cohen, John Dewey, R. M. MacIver, and Bertrand Russell — live with a sense of tragedy, a realistic perception of the risks attendant upon a free society. They see, as the neo-conservatives do not, that growth and, let it be added, virtue, come only from free choice. And if men are to be free to choose, they must be free to examine alternative possibilities, and to act on the basis of their own best judgment.

V

Given Berns's views on the nature of freedom, justice, and government, how does he conceive the role of the Supreme Court in the American democracy? He wants the judge (1) to assume the role of legislator, and subordinate even the Constitution to "justice"; and (2)) to control, through appropriate censorship, the inner life of the citizens so as to develop "good character." If the Supreme Court were to attempt these things, it would cease to be a court and would become a body of philosopher-kings. Such an attempt is hardly feasible politically, but it would also be highly undesirable — even if those philosopher-judges held more advanced social views than those of Professor Berns.

If an elected assembly is deprived by a censorial interventionist judiciary of its power to make the major policy decisions of government, it becomes a subordinate rather than a primary power in the process of legislation. It also, at the same time, loses its creativity and sense of responsibility. Why, in those circumstances, should the legislature reflect seriously on the pressing issues of the day? Why, indeed, should it think at all? Surely the Court will do all that needs to be done.

Berns nowhere considers the consequences to the American system of government of his argument for judicial, rather than legislative, philosopher-kings. He assumes a judiciary with a will of its own and the power to implement that will. Yet in all the cases that Berns cites, the Court acts only when the issues are brought to it; the Court does not *initiate* actions. To be sure, when the Court acts on cases brought before it, it in some sense establishes policy — either negatively, by telling the Congress and the Executive what they may not do, or positively, by interpreting statutes so as to spell out the nature and limits of legitimately exercised power. But such power, great as it is, constitutes no more than the controls of a nocturnal council; it does not convert the Court into a daytime government. For the Court to become such a government, to become a true body of philosopher-kings, the American system of government would have to be transformed. It seems curious that Berns never recommends, or confronts the consequences of, such a transformation.

In general, Berns tends to obliterate the necessary distinction between the role of a legislator and that of a judge. No one would seriously deny that a judge, in interpreting law, makes law; but there is a difference between law-making within the contours of policy set by high constitutional compromises, and law-making without regard to the legislative will. As the English system exemplifies even more than does the American, the legislator and judge are different persons holding different

171

offices with different duties. Legislators must, in principle, look forward and promulgate rules designed to govern the conduct of men in future relationships. Judges, on the other hand, must look backward, to see whether men have broken rules already established; they can punish men only in terms of penalties assigned by the law for violations of those rules. American judges occasionally — and, because of judicial review, to some extent necessarily — confuse the two functions of judge and legislator, but to have them assume a completely legislative role, as Berns proposes, is to remove all certainty from the law. It is to convert the law into a series of *ex post facto* edicts that reflect no more than the changing whims of irresponsible judges.

It seems odd that a neo-conservative like Berns, who might be expected to approach traditional institutions with piety, if not reverence, should be so cavalier when it comes to the Constitution. Yet he writes: "The purpose of the Supreme Court cannot be described as making justice conform to the Constitution. It is rather to make the Constitution conform to justice."[19] Now judges in the American system take an oath to support the Constitution, not Berns's conception of justice; and it would be not only presumptuous, but unlawful, for those judges to do as Berns demands.[20] In this sense, his proposals are not at all conservative, but quite reactionary.

Reactionary, too, are Berns's views on the necessity of censorship to bring about right thinking. To control inner belief through law, as Berns proposes, is not only to confound the realms of ethics and politics; it is effectively to prevent changes in the law through criticism from below. For if men are so educated, to use Berns's terms, "that suppression and persecution become unnecessary,"[21] it can only be because their minds have been denuded of all creative and dissident ideas. This demands both positive instruction in the right, as Berns conceives it, and the exclusion of ideas that might lead people to entertain and act on notions that are deemed wrong.

Berns is so concerned to censor "evil" publications that he slights, even as he grants, the dangers inherent in censorship — in particular, that the censors may be bigoted and incompetent men. This becomes ironic when he condemns the judges whom he would make philosopher-kings for approving the sale of certain "obscene" publications like *Headquarters Detective* and disapproving Edmund Wilson's novel, *Memoirs of Hecate County*. And what shall we say of those censors who would prohibit from the mails D. H. Lawrence's *Lady Chatterley's Lover* and Aristophanes' *Lysistrata,* the latter (if we are to believe our Postmaster) because certain passages are "well calculated to deprave the morals of persons . . . and almost equally certain to arouse libidinous thoughts in the minds of the average normal reader"?

For the Court — or government generally — to assume the obligation of forming "good character" is to move far beyond its proper province. For this is to invade the sphere of social prerogatives — of the family and religious congregation and voluntary association of every sort — and to transform a democratic into a totalitarian state.

VI

I have not dwelt here on the more technical aspects of Berns's argument, in particular his use of case materials; for these have received their appropriate corrections in the legal journals.[22] Nor have I considered the important application of Berns's argument on freedom for "good speech" only, in which he calls for the outright suppression of the Communist Party. To point out his misunderstanding of Marxist teaching, and his failure to draw the necessary distinction between the lawful activities and beliefs of that party, on the one hand, and its unlawful practices, on the other, would require more space than is warranted here.[23] But these and other deficiencies[24] testify to the fact that Berns's moral earnestness is no substitute for empirical knowledge and logical reasoning.

This is not, however, to say that Berns's book lacks merit. Its value is not as a work of constitutional law, but as a statement of a significant — though relatively small — school of political philosophy that is currently challenging the liberal conception of society. Berns's book also reminds us that some of our Justices have not been wise men, and that some of the Court's decisions have actually been foolish. Finally, it emphasizes once again that judicial review is an undemocratic institution; but here Berns draws not the inference that judicial review should therefore be abandoned, but rather the contention that it should therefore be retained: "for judicial review provides virtue with, as it were, a final chance."[25]

What Berns and other neo-conservatives value above all is a regime that would reduce the bulk of humanity to the status of children, if not of subjects or slaves. Under the pretense that they are being ruled by a body of wise men, of philosopher-kings, he would have citizens who lack "good character" and the "right morality" restrained from exercising the democratic rights of citizenship. He would manipulate and coerce them so as to make them "truly free." And his conception of "true freedom" is essentially that of submission to the true religion, a civil or secular morality in which Nature is substituted for God.

We are fortunate that no Justice has yet succumbed to the appeals

173

of this "new" scholasticism. If one should do so, the winds of doctrine that now beset the Supreme Court would be so agitated as to threaten the very foundations of our democratic system; for it is one of the striking paradoxes of neo-conservative thought that its utopian view of "justice" always seems to lead to a narrow view of civil liberties.

Afterword:

Why Communists Are Not of the Left

One of the depressing facts of history is the tenacity with which men cling to labels long after the meaning has changed. The liberalism of John Stuart Mill is not quite that of Bertrand Russell and Morris Cohen. The communism of Karl Marx is in important respects different from that of Stalin. Yet a proclivity for loose thinking and heated argumentation leads men to blur the distinctions for the sake of a common identification. This is bad logic and bad history. It also ensures bad results.

One such result is the confused notion that communists belong to the left. Why this should be so is not difficult to understand, for when Marx and his disciples attacked the injustices of the economic and, more broadly, the social order, they aligned themselves with those rebellious souls who were championing the cause of human decency and human rights. And whatever the factors that kept communists and Trotskyites, socialists and anarchists, Fabians and syndicalists, apart, they were as one in their insistence that the servant has as much claim to freedom and security as his master, that the ordinary man is not destined to dwell eternally at the base of a pyramid which he has not constructed but which he is commanded to maintain.

In their adherence to this cause communists have been both loud and vigorous. By word and by deed they have set themselves forth as the assailants of the rich and the defenders of the poor. They have sought to lay bare the intricacies of the economic system, so as to account for the causes, and make plain the correctives, of poverty and insecurity. They have noted, with much insight, the paradox of certain Western countries that possess undemocratic institutions and permit undemocratic practices yet profess democratic ideals. They have pleaded, in those same countries, for an educational system divorced from the injustices of minority discrimination and bigoted controls. Through these and other approaches they have endeavored to justify their inclusion among the forces of the left.

But if any one thing is clear, it is that communists today are in spirit, thought, and action alien to the tenets of the left. This raises the questions: What is a communist? And what is meant by "the left"?

II

At the outset, let us be clear that there are many things that a communist is not. He is *not* simply a radical, nor is a radical necessarily a communist. This is a common but dangerous confusion. If by radical we mean one who would do away with the existing order for some conception of what ought to be, one who seeks drastic, all-encompassing change, then socialists, anarchists, and indeed fascists, are radical; but they are not communists.

Nor are communists always radical. In the Soviet Union a communist is a conformist, a defender rather than an attacker of the *status quo,* which in its authoritarian practices and denial of political and intellectual freedoms bears little resemblance to the historical aspirations of the left. Outside the Soviet Union a communist is a radical only with respect to the policies of noncommunist governments, and then only when these policies are not in harmony with the interests of the USSR.

In Britain and the United States during the Second World War, for example, communists sought to suppress criticism of the "capitalist democracies" on policies they themselves attacked prior to Soviet participation on the side of these countries and since the end of the war. More recently, in postwar Austria, local Communist Party officials joined Soviet commanders in opposing the nationalization of Austrian industries, because control of those industries would then go to the Austrian government rather than to the USSR, which has been claiming them for itself. In Italy the communist leader Palmiro Togliatti supported the union of Roman Catholic church and state in the new constitution; while in Czechoslovakia the Communist Party denounced the "bourgeois" five-day work week and instituted a six-day work week, reverting, in justification of this act, to very much the same arguments advanced by capitalists in early nineteenth-century England against higher wage rates and shorter hours.

To equate communism with radicalism, therefore,, is to ignore the profound sense in which communists are conservative. More important, labeling as communists those noncommunists who seek substantial change is to pave the way for reactionary attacks on liberals and socialists; for a radical may be many things, including a communist.

It is equally misleading to identify a communist as one who advocates the overthrow of the government by force. Many non-Stalinists — Trotskyites, some anarchists, some fascists — fall into this category. More important, except where they are a substantial minority with a real chance of achieving power through revolution, communists as a matter of strategy rarely, today, advocate the overthrow of the government by force. What they contend is that a communist victory at the polls will lead to opposition by reactionary groups which will refuse to surrender control of the state machine, in which case the then constitutionally elected (communist) government will be compelled to seize power and suppress the rebellion by force. This, they note, is the business of any government that is properly elected and desires to survive.

A communist, again, cannot be defined simply as a Marxist. It is possible to claim adherence to a substantial part if not all of Marx's thought without accepting the interpretations of Lenin, just as one may subscribe to Marxism-Leninism without rendering obeisance to Stalin's several versions. Marxism and Marxism-Leninism are part of the baggage of a communist, but in some degree they also make up the intellectual inheritance of Trotsky, the social democrats of pre-Hitler Germany, and the Socialist Labor Party of Daniel de Leon, not to mention the numerous individuals and splinter groups that everywhere profess varying degrees of allegiance to Marx.

A communist is not simply a member of the Communist Party. Many who are communists do not hold membership cards: the party may think it more strategic that they not be known as party members; they may be communists who fear to avow it; or they may be communists without realizing it. In addition, some who hold membership cards are not communists. This is a delicate distinction and one that is not always easy to establish. Ordinarily, one who holds a membership card is a communist. But there are exceptions. It is too obvious and inconsequential, perhaps, to call attention to the espionage agent who joins the party for anticommunist purposes. It is less obvious but more common, however, that some are members only temporarily because of the party's stand on a particular issue. Thus for many Negroes the Communist Party is like a sieve: they join in the belief that the party stands for the betterment of their race and in the hope that by joining they will help the party to improve their condition; but after a short while they learn that the party is more interested in using them to achieve its special goals, which may not coincide with the purpose for which they have joined, and they get out. Similarly, there are at all times within the party men who, for one reason or another, do not go along with the Politburo on all policies or details. These "deviationists" periodically become the subjects of the mass purges whereby the party seeks to cleanse itself of all recalcitrants and ensure absolute conformity.

A communist, finally, is not one who occasionally or even frequently speaks with admiration for the achievement of the USSR, or more commonly for certain features of the USSR, or who stands for certain policies with which the Communist Party may at any one time happen to agree.

177

It is possible to commend certain economic and judicial reforms instituted by the Soviet Union, or to applaud the great strides that have been made in that country in the conquest of illiteracy, without being a communist. And it is possible to support legislation designed to promote equality of citizenship and of opportunity for all the people, without being a communist, even if the Communist Party should commit itself to the same measure. A cause does not cease to be just because the wrong people affiliate themselves with it.

Who, then, is a communist? He is one who accepts *and consistently follows* the policies and tactics set forth by the Cominform, or, in the formal absence of a Cominform, by the rulers of the Soviet Union. This definition draws no sharp distinction between fellow-travelers and members of the party. They are cut from the same cloth though they display slightly different garb; a membership card hidden in the pocket is no real mark of distinction. On the other hand, this does permit a distinction to be drawn between those party members who are communists and those who are temporarily there because of error or misunderstanding. It includes communists who advocate the overthrow of the government by force when the Kremlin desires to avow this policy, and those who dissemble by advancing the same thesis under the guise that they are preparing to defend the government (when it is *their* government) from those who would use violence to overthrow it. It includes communists who are conservative and communists who are radical, depending on whether it is loyalty to the USSR or rebellion against noncommunist states that is the standard by which they are to be judged.

In every case, what is central in the delineation of a communist is that he accepts not simply Marx but Marx as amended by Lenin; and not simply these but both as revised by Stalin, even and indeed especially where Stalin chooses to reverse his policy and his direction. Fidelity to the Kremlin, in a word, is the crucial determinant.

III

When we turn to the problem of left and right we move to more difficult ground. This is because the passion for simplicity has led men to draw a dichotomy between left and right on the basis of a single standard. Most commonly, this standard has been acceptance of or opposition to the established order. The right has been identified with those who wished to preserve the established order and the left with those who wished to change it. This simple division, however, does not correspond to historical reality; nor is it logically sound.

This becomes evident when we reflect that opposition to the established order merely indicates a desire for change; it does not indicate the direction of the change. Reactionaries are opposed to the *status quo,* but their desire to return to the *status quo ante* scarcely warrants their inclusion in the forces of the left. Fascists, too, are opposed to the established order, but their revolutionary appeal is to an authoritarianism that can in no way be identified with the methods and objectives of the left. Moreover, if we identify the right with the existing order and the left with the attack on it, we produce a paradoxical situation in which, after a political revolution, left and right assume reverse roles. On the other hand, where the left achieves power and pursues the policies it had formerly espoused, as was the case with the Labor government in England after 1945, support of the established political order is in no sense a deviation from the precepts of the left.

Can we then define the right as the group which favors private property and individual enterprise, in contradistinction to the left which opposes private property and urges collectivist controls? If we do, we are embarrassed by the fact that the fascist right is quick to adopt collectivist measures and to do away with private property when it is deemed expedient or necessary; while the concept of individual enterprise held by the reactionary and even conservative right is increasingly one which restricts that enterprise to those few who share in the ownership or management of the huge concentrations of capital and industry. The allegedly communist left, on the other hand, does away with the system of private property, but in doing so it creates a new economic elite based on the control rather than the ownership of property, and abrogates those political and cultural freedoms that the liberal and radical left have historically cherished.

Is the left, then, the home of those who would increase the area of freedom, and the right the refuge of those who would destroy it? Historically, there is much substance to this view, for one of the hallmarks of the left has always been its refusal automatically to conform to customary ways and traditional beliefs. But here again we are confronted with the paradox that undemocratic practices and authoritarian programs are common to communists and Trotskyites as well as to some political parties of both the left and the right, while the espousal of civil liberties frequently cuts across the left-right dichotomy.

These considerations make plain the difficulty of a linear conception in which left and right represent the polar extremes. If we take property as our line of division, communists are indeed on the left but so too are the fascists of Nazi Germany, even if in varying speed and degree. If we use liberty as our point of departure, elements of the conservative right

179

assume some of the attributes of the left while the communists join the fascists on the right.

A solution to this dilemma has been suggested by some writers who urge the substitution of a circle in place of a line, with the extreme (fascist) right and the extreme (communist) left meeting at the bottom. Then the circle can be viewed in two ways: from the standpoint of property, fascism and the moderate right are aligned against communism and the moderate left; from the standpoint of liberty, fascism and communism stand together against the moderate right and moderate left.

This conception has the virtue of joining the two authoritarian systems on the basis of their common opposition to liberty. But it overlooks the fact that in Nazi Germany and increasingly in Mussolini's Italy, the demands of the state took priority over the perquisites of private property. Moreover, the position of some sectors of the moderate right on questions of freedom of speech for dissenters, or of civil liberties for Negroes and other minority groups, is hardly calculated to unite them with the noncommunist left.

Once again, therefore, we must reject the attempt to reduce complex social phenomena to a simple mathematical symbol, whether it be a line or a circle. In both cases the kind of distinction that is offered fails to give us the precision we seek: a category that will enable us somehow to distinguish left from right with some semblance of consistency.

The basis for such a category appears if we abandon the idea of a single standard and think instead in multidimensional terms. We must take not liberty *or* property but *both,* and on three levels at least — the political, the economic, and the intellectual.

On the political level, the tradition of the left is clear. It has always been associated with the fight against authoritarianism in government, with the attack on limited suffrage and oligarchical rule. Apart from the anarchists who reject all forms of organized coercion and thus government itself, the left has been the party of democracy, the sector of the population that has denied the claim of any special group permanently to control the government and to determine public policy. Where elements of the right have sought to restrict the exercise of political power to the allegedly superior few, the left has denied that racial composition, or economic or physical advantage, is a rational criterion of political competence. The fallibility of men in power, and the tendency they demonstrate to abuse that power, has convinced the left that whatever else a proper political system requires, the mechanism for the correction of error must always be present. Only democracy offers such a constitutional mechanism for the correction of error, for only democracy provides for the periodic election *and removal* of the rulers by the ruled.

Economically, the left has always represented the interests of the lower classes, while the right — revolutionary fascists apart — has tended to defend the interests of the upper or ruling classes. The left has been opposed to private property because it has believed that private ownership gives power without responsibility; he who owns property has the legal right to use it for his own interests, even at the sacrifice of the welfare of others. Accordingly the left has supported the efforts of labor unions, through collective bargaining, to curb the great economic powers of the owners and managers, and to give workers a voice in the formulation of the conditions under which they labor. It has sought the intervention of government, both to curtail the growth of monopoly, which dooms individual enterprise and economic freedom, and to prevent the use of discriminatory practices in employment. More, it has encouraged government to move directly into the economic sphere through the public ownership and operation of industry. Through all these devices, the left has endeavored to equalize opportunity and to eliminate what it regards as unmerited privilege and advantage. It has tried to establish in the economic, as in the political, sphere, those conditions that free men can respect and find adequate to the fulfillment of their capacities and their dreams. In this the left, unlike the right, has fought for man's emancipation from arbitrary command.

On the intellectual level, the left has consistently stood for intellectual freedom and the right of all men to pursue their chosen ways of life. It has attacked the dictates of authority and the theory of the closed mind, arguing instead that only where men are free to examine the pronouncements of others can reason emerge to lead the way. The left does not claim that the opinions of those in authority are inevitably wrong; it insists only on the freedom to examine them. Since it denies that any one system or group of men embodies final truth, it refuses to accept the principle of conformity but defends the principle of free inquiry and free expression — in art, in music, in scholarship, in religion. The left is rebellious, not against everything, but against authoritarianism of the mind.

In brief, the left — liberals, socialists, and anarchists alike — is that group which stands for emancipation from authoritarian government and arbitrary command, for equality of opportunity and the elimination of artificial privilege, for freedom of the mind to pursue truth and even error as one's reason, capacities, and interests may indicate. The left has always been, and still remains, that sector associated with the fight for political and intellectual freedom, and for economic change, where necessary or desirable, in the interests of the many rather than the few, of the lower rather than the upper classes.

IV

How do the communists meet this threefold criterion of the left? At first blush, there is no simple answer to this question. It depends on whether the communists are in power or out of power, and if out of power on the position currently held by the Soviet Union. But closer examination will reveal that underlying all the shifts in policy there is a common purpose and a common theme. If we look at the political, economic, and intellectual phases of communist philosophy and tactics, we may find our answer.

On the political side, wherever the communists are in power, as in the Soviet Union and its satellite countries, they deny the principle of democracy and affirm the right of the party elite to rule. Stalin, to be sure, contends that the Soviet constitution and political system are the most democratic in the world. He bases this claim on the fact that electoral results regularly show the people to be almost unanimously agreed in support of the government, as in the 1946 elections to the Supreme Soviet, where 96.8 per cent of those eligible to vote actually voted, and of those voting 99.7 per cent voted for the "bloc" of party and nonparty Bolsheviks.[1]

Apart from the dubious validity of these figures, this is clearly a spurious argument. In the absence of free elections, of a choice of alternatives, of a legal opposition, there can be no democracy.. And when we look carefully at the institutions and practices of the USSR the lack of democracy is precisely what we find. Instead of rule by a popularly elected legislature, the Soviets employ rule by the Politburo, by executive decree. For a political party system in which, in England at least, the parties represent different conceptions of public policy, the Soviets have instituted a single party, the Communist Party, whose role it is to execute the will of the Politburo. For the free play of conflicting ideas, the Soviets have substituted a single creed, Marxism-Leninism-Stalinism, under which criticism of the government is construed as treason. In place of a responsible executive, there is a Leader, Stalin, whose will, unchallengeable, is law. These, however else we may regard them, do not add up to democracy.

Where the communists are out of power, as in the United States, their position is greatly confused. They are quick to defend the political institutions of the USSR and to insist that these are democratic. More than that, they maintain within their own communist party organizations the same rigid controls, the same hierarchy of authority, the same intolerance of dissent. Nevertheless, they do not hesitate to condemn these principles when practiced by others. Thus they point to the denial in certain communities of the right to freedom of speech for dissenting groups, to the perversion of democracy embodied in boss-rule, to the restriction of suffrage in southern states, and the like. If any conclusion from this double system of bookkeeping is possible, it can only be that communists, when seeking power, represent themselves as the champions of democracy; but once in power they pursue the very authoritarian practices they applaud in Georgia, USSR, but denounce in Georgia, USA. In this they remain true to Lenin who said: "There are no morals in politics; there is only expediency."[2] But they are not thereby true to the left.

The position of the communists in the economic sphere is less clear. In the Soviet Union much has been done, through a broad system of social services, to establish certain minimum standards for the great masses of the people. Much also has been done to eliminate the class of the idle rich and, in lesser degree, to seek to narrow the gap between the economically favored and the lower social classes. Everybody not only has a right to a job, everybody works; and this includes both the powerful and the privileged.

But the system of disproportionate rewards remains. The new upper classes of party officials, bureaucrats, managers, and technicians, scientists and artists, army and navy officers and the chieftains of the secret police, enjoy a standard of living far greater than that of the people over whom they rule. Between manager and worker there is a chasm of privilege exceeded only by that of power. The Russian worker who in any way expresses dissent on questions of political or economic policy finds his opportunity to rise severely limited; and there are no alternatives to government employment. His wage rates are set by the agencies of the government, and the leaders of his trade unions are responsible not to him but to the Communist Party. Since the abortive attempt of the Kronstadt sailors in 1921, there have been no strikes over wages and related matters in state industries; the Russian worker knows that a strike is liable to prosecution as a counter-revolutionary measure or an act of sabotage. He carries a card or "labor passport" which bears much of his life and occupational history and without which he cannot be employed. He can change his job only with permission of the manager of his industry, and if he is frequently late or absents himself from his place of employment he is guilty of a crime punishable by imprisonment. The economic freedoms and opportunities traditionally defended by the left are not, it would appear, defended by the communists in the USSR.

What of communists outside the Soviet orbit? Do they not speak for the interests of the many rather than the few? Here the record is equally blurred. The Communist Party in the United States, for example, has a long history of opposition to economic privilege, to big business and monopoly; it has a long history too in support of the economic struggles of the wage-earners, the unemployed, the consumers. Indeed, communists have sacrificed their very lives as they have fought in the forefront of many struggles for more humane treatment and a greater share of economic wealth for the underprivileged.

However, a study of the history and functioning of communists in such struggles reveals that their underlying policy is always that of rule-or-ruin. They have become active in labor organizations, unemployed leagues, farm groups, consumer councils, and the like, in an effort to secure positions of leadership in them. Once in control, they use these organizations not simply for the avowed purposes for which these organizations were designed but as a springboard from which to proclaim communist doctrine on all subjects, and especially to propagandize for the Soviet Union and its policies. After the disruption of the Nazi-Soviet Pact, for example, and the entrance of the Soviet Union into the war, communist-dominated unions vigorously promoted the institution of industry wage incentives to increase production, a program they bitterly opposed during the pact and since the end of the war. Communist-dominated unions in France and Italy opposed Marshall Plan aid which would give their members jobs and aid their countries economically, thereby demonstrating that communists will not hesitate to sacrifice the economic ends of organizations they control for the political ends of the USSR.

Where communists have not been able to control the economic organizations of the lower income groups, they have followed, in the main, two alternative patterns of strategy. One has been to promote internal dissension and thus prevent the organization from effectively pursuing its avowed purposes, while at the same time calling for "internal democracy" so as to maintain the conditions that will enable them to continue their activities and eventually to achieve control. Along with this there is generally involved the most extreme type of personal vilification of non-communist leaders, in an effort to discredit them and alienate their following. The other pattern has been to sabotage the organization by setting up a rival group under their control to combat it, or to prevent it from functioning by attack from without. This takes the form of name-calling, of labeling the organization a fascist tool, of denying it any assistance and urging those whom it influences not to support it, and so on. In every case, from the communist standpoint, either it shall be communist-ruled or it shall be communist-ruined.

Communist abdication from the principles of the left is nowhere more clear than in the intellectual sphere. In the Soviet Union the body of thought we call communism has become a theology, to be accepted in all its details and to be removed from the area of scrutiny. There is the bible, containing the old testament of Marx and Engels and the new testament of Lenin. There are the high priests — Stalin and the Politburo —to interpret the bible. And there are the inquisitors, swift to castigate those who deviate from the true path and to place their books and their theories on the Soviet Index. Whether it is political doctrine or economic analysis, architecture or biology, musical composition or the drama, mathematics or statistics, history or literature, conformity to the Communist Party position is the necessary prerequisite to survival.

It is not important to ask whether the particular position of the Soviets on a question of art or genetics is the right one. What is important to note is that, whether right or wrong, it is a *political* decision and must be obeyed, even if one's knowledge and reason were to dictate otherwise. Consider, for example, the revealing remark of Professor Anton Zhebrak, a distinguished Soviet geneticist: "I, as a party member, do not consider it possible for me to retain the views [on genetics] which have been recognized as erroneous by the Central Committee of our party." Were a scientist in England or the United States to utter such a statement with reference to the noncommunist political parties of his country, he would almost certainly be regarded as ready for incarceration in a home for the mentally deranged.

It is interesting to note that this intellectual authoritarianism — what the communists call "democratic centralism" — is not a new but a very old article in the communist theology. Lenin "proves" many of his arguments by quotation from Marx and Engels; Stalin "proves" his theses in the same way. Thus, with reference to the once controversial issue of equalitarianism, Stalin observed that Marx and Lenin had said one thing, their critics another. "Who is right," Stalin then asked, "Marx and Lenin, or our equalitarians? We may take it that Marx and Lenin are right."

What emerges from this pattern of faith is a slavish obedience to presumed first principles. In place of scientific method, experimentation, and the inductive process, we have a closed system in which one reasons by simple deduction from truths already established or newly proclaimed by those who have the power to do so. That these truths are altered or reversed as the contingencies of the moment seem to dictate, only to be restored again, is no cause for concern to the faithful. The truth is always true, even if it had once been false.[3]

This applies equally to communists outside the USSR. Nothing in modern history is so striking as the consistency with which communists in England, the United States, France, and other noncommunist states, have changed their ideas and their positions at the dictates of the Soviet

Union. Before the Nazi-Soviet Pact, the fascists were "beasts" who had to be crushed.[4] After the pact, in accordance with Molotov's declaration, a war against fascism was held to be a crime against humanity, a barbaric medieval crusade; for fascism, Molotov said, was only "a matter of political views."[5] When the Soviets were invaded by Germany, the war changed into a people's struggle for democracy and freedom. And now that the war is over, only the Soviet Union is pursuing the right foreign policy, and only the "capitalist democracies" are imperialist aggressors. These intellectual gyrations have recently been displayed on questions of Zionism, the acceptance or rejection of Western culture, nationalism versus internationalism, cooperation with liberal forces in politics, and the like, *ad infinitum.*

What is fascinating in this process to the noncommunist observer is the way in which all but a very few communists — who are promptly vilified as renegades — change their minds concurrently. In all countries and within a few days, the new "line" is adopted and the old "line" cast aside. The rapid succession with which Togliatti in Italy, Pollitt in England, and Foster and Dennis in the United States parrotted Maurice Thorez's declaration of allegiance to the Soviet Union in the event of war between the USSR and his own country, France, is only one of the more recent of many cases in point. In a habitat of intellectual freedom and intellectual respect, would not some express skepticism that what had been true on Monday should be false on Tuesday?

But what we have here is an authoritarianism of the mind based on a conviction that the leaders of the party are both omniscient and unerring. If communists ceased to have this conviction, they would be compelled to say, with Rubashov, the tragic hero of Koestler's *Darkness at Noon:* "The fact is : I no longer believe in my infallibility. That is why I am lost."

V

The conclusion is inescapable: communists are not of the left. They are not democrats but totalitarians, not radicals but conformists, not fighters for freedom and the economic welfare of the ordinary man but harbingers of a new slavery and a new privileged class. For the liberal who cherishes individual judgment and the freedom to choose between alternative possibilities, for the democratic socialist who seeks more quickly to alter the economic foundations of the social order so as to effect a more desirable distribution in economic power and economic goods, for the anarchist who rejects political and economic coercion so as to establish the conditions for the free flowering of the individual personality, there is no kinship with communism.

The myth of communist leftism cannot long survive contradictions. Until it is completely dead, liberals and their brethren of the left must guard against those who would stand in disguise alongside them.

Notes

FOREWORD

1. See, among other works, his *Modern State* (London, 1926).
2. See, typically, his *Human Society in Ethics and Politics* (New York, 1955).
3. See especially his *Faith of a Liberal* (New York, 1946).

CHAPTER 1

1. M. R. Cohen, *Reason and Law* (Glencoe, Ill., 1950), p. 79.
2. Since the "ins" and the "outs" are both held to be elite, oligarchical theorists have tended either to ignore this distinction or to term it a pseudo-problem. But it is the reality of this division within the alleged elite that (1) destroys the illusion of the elite as a ruling *class,* and (2) compels competing elites to seek popular support. On this point Dennis in his *Dynamics of War and Revolution* (New York, 1940) evidences a degree of perception lacking in Mosca, Burnham, and other elite writers.
3. *Political Parties: A Sociological Study of the Oligarchical Tendencies of Modern Democracy* (trans. E. and C. Paul, New York, 1915).
4. A difficult but rewarding task — that of empirically investigating democratic or anti-oligarchical tendencies in modern trade union and political organizations on a scale as broad and exhaustive as Michels employed in his study of oligarchical tendencies — remains still to be done. [Since this was written, such investigations have begun to be made. See, for example, S. M. Lipset et al, *Union Democracy* (Glencoe, Ill., 1956).]
5. Similarly, an empirical study of the increasing rigidity of oligarchies, frequently but not necessarily accompanied by a progressive narrowing of the base of the ruling "elite," would, I think, shed considerable light on this largely neglected aspect of the "iron law" theory.
6. See also Montesquieu, *The Spirit of the Laws,* Book XI, chap. 4, and John Stuart Mill, *Representative Government,* chap. 6.
7. See my *Patterns of Anti-Democratic Thought* (New York, 1949).
8. See his *Power and Personality* (New York, 1948), pp. 186f. and *passim.*
9. I have subsequently developed these and other arguments relating to the control of power in my *Democracy and the Challenge of Power* (New York, 1958), Part Two.

CHAPTER 2

1. Karl Loewenstein, *Political Power and the Governmental Process* (Chicago, 1957).

CHAPTER 3

1. *Leviathan,* chap. x.
2. *Gorgias,* 466.
3. Compare *Republic,* Book IX, especially 579–80.
4. *Leviathan,* chap. xi.
5. *Ibid.*

CHAPTER 4

1. So restricted an approach violates Montesquieu's injunction that his work be judged entire, on the basis of its total design, and not on a few particular phrases (*The Spirit of the Laws* [1748], trans. Nugent [New York, Hafner edition, 1949], Preface) (hereinafter referred to by book number only). But a man's ideas, if not

misrepresented, can generally be sufficiently distinguished to permit critical scrutiny even in part.

2. Despite the bias with which a Roman Catholic like Lord Acton might approach Montesquieu, there is much justice in his reference to Montesquieu as "an intelligent Tory," a man who "knows so many pleas for privilege that he almost overlooks the class that has none" *(Essays on Freedom and Power* [ed. Himmelfarb, Boston, 1948], pp. 257, 268). For a generally appreciative view of Montesquieu as a political and legal thinker see Eugen Ehrlich, "Montesquieu and Sociological Jurisprudence," *Harvard Law Review,* XXIX (1916), 582–600, and the Introduction by Franz Neumann to the Hafner edition of *The Spirit of the Laws,* pp. ix–lxiv. For a critical account see G. H. Sabine, *A History of Political Theory,* rev. ed., New York, 1950), pp. 551–60.

3. As. W. E. H. Lecky in his *Democracy and Liberty* (London, 1896), II, 196, seems to suggest when he speaks of Montesquieu "valuing highly liberty in all its forms."

4. Book XI, chap. iii.

5. *Ibid.,* chap. vi.

6. *Ibid.,* chap. iii; Book XIX, chap. xxvii.

7. But cf. the cautionary note in H. J. Laski, *A Grammar of Politics* (4th ed., London, 1938), p. 104.

8. "Freedom and Government," in *Freedom: Its Meaning* (ed. Anshen, New York, 1940, p. 250.

9. Montesquieu's later books on commerce are but a seeming exception to this statement, for he is there more concerned with legal constraints on commerce itself, less so with constraints on the merchant, and hardly at all with constraints on the individual. In fact, as Ehrlich, *op. cit.,* p. 598, properly notes, when Montesquieu inquiries into the social and economic situation, "he is not capable of pointing out their consequences in law because he misses the social institutions through which they operate. The history of the world's commerce . . . appear[s] in some measure suspended in the air."

10. See, for example, Book I, chap. iii, where Montesquieu in writing of positive laws declares: "Law in general is human reason, inasmuch as it governs all the inhabitants of the earth: the political and civil laws of each nation ought to be only the particular cases in which human reason is applied." Cf. the characteristic attack by Bentham (who termed Montesquieu's book a work of "pseudo-metaphysical sophistry") in Elie Halévy, *The Growth of Philosophic Radicalism* (trans. Morris, New York, 1949), pp. 54–55. For the special sense in which Montesquieu talks of the law of nature and for the vagueness of his wording see Ehrlich, *op. cit.,* pp. 582–83.

11. Book XXVIII, chap. i. This is not a unique reference. Throughout this and the following books, for example, Montesquieu emphasizes that "laws always conform to the passions and prejudices of the legislator" (Book XXIX, chap. xix) and that "there are laws so little understood by the legislator as to be contrary to the very end he proposed" (Book XXIX, chap. iv).

12. Book XIX, chap. v.

13. Book XXVII, chap. i.

14. Book XIX, chap. v.

15. Book XVI, chap. ii; see Book XXVI, chap. iii, for further illustrations of civil laws contrary to the law of nature.

16. Book XVII, chap. v.

17. Book II, chap. ii.

18. *Ibid.*

19. See n. 7 above.

20. Book XXIV, chap. vii.

21. Book XXVI, chap. ii.

22. *Ibid.,* chap. xi.

23. In terms of the sociological foundations of Montesquieu's jurisprudence, this may be interpreted to mean that "laws are not the arbitrary products of reason but are largely the result of the social forces obtaining in the community" (Huntington Cairns, *Law and the Social Sciences* [New York, 1935], p. 134).

24. Book XI, chap. vi. Curiously, Montesquieu holds that the imprisonment of persons suspected of conspiracy against the state *is* a loss of their liberty; but only, he adds, "for a while, to preserve it forever" *(ibid.).*

25. Book III, chap. iii.
26. Montesquieu's somewhat ambivalent views on freedom of speech may serve to illustrate this difficulty. He argues strongly that "the laws do not take upon them to punish any other than overt acts"; that "words do not constitute an overt act; they remain only in idea"; and that wherever law is established declaring people guilty of high treason for indiscreet speeches, "there is an end not only of liberty, but even of its very shadow" (Book XII, chaps. xi-xii). But he also affirms that "there are cases in which a veil should be drawn for a while over liberty" *(ibid., chap. xiv)* and that censorship is necessary in a republic lest virtue be destroyed "by omissions, by neglects, by a certain coolness in the love of our country, by bad examples, and by the seeds of corruption: whatever does not openly violate but elude the laws, does not subvert but weaken them, ought to fall under the inquiry and correction of the censors" (Book V, chap. xix).
27. See his Introduction to *The Spirit of the Laws,* p. 1.
28. Book XI, chap. vi; see also Book XII, chap. i. In Russell's judgment this is the most perceptive and meaningful of Montesquieu's definitions of liberty, though Russell cautions that governors as well as subjects require safety *(op. cit.,* pp. 250 ff.). But see the criticism of Montesquieu's view in Francis Lieber, *Civil Liberty and Self-government* (ed. Woolsey, 3d ed., rev., Philadelphia, 1875), pp. 33–34.
29. It is to be noted that Montesquieu now assumes that, given the laws, liberty can be secured through a proper administration of them. He leaves aside the element of will. This is an important departure from his other definition, but it makes possible the greater insight that all men can will the law yet be deprived of their liberty through faults in the mechanism of government.
30. For the distinctions between Locke's doctrine of divided powers and that of Montesquieu see J. W. Gough, *John Locke's Political Philosophy* (Oxford, 1950), chap. v, and Neumann, *op. cit.,* pp. lv–lvii.
31. See, for example, the correspondence between Justice Holmes and Frederick Pollock in the *Holmes-Pollock Letters* (ed. Howe, Cambridge, 1942), II, 265–67. Holmes had written, in his introduction to a reprint of *The Spirit of the Laws,* that Montesquieu's "England — the England of the threefold division of power into legislative, executive, and judicial — was a fiction invented by him." See Holmes, *Collected Legal Papers* (New York, 1920), p. 263. Pollock's refutation of this statement convinced Holmes that he had been insufficiently informed and led him to accept Pollock's remarks "in respectful silence." The opposite view — generally encountered in most discussions of the subject — is affirmed in Neumann, *op. cit.,* pp. liii–lv.
32. Book XI, chap. iv.
33. *Ibid.,* chap. vi.
34. Gaetano Mosca, however, attributes this failing less to Montesquieu than to the writers who have drawn on him. *The Ruling Class* (ed. Livingston, New York, 1939), p. 138.
35. *Ibid.* See also Neumann, *op. cit.,* pp. lviii and lxiv, and P. R. Rohden, "Montesquieu," *Encyclopaedia of the Social Sciences,* X, 638.
36. Cf. Bertrand Russell's argument that this is also an inefficient method of controlling arbitrary power, in *Power: A New Social Analysis* (New York, 1938), pp. 281–82.

CHAPTER 5

1. *Dominations and Powers: Reflections on Liberty, Society, and Government* (New York, 1951).

CHAPTER 6

1. Where, as in the first two sections of this paper, I have largely limited myself to an exposition of MacIver's ideas, I have made liberal use of his own language, unburdened, however, by the apparatus of quotation marks and page references. For his social philosophy, I have relied most heavily on *Community* (3d ed., London, 1924), and *The Elements of Social Science* (9th ed., London, 1949), and to a lesser degree on *Society: A Textbook of Sociology* (New York, 1937). His political theory is systematically developed in *The Modern State* (London, 1926), and *The Web of Government* (New York, 1947); but I have also found useful "The Meaning of Liberty and Its Perversions," in *Freedom: Its Meaning* (ed. Anshen, New York, 1940), pp. 278–287, *Leviathan and the People* (Baton Rouge, Louisi-

ana, 1939), *Towards an Abiding Peace* (New York, 1945), and *The Ramparts We Guard* (New York, 1950). For his methodology, the major item is *Social Causation* (Boston, 1942), but I have gained much illumination from two articles — "Sociology," in *A Quarter Century of Learning, 1904–1929* (New York, 1931), pp. 62–91, and "The Historical Pattern of Social Change," in *Authority and the Individual* (Cambridge, 1937), pp. 126–153 — and from his book, *The Contribution of Sociology to Social Work* (New York, 1931).

2. Generally MacIver has been careful to distinguish the state as an abiding association from its temporary administrative agent, the government. In *The Web of Government*, however, he reverses the usual order of definitions and employs the term "government" more broadly to refer to the organization of men under authority. On this basis the state becomes a form of government.

3. I have followed here the conspectus given in *The Web of Government*, p. 151; cf. also the conspectus in *The Modern State*, p. 363.

4. This point would be too obvious to mention were it not for the fact that the bulk of what is called social science research in this country — not least in sociology and in politics — has shifted from the quest for knowledge to the proliferation of measurements, forgetting that measurement alone is not knowledge and that the things most knowable — the nature and purposes of man, movements of thought, social relations and social institutions, and the like — are the data which are least amenable to quantification. Indeed, as MacIver has argued, since what can be measured is only the external, only that which lies outside the grasp of the imagination, men can measure only what they cannot understand. This may help to explain why American social scientists generally avoid causal analysis and take refuge in correlations.

5. Reasoning along these lines, MacIver arrived at the conclusion in *The Modern State*, pp. 339–340, that the historical trend of political evolution, in spite of reversions, was in the direction of democracy. It is to be noted, however, that *The Modern State* was published in 1926, when prevailing conditions were charitable to such a view. It is at least questionable, in the light of subsequent developments, whether history can sustain the argument. MacIver's conclusion would be more plausible were it based solely on logical rather than historical considerations, for then the state as he defines it most truly approximates itself — that is, its true nature or end in the Aristotelian sense — as it moves toward democracy. But unless one is prepared to deny that dictatorships and other forms of oligarchy are states — and MacIver does not of course entertain such a notion — there are limitations even to the logical argument. MacIver's inference from history is attacked, though crudely and without the necessary analysis, in E. M. Sait, *Democracy* (New York, 1929), pp. 16–18.

6. This special problem of federalism is treated most directly in *Community*, pp. 264–266, and *The Modern State*, pp. 378–381.

7. For MacIver's ideas on the relation between the state and the economic order, see his *Labor and the Changing World* (New York, 1919); *The Modern State*, chap. ix; *The Web of Government*, pp. 125–143, 331–359; and *Democracy and the Economic Challenge* (New York, 1952).

8. See, for example, Morris Ginsberg, *Reason and Unreason in Society* (London, 1947), pp. 115–121; J. D. Mabbott, *The State and the Citizen* (London, c. 1948), pp. 79–85; P. A. Sorokin, *Society, Culture, and Personality* (New York, 1947), pp. 116–118; D. B. Truman, *The Governmental Process* (New York, 1951), pp. 49–52, 351; and the article by J. H. Muirhead in *Mind*, XXXVII (1928), 82–87.

9. The argument is concisely put in *The Elements of Social Science*, p. 166. See also note 6 above.

10. *Community*, p. 265.

11. *The Modern State*, p. 150.

12. *Ibid.*, p. 219; *The Web of Government*, pp. 200–201.

13. So concerned is MacIver with the security of the social order that at one point he even defends the right of the state to forbid the teaching of certain religious doctrines that are calculated to undermine the social order, provided the state is right in its conception of the social danger and commits no counterbalancing evil by interfering. *Community*, p. 40. Apart from the ambiguities (e.g., the definition of a "counterbalancing evil") and the dangers (e.g., granting to the state the responsibility for determining the rightness of its own judgment) in this doctrine, Mac-

Iver has himself, in his later books, shifted the emphasis to the democratic principle of religious liberty.

14. *The Modern State*, p. 228.

CHAPTER 7

1. John Dickinson, "A Working Theory of Sovereignty," *Political Science Quarterly,* XL (1928), 32–63, at p. 50. Taken by itself, the argument of the *Crito* (50–51) does, I think, support Dickinson's interpretation. But there are strong grounds for holding a contrary view of what Socrates actually believed. It is clearly the teaching of the *Apology* (and other Socratic dialogues of Plato) that it is never right to do wrong, regardless of personal consequences. For this reason Socrates refused to obey the command of the Thirty to bring Leon the Salaminian to Athens to be put to death by the oligarchy; and he refused to remain silent when, "as I conceive and imagine, the god orders me to fulfill the philosopher's mission of searching into myself and other men" *(Apology, 32, 28)*. Plainly, Socrates would disobey a law that required him to do an unjust thing. From this standpoint, the argument in the aforesaid passage of the *Crito* can be read as no more than a demonstration to Crito that none of his arguments is sufficient to persuade Socrates to flee prison. This leaves open the question whether Socrates might not have been persuaded by other reasons — e.g., by a refutation of his own implicit thesis that death was really preferable to him than exile, in view of all the circumstances. Such a refutation might have been convincing if there were a diffferent set of circumstances surrounding such factors as his age, the suffering he might cause his friends in Athens, the treatment he might expect in the place or places of his exile, and above all the effect that escape would have had upon Socrates' life-work, his philosophic mission, the thing which was more precious to him than life.

For another argument in support of the thesis that Socrates would have approved Antigone's action, see R. N. Cross, *Socrates: The Man and His Mission* (Chicago, no date), pp. 168–172. Aspects of the general problem are discussed in Harry V. Jaffa, *Thomism and Aristotelianism* (Chicago, 1952), pp. 29–30, 199, and Jerome Hall, *Living Law of Democratic Society* (Indianapolis, 1949), pp. 21–22.

2. Dickinson, *op. cit.,* p. 50.

3. Aristotle, *Politics* (trans. Ellis, Everyman's ed., London, 1912), 1281a.

4. It seems hardly necessary to add that while the analysis of this problem is motivated by certain consequences which have ensued from the intense activities of congressional investigating committees in recent years, I am concerned not with the specific conduct of individuals who have appeared before such committees or with the behavior of the committee members themselves, but with the *principles* of political obligation that are relevant to such conduct.

5. For a contemporary view, see the argument by Peter Viereck in *Conservatism Revisited* (New York, 1949), pp. 10–11; but note his argument for the reverse position, pp. 20–21.

6. Henry David Thoreau, "Civil Disobedience," in *Walden and Other Writings* (ed. Atkinson, Modern Library ed., New York, 1937), p. 646.

7. "Antigone," in Sophocles, *The Theban Plays* (trans. Watling, Penguin ed., London, 1947), pp. 142–143.

8. But if in such an instance the state cannot prevent moral disapproval, and even perhaps the imposition of social and economic sanctions, by those whose sentiments may have been outraged, it can at least assume the obligation not to leave the acquitted man impoverished if in establishing his innocence he has been compelled to exhaust his funds.

9. See, for example, Morris R. Cohen, *Law and the Social Order* (New York, 1933), especially pp. 41–68, 102–111; Edgar Bodenheimer, "Power and Law: A Study of the Concept of Law," *Ethics,* L (1940), 127–143, at pp. 133–135; Alexander H. Pekelis, *Law and Social Action* (ed. Konvitz, Ithaca, N.Y., 1950), pp. 91–127; and Robert L. Hale, *Freedom through Law* (New York, 1952). On the mutual dependence of legal and non-legal social controls, there is, of course, a vast literature — e.g., the writings of Ihering and Gierke, Edward A. Ross and Max Weber, Robert M. MacIver and Bertrand Russell. Some of the juristic thinkers are considered in Julius Stone, *The Province and Function of Law* (2d printing, Sydney, Australia, 1950), chaps. 11 and 24.

10. 313 U.S. 299 (1940). See further the cases and discussion in Robert K. Carr, *Federal Protection of Civil Rights* (Ithaca, N.Y., 1947), chap. 4.

11. It is not without interest that even a near-absolutist like Hobbes would in the immediate circumstances seem to sanction a man's refusal to obey. "No man," Hobbes declared, "is tied by any compacts whatsoever to accuse himself, or any other, by whose damage he is like to procure himself a bitter life . . . yet in a public trial he may, by torture, be forced to make answer. But such answers are no testimony of the fact, but helps for the searching out of truth; insomuch that whether the party tortured answer true or false, or whether he answer not at all, whatsoever he doth, he doth it by right." *De Cive,* II, 19.

12. Cf. T. H. Green, *Lectures on the Principles of Political Obligation* (London, 1924 ed.); J. P. Plamenatz, *Consent, Freedom and Political Obligation* (London, 1938), chaps. 1–4; Max Weber, *The Theory of Social and Economic Organization* (trans. Henderson and Parsons, New York, 1947), pp. 324–373, 382–392; and Ernest Barker, *Principles of Social and Political Theory* (Oxford, 1951), Book V.

13. *Crito* (trans. Jowett), 50–51.

14. The fact that Socrates was in prison at the very moment he was thus arguing against Crito's plea that he disobey the law, reinforces the contention in note 1 above that Socrates did not actually accept this position; that he was in fact prepared to yield only a qualified obedience to the laws.

15. For this reason skeptics have put the argument for social order not in terms of right but in terms of convenience. The difficulty here, of course, is that it then becomes "right" to disobey whenever the social order ceases to be convenient.

16. I do not mean to imply that Mr. Dennis accepts the logic of his own position. See my *Patterns of Anti-Democratic Thought* (New York, 1949), chap. 3. For the absurdity of the "principle" that might makes right see the classic argument in Rousseau, *The Social Contract,* Book I, chap. 3. Compare, however, Spinoza, *Tractatus Theologico-Politicus,* chap. 16, and *Tractatus Politicus,* chaps. 2–4.

17. Some writers have sought in intuition or in natural law an "objective" criterion in terms of which they could show that democracy is intrinsically and not merely instrumentally best — e.g., Walter T. Stace, *The Destiny of Western Man* (New York, 1942) and Mortimer J. Adler and Walter Farrell, "The Theory of Democracy," *The Thomist,* III–VII (July, 1941–Jan., 1944) — but all such efforts rest ultimately on certain assumptions which cannot be *proved.* See further my "Power, Law, and Freedom of Inquiry," chap. 8, sec. III below.

18. For a recent (though qualified) restatement of this position, see Gray L. Dorsey, "The Necessity of Authority to Freedom," in *Freedom and Authority in Our Time* (ed. Bryson *et. al.,* New York, 1953), pp. 317–333, at pp. 329–331.

19. See her autobiography, *Living My Life* (2 vols., New York, 1931), II, 726–927.

20. This was clearly perceived by Justice Holmes, who with typical frankness wrote to Frederick Pollock: "I do think that man at present is a predatory animal. I think that the sacredness of human life is a purely municipal ideal of no validity outside the jurisdiction. I believe that force, mitigated so far as may be by good manners, is the *ultima ratio,* and between two groups that want to make inconsistent kinds of worlds I see no remedy except force." *Holmes-Pollock Letters* (ed. Howe, 2 vols., Cambridge, 1942), II, 36. And again, in letters to Harold J. Laski: ". . . all law means I will kill you if necessary to make you conform to my requirements." ". . . there is no superior arbiter — it is one of taste — but when men differ in taste as to the kind of world they want the only thing to do is to go to work killing." *Holmes-Laski Letters* (ed. Howe, 2 vols., Cambridge, 1953), I, 16, 116.

21. I am not unaware of the objection that the state cannot regard as irrelevant the effects of such disobedience on others. There is an immense difference, it is said, between disobeying the law when it conflicts with my principles or preferences if such disobedience does not injure others, and disobeying the law at the cost of injury to others. This argument has great force, and in general I think it proper that men should obey even unjust laws when disobedience has the effect of worsening, rather than improving, the situation. But the argument seems to me also to beg two of the very questions at issue: whether the law (and more important the system itself) does in fact injure others, and whether the numerical calculus is a proper principle of justice. In disobeying the law under the circumstances cited here, the dissident takes the position that it is the law (and the system of

order as well) which inflicts the injury, and that by disobeying the law he is calling the attention of the people to the injustice of the state. Moreover, if justice involves injury to others, then it is "just" that such injury be inflicted upon them. (In this event, of course, the dissident might well contend that the injury is apparent rather than real.) In any case, the objection does little more than return us to the fundamental issue at stake: which of the conflicting value systems is truly best or just?

22. *Politics*, 1292b.

23. There is substantial though not complete truth in Aristotle's dictum that "a well-formed government will have good laws, a bad one, bad ones." *Ibid.*, 1282b.

24. See R. M. MacIver, *The Modern State* (London, 1926), p. 154. This is not to argue that reason is the only, or the decisive, factor in leading men to obey laws which they regard as unjust. Habit, indolence, deference, fear, and the like, are in most cases the crucial determinants of obedience. See James Bryce, *Studies in History and Jurisprudence* (New York, 1901), pp. 467 ff., and R. M. MacIver, *The Web of Government* (New York, 1947), pp. 73–81.

25. "My problem," Laski wrote to Holmes, "is to take away from the state the superior morality with which we have invested its activities and give them [*sic*] back to the individual conscience." *Holmes-Laski Letters* (cited in note 20), I, 23. See further his *Authority in the Modern State* (New Haven, 1919), chap. 1, especially pp. 43, 46, 55; *A Grammar of Politics* (4th ed., London, 1938), Part I; and *Studies in Law and Politics* (New Haven, 1932), chap. 11. So also Thoreau: "Must the citizen ever for a moment, or in the least degree, resign his conscience to the legislator? Why has every man a conscience, then? I think that we should be men first, and subjects afterward. It is not desirable to cultivate a respect for the law, as much as for the right. The only obligation which I have a right to assume is to do at any time what I think right." Thoreau, "Civil Disobedience" (cited in note 6), pp. 636–637.

26. This is convincingly demonstrated in Felix S. Cohen, *Ethical Systems and Legal Ideals* (New York, 1933), pp. 62–65.

27. There is, however, a certain ambiguity in Hegel's absolutism, stemming from his apparent insistence that Antigone in refusing to obey the law of the state was both right and wrong. Cf. Georg W. F. Hegel, *The Phenomenology of Mind* (trans. Baillie, 2 vols., New York, 1910), II, 453 ff., and Georg W. F. Hegel, *Philosophy of Right* (trans. Knox, Oxford, 1942), pp. 3–10, 100, 114–115, 165–173, and the relevant translator's notes on pp. 299, 301, and 351. Hegel's subordination of the state (the highest reality within the realm of right) to philosophical truth (the highest reality within the whole system) is emphasized in Herbert Marcuse, *Reason and Revolution* (New York, 1941), p. 178.

28. For Hobbes's denial that political obligation requires an absolute obedience to all laws, see for example *De Cive*, VI, 13; VIII, 1; and XV, 18.

29. "A Working Theory of Sovereignty" (cited in note 1), pp. 50–51.

30. See also Elijah Jordan, *Theory of Legislation; An Essay on the Dynamics of Public Mind* (Chicago, 1952).

31. Cf. MacIver, *The Modern State*, p. 482; Dorothy Fosdick, *What is Liberty?* (New York, 1939), p. 128; and the writer's *Patterns of Anti-Democratic Thought*, pp. 204–206, 247–248.

32. As Mr. Justice Jackson so aptly put it in *West Virginia State Board of Education v. Barnette*, 319 U.S. 624, 642 (1943). See also the interesting argument of Charles R. Nixon, "Freedom vs. Unity: A Problem in the Theory of Civil Liberty," *Political Science Quarterly*, LXVIII (1953), 70–88.

33. This, indeed, is what Lincoln frankly urged in his address in 1838 on "The Perpetuation of Our Political Institutions": "Let every American, every lover of liberty, every well wisher to his prosperity, swear by the blood of the Revolution, never to violate in the least particular, the laws of the country; and never to tolerate their violation by others. . . . let every man remember that to violate the law, is to trample on the blood of his father, and to tear the character of his own, and his children's liberty. Let reverence for the laws, be breathed by every American mother, to the lisping babe, that prattles on her lap — let it be taught in schools, in seminaries, and in colleges; let it be written in primers, spelling books, and in Almanacs; — let it be preached from the pulpit, proclaimed in legislative halls, and enforced in courts of justice. And, in short, let it become the *political religion* of the nation; and let the old and the young, the rich and the

poor, the grave and the gay, of all sexes and tongues, and colors and conditions, sacrifice unceasingly upon its altars." *Abraham Lincoln: His Speeches and Writings* (ed. Basler, Cleveland, 1946), pp .80–81.

34. In employing here a modified phrase from Professor Stone, *The Province and Function of Law* (cited in note 9), p. 228, I do not mean to associate him with the doctrine in the text.

35. Eric Voegelin, "The Oxford Political Philosophers," *The Philosophical Quarterly,* III (1953), 97–114, at p. 100.

36. This is not, perhaps, inconsistent with Aristotle who, while he defines a citizen as "one who obeys the magistrate" *(Politics,* 1277a), also affirms that the one care common to all the citizens — that which *describes* a citizen — is "the safety of the community"*(ibid.,* 1276b).

37. Despite certain phrases in which Professor Barker seems to argue that obedience to the law is the highest political obligation *(op. cit.,* p. 194), I take his general position to be in accord with the proposition affirmed here: that it is the state, not the law, which merits that obedience. Clearly, he concurs with the further judgment that since the state is less than society, obedience to law must be subordinate to obedience to right, the highest moral obligation. *Ibid,* pp. 193, 221 ff.

38. So Lincoln in the address cited earlier (note 33, above), p. 81: ". . . bad laws, if they exist, should be replaced as soon as possible, still while they continue in force, for the sake of example, they should be religiously observed."

39. It is well to recall the insight of Spinoza: "All men are born ignorant, and before they can learn the right way of life and acquire the habit of virtue, the greater part of their life . . . has passed away." Spinoza, *Tractatus Theologico-Politicus* (trans. Elwes), chap. 16.

40. "Slavery in Massachusetts," in *op. cit.,* p. 669. Compare the principles and grounds of justifiable disobedience in Franz L. Neumann, "On the Limits of Justifiable Disobedience," in *Conflict of Loyalties* (ed. MacIver, New York, 1952), pp. 49–56.

41. Apart, of course, from the submission that looks to God. So Hobbes argued *(De Cive,* XVIII, 13): "Must we resist princes, when we cannot obey them? Truly, no; for this is contrary to our civil covenant. What must we do then? Go to Christ by martyrdom. . . ." And so the author of the *Vindiciae contra tryannos* (trans. as Hubert Languet, *A Defence of Liberty against Tyrants* [ed. Laski, London, 1924], p. 210), who, in the silence of the magistrates and the failure of men to run away, insisted that "there are no other weapons to be used, but bended knees and humble hearts."

42. M. R. Cohen, *The Meaning of Human History* (La Salle, Ill., 1947), p. 296.

43. To rely on conscience, integrity, and the capacity of man to judge rationally the probable consequences of his act of disobedience is insufficient, perhaps, to meet the objection of those who demand proof both of moral inescapability and of intellectual adequacy. But in the absence of an ethical absolutism and of a determinate aristocracy that embodies this alleged moral and intellectual superiority — and clearly democracy cannot in principle admit either alternative — I see no way to escape this trust.

CHAPTER 8

1. Cf. Felix S. Cohen, *Ethical Systems and Legal Ideals* (New York, 1933).

2. See Frank H. Knight, *Freedom and Reform* (New York, 1947), chap. i.

3. In this sense there is a real element of truth in Thrasymachus' forceful argument that justice is the interest of the strongest. For when Socrates in the *Republic* denies the rightful equation of justice with power, he opposes an ethical judgment to a sociological fact; and this is not a refutation. Both Socrates and Thrasymachus, indeed, are correct, though on different levels of discourse, if we understand or interpret Thrasymachus' statement as an assertion of what *is* rather than a prescription of what ought to be, as a reference not to any ideal concept of justice but to the conventional view which identifies justice — i.e., what ought to be — with legal rather than with moral right. There are, of course, serious questions concerning the meaning of "justice," "interest," and "strongest," but these must go unexplored here. For purposes of this analysis, "interest" is taken as that which men conceive or profess their interest to be, not what their interest logically or actually is; while "strongest" is identified with that group or coalition

of groups which actually, in a particular community, has the final say as to what may or may not be done.

4. The freedom to think, but not to speak, is Hobbes's classic exception. Were it not for George Orwell's graphic portrayal of thought control in *Nineteen Eighty-Four*, one would be tempted to add that this is an unavoidable exception.

5. In another context, equal or greater importance might well be placed on the dangers of free inquiry to others — to the individual who may come to doubt or even to abandon his basic values without discovering an acceptable substitute; to the community which may find itself confronted with disillusioned and unhappy, even contemptuous and rebellious, men.

6. Cf. Harold J. Laski, *Liberty in the Modern State* (rev. ed., New York, 1949), pp. 172–173 and *passim*.

It would be easy to conclude that men who resort to suppression are neither learned nor wise. History is a romantic fantasy for them, even a picaresque tale. They have not profited from the grim experiences of civilizations which undertook to persecute dissenters and discovered that they were in fact destroying themselves. But while such an interpretation would in many cases be correct, we must not forget that suppressors have also been thoughtful men who felt that momentary gains were sufficient to offset whatever losses might accrue over the long run. And in rare cases it may even be argued that suppressors employed the technique of suppression precisely because they sought to give greater currency to the seemingly outlawed doctrine. But however we explain motivation, the fact persists that throughout history men in power have on the whole sought to stigmatize, and legally to exclude, "dangerous" ideas.

7. For an effective recent statement of this position (as well as a critique of the legalistic and natural rights schools), see Henry Steele Commager, "The Pragmatic Necessity for Freedom," in *Civil Liberties Under Attack* (ed. Wilcox, Philadelphia, 1951), pp. 1–22.

8. It may, of course, be objected that the value of democracy cannot be assumed but must itself be demonstrated, that process without regard to ideal end or purpose cannot have intrinsic or instrumental value since it lacks a criterion other than itself by which it may be judged. This objection implies that democracy as a method of tentative power must be validated by a value outside itself and somehow absolute. Within the limitations of this discussion, I can only indicate my belief that this validation is impossible. Values cannot be intellectually reconciled because they are not intellectual in origin or in effect. Indeed, any attempt to justify a preference for democracy as against a system of absolute and final power would necessarily be supported by arguments which are themselves based on other value judgments, and so on.

9. Some of the implications of this bizarre circumstance are perceptively explored in Walter Lippmann, *American Inquisitors* (New York, 1928). It seems hardly necessary to add that precisely this sort of shift goes on in the Soviet Union, as events compel the ruling oligarchy continually to rewrite history.

10. Cf. Robert M. Hutchins, "The Freedom of the University," *Bulletin of the American Association of University Professors,* XXXVII (Summer, 1951), 238–252.

11. See the analysis in Alan Barth, *The Loyalty of Free Men* (New York, 1951).

CHAPTER 10

1. When I wrote these lines (as well as the first two sentences of §VI below), it did not occur to me that I might someday be attacked for *not* having written them. Yet a recent writer has inveighed against this article on the ground that it misrepresents Milton as a "principled defender of freedom," ignoring (so he says) the fact that Milton excluded certain categories of persons from the protection of freedom of opinion. See John P. Roche, "American Liberty: An Examination of the 'Tradition' of Freedom," in *Aspects of Liberty* (ed. Konvitz and Rossiter, Ithaca, N.Y., 1958), p. 132 note 6.

CHAPTER 12

1. Isaiah Berlin, *Two Concepts of Liberty* (Oxford, 1958), and David Fellman, *The Limits of Freedom* (New Brunswick, N.J., 1959).

CHAPTER 13

1. Clinton Rossiter, *Conservatism in America* (New York, 1955), pp. 48, 51.
2. Cf. David Spitz, *Democracy and the Challenge of Power* (New York, 1958), chap. ix.
3. What is also curious is that conservatism, and in particular that form of conservatism termed "philosophic conservatism" — by way of distinguishing it from materialistic or non-moralistic conservatism — involves a basic confusion of terms. For if by philosophy we mean the love of and quest for wisdom, the commitment of the philosopher is primarily to the method by which he pursues this quest and only secondarily, if at all, to the specific solutions or values that at a particular moment in time appear to him to constitute the nearest approximation to the ideal or ultimate best. Yet it is on this very point that those who call themselves conservatives most sharply divide.
4. I exclude from consideration here those whose conservatism derives not from philosophical or theological grounds but from apathy, timidity, or a presumed self-interest; for to the extent that such men may be said to have principles, their principles reflect no more than the patterns and mores of the existing social order. They view the social order as "good" because it makes them happy, or at least not uncomfortable; they are not happy because the social order is demonstrably "good."
5. Barry Goldwater, *The Conscience of a Conservative* (New York, Hillman Books ed., 1960), foreword.
6. Goldwater's peculiar conceptions of American educational problems and of the teachings of John Dewey are nowhere more strikingly revealed than in his assertions that "In the main, the trouble with American education is that we have put into practice the educational philosophy expounded by John Dewey and his disciples" and that we subscribe "to the egalitarian notion that every child must have the same education." *Ibid.*, p. 85. Nor does Goldwater seem to grasp the elementary distinction between the task of the primary school teacher as distinct from that of the university teacher; the former is by the very nature of things compelled to be more pupil-oriented than subject-oriented, a fact which someone concerned with the whole man should hardly deplore.
7. According to Stephen Shadegg, one of Goldwater's principal speechwriters and author of a fulsome biography of the Arizona Senator *(Barry Goldwater: Freedom Is His Flight Plan* [New York, 1962], Goldwater said "Keynesianism," not Communism. If this is true, the correction is the more damaging — because more ludicrous — remark. Moreover, it is questionable that Goldwater has ever read, much less studied, Keynes's works. Among other things, we have his younger sister's remark that "I don't think he [Goldwater] ever read a book growing up." And we find in Shadegg's biography that, apart from his voracious consumption of *Popular Mechanics,* Goldwater seems to have read but one book during his formative years — Gibbon's *Decline and Fall of the Roman Empire* — and this before he was eight years old! (I have commented briefly on Shadegg's book in a review in *Arizona Frontiers,* II [April, 1962], 21–22.)
8. "Three on the Line," *National Review,* IV (August 31, 1957), 179–181, 191.
9. Kendall has written elsewhere, and at greater length, on what he conceives to be Mill's rebellious and "evil" teaching in *On Liberty.* See his essay, "The 'Open Society' and Its Fallacies," *American Political Science Review,* LIV (December, 1960), 972–979.
10. Cf. Spitz, "Loyalty, Security and Freedom," *New Republic,* CXXVI (January 21, 1952), 17–18.
11. As published in the Columbus (Ohio) *Dispatch,* July 19, 1961.

CHAPTER 14

1. Peter Viereck, *Conservatism Revisited: The Revolt against Revolt, 1815–1949* (New York, 1949); see also his *Conservatism from John Adams to Churchill* (Princeton, 1956).
2. *Conservatism Revisited,* pp. 11, 21.
3. See, for example, Cram's book, *The Nemesis of Mediocrity* (Boston, 1917).
4. F. L. Wright, *Genius and the Mobocracy* (New York, 1949).
5. English translation from the fifth Swiss edition (Chicago, 1950).

6. See, among other books, his *The Conservative Mind* (Chicago, 1953) and *A Program for Conservatives* (Chicago, 1954).
7. Chicago, 1957.
8. E. Jordan, *Theory of Legislation: An Essay on the Dynamics of Public Mind* (Chicago, 1952).
9. *Conservatism from John Adams to Churchill,* p. 187.

CHAPTER 15

1. Bertrand de Jouvenel, *Sovereignty: An Inquiry into the Political Good* (trans. Huntington, Chicago, 1957).
2. I note in passing that Jouvenel's idea of sovereignty is consistently entangled in technical and vacuous language, almost to the point where it defies comprehension. He defines sovereignty, for example, as "the visible sign of an inner conviction held by the members of an aggregate that their aggregate has an absolute value" (p. 21). This is clearly meaningless; it does not enable us to identify the sovereign and it raises rather than answers questions. If we seek elsewhere to discover what the author of this verbal nonsense means, we find little to help us other than the contention that sovereignty is not to be located in a man or a group from which decisions emanate but in a quality of will. Not any will, however; only that will which is reasonable. And if we ask what is the mark of the reasonable as distinct from the arbitrary will, we learn that it is the will which recognizes and respects the "right" moral code. The sovereign, says Jouvenel, is he who rules in accordance with the natural law, which is anterior to and coexistent with him; and if, perchance, the sovereign does not will what is reasonable and just, why, alas, he must be deemed not to have willed it (pp. 209–210).

CHAPTER 16

1. "When the Public Judges the Court," *New York Times Magazine* (May 31, 1959), pp. 16, 41–42; see also his article "Liberals and the Supreme Court," *Commentary,* XXII (July, 1956), 20–26.
2. Baton Rouge, La., 1957.
3. By which Strauss means the "unchangeable standards founded in the nature of man and the nature of things." See his article, "The Liberalism of Classical Political Philosophy," *Review of Metaphysics,* XII (March, 1959), 393, 439.
4. *The Moral Foundation of Democracy* (Chicago, 1954), p. 112.
5. Leo Strauss, *Natural Right and History* (Chicago, 1953), p. 7.
6. Walter Lippmann, *The Public Philosophy* (Boston, 1955), pp. 165, 115.
7. *Ibid.,* pp. 123, 160; my italics.
8. To say that Strauss rejects God is simply to recognize that Strauss subordinates theology to philosophy. He understands, of course, that theology has been historically important and politically useful; but he holds it to be philosophically irrelevant, that is, untrue. In his view, philosophy and theology cannot be harmonized or synthesized in any ultimate sense; one must be servant and the other master. And nowhere in his work is there any suggestion that philosophy can be the handmaiden of theology; instead, there is abundant evidence that philosophy is the autonomous or master discipline. Strauss always appeals to nature, or to the classical idea of natural right, never to divine revelation or God.
9. *Anarchy or Hierarchy* (London, 1937), pp. 169–170.
10. Berns, *op. cit.,* p. 250.
11. *Ibid.,* pp. 251, 256.
12. *Ibid.,* p. 228. Some additional sentences from Winthrop's argument, not given by Berns, are revealing. Winthrop says: "This liberty is maintained and exercised in a way of subjection to authority; it is of the same kind of liberty wherewith Christ hath made us free. The woman's own choice makes such a man her husband; yet being so chosen, he is her lord, and she is to be subject to him, yet in a way of liberty, not of bondage; and a true wife accounts her subjection her honor and freedom, and would not think her condition safe and free, but in her subjection to her husband's authority" (from *A Speech to the General Court,* July 3, 1645).
13. Berns, *op. cit.,* pp. 257, 251, 255, 232.
14. *Ibid.,* pp. 126, 214, 207, 173.

15. *Ibid.,* p. 27.
16. He must, that is to say, be a Socratic philosopher, possessing both theoretical wisdom (knowledge of what is absolutely best) and practical wisdom (knowledge of what is politically possible, what is best in the particular circumstances).
17. Berns, *op. cit.,* pp. 253, 238–243 252, 256.
18. *Ibid.,* p. 222.
19. *Ibid.,* p. 162.
20. What Berns in effect proposes is that the justices ignore the motto — Equal Justice Under Law — they have had etched in stone over the entrance to the Supreme Court building, and replace it with the legend — Equal (or Unequal) Law Under Justice.
21. Berns, *op. cit.,* p. 252.
22. See, for example, the reviews by Carl A. Auerbach in the *Northwestern University Law Review,* LIII (March-April, 1958), 122–126, and Kenneth L. Karst in the *Harvard Law Review,* LXXI (May, 1958), 1387–1392).
23. Cf. the discussion in David Spitz, *Democracy and the Challenge of Power* (New York, 1958), chap. iv.
24. A few observations on Berns's methods would seem in order, in view of the pride which neo-conservatives take in their scholarship and rigorous logic:

1. Berns, a True Believer, sees complex questions primarily in simple and extreme terms. No sophisticated student of American constitutional law, for example, would pretend that a case is susceptible of only one interpretation; yet time and again Berns cites a judicial ruling, e.g. the Murray Winters obscenity case, as if the judge were there concerned with but a single issue — bad books — to the exclusion of other issues, such as requiring the New York legislature to draft careful, non-blunderbuss legislation.

2. He is frequently guilty of distortion. One of his key propositions, for example, is that jurisprudence is concerned with knowledge of what is right and how that right is to be done. He seeks to establish this by quoting the definition given in the Oxford Dictionary: that "jurisprudence is 'knowledge of and skill in the law or the right.'" But then, though he warns us of the need to emphasize each element of this definition, he promptly omits the terms "law" and "or" so as to make the definition refer only to "the right" (see p. 27). Later, he renders the quotation from the Oxford Dictionary differently, as "knowledge of and skill in law," but *jus,* he tells us, means law or right, and since *lex* means law, *jus* should be rendered as right, or the right (p. 161). Thus Berns achieves a linguistic leap that enables him to condemn jurists for being what they are — practitioners in or students of law — instead of the philosophers that he wants them to be. (My own copy of the Oxford Universal Dictionary — 3rd ed. revised, 1955 — defines jurisprudence as "knowledge of *or* skill in law." The word "right" nowhere appears in the definition.)

3. Berns plays fast and loose with the rules of argument. To support his contention that judges must concern themselves with moral considerations, for example, he asserts that "judges cannot be amoral because law is not amoral." But he immediately adds, "Amoral law is bad law" (p. 250). Now clearly, if law is not amoral, there cannot be, in this sense, bad law; while if there is amoral law that is therefore, bad, it is false to say that law is not amoral. What is involved here and elsewhere, of course, is Berns's confusion of the actual and the ideal; when he writes "is," he means "ought."
25. Berns, *op. cit.,* p. 254.

AFTERWORD

1. In 1950, 99.98 per cent of the eligible voters went to the polls; of these, 99.72 per cent supported the Party list. In 1954, 99.98 per cent again voted; of these 99.84 per cent supported the officially-approved list.
2. Lenin once told a gathering of Young Communists: "In our opinion, morality is entirely subordinate to the interests of class war. Everything is moral which is necessary for the annihilation of the old exploiting social order and for uniting the proletariat. Our morality, then, consists solely in close discipline and in conscious war against the exploiters. We do not believe in external principles of morality and we will expose this deception. Communist morality is identical with the fight for strengthening the dictatorship of the proletariat." David Shub, *Lenin* (Garden City, N.Y., 1948), p. 369.

3. For Stalin's disingenuous defense of such "revisionism," see his *History of the Communist Party of the Soviet Union (Bolsheviks)* (New York, 1939), pp. 355–358; also his "Reply to A. Kholopov," in his *Marxism and Linguistics* (New York, 1951), pp. 42–47.
4. So Harry Pollitt, leader of the Communist Party in England, on September 14, 1939: "To stand aside from this conflict, to contribute only revolutionary-sounding phrases while the Fascist beasts ride rough-shod over Europe, would be a betrayal of everything our forebears have fought to achieve in the course of long years of struggle against capitalism."
5. An editorial in *Izvestia* (October 9, 1939) put it this way: "Every one is entitled to express his attitude toward one or another ideology, defend it or reject it. But extermination of a people for the reason that some one does not like certain views and an ideology is senseless and absurd cruelty. It throws us back to the dark medieval epoch of devastating religious wars for extermination of heretics and dissentients. . . . One may respect or hate Hitlerism, just as any other system of political views. This is a matter of taste. But to undertake war for 'annihilation of Hitlerism' means to commit criminal folly in politics."

David Spitz is a well-known writer on social and political subjects, as well as a distinguished scholar in political science. His books include *Patterns of Anti-Democratic Thought* (MacMillan, 1949) and *Democracy and the Challenge of Power* (Columbia University Press, 1958). A professor of political science at the Ohio State University, he writes articles frequently for *Harper's Commentary,* the *New Republic,* the *Antioch Review, Ethics,* and journals of political and social science. He has been a visiting professor at Cornell University, Hunter College, and Kenyon College and spent 1962–63 teaching in Italy at the Johns Hopkins University Bologna Center of the School of Advanced International Studies.

Acknowledgments

For permission to reprint here essays and reviews that originally appeared in their books or journals, I am grateful to the editors and publishers listed below.

Foreword: The remarks on liberalism were incorporated in a paper read at the annual meeting of the American Political Science Association, New York City, September 6, 1957.

Chapter 1: A paper read at the annual meeting of the Midwest Conference of Political Scientists, in Ann Arbor, Michigan, April 22, 1950.

Chapter 2: This essay, originally entitled "On Power and the Unification of Politics," was published as a review of Karl Loewenstein, *Political Power and the Governmental Process,* in the *Antioch Review,* XIX (Spring, 1959), 122–126.

Chapter 3: The substance of these remarks has been taken from a paper "On Power and Charismatic Leadership," read at the annual meeting of the American Political Science Association, in New York City, September 9, 1960.

Chapter 4: This essay was originally published in *Ethics,* LXIII (April, 1953), 207–213, as "Some Animadversions on Montesquieu's Theory of Freedom."

Chapter 5: This essay was originally published in *Ethics,* LXII (January, 1952), 122–127, as "George Santayana: Politics as a Secular Theology." I have dealt more fully with Santayana's political theory, as extrapolated from his other writings, in my *Patterns of Anti-Democratic Thought* (New York, 1949), chap. 8.

Chapter 6: This essay, originally entitled "Robert M. MacIver's Contributions to Political Theory," was first published in M. Berger, T. Abel, and C. H. Page (eds.), *Freedom and Control in Modern Society* (New York: D. Van Nostrand Co., 1954), pp. 293–312.

Chapter 7: A paper read at the annual meeting of the American Political Science Association, in Washington, D. C., September 12, 1953, and published in the *American Political Science Review,* XLVIII (June, 1954), 386–403. Despite the fact that no scholarly article I have written seems to have attracted as much attention, or produced so violent a reaction — in non-academic even more than in academic circles — I see no reason to revise any of the opinions or judgments, or to alter any of the analysis, in that printed record.

Chapter 8: This essay was extracted from me by the gentle persuasion of H. Gordon Hullfish, friend and colleague and editor of the Twelfth Yearbook of the John Dewey Society, *Educational Freedom in an Age of Anxiety* (New York: Harper & Bros., 1953), in which it appeared (pp. 52–69). It is difficult to accept the fact that one who so effectively combined leadership with compassion is no longer with us; his death (in June, 1962) leaves those of us who knew him a little less than what we were before.

Chapter 9: This essay was originally published under the title "Politics and the Realms of Being," *Dissent,* VI (Winter, 1959), 56–65, as a critique of Hannah Arendt's "Reflections on Little Rock," *ibid.,* pp. 45–46. For Miss Arendt's reply, see *ibid.,* VI (Spring, 1959), 179–181.

Chapter 10: First published in the *Antioch Review,* XIII (Fall, 1953), 290–302, under the title "Milton's Testament," and reprinted in Robert B. Downs (ed.), *The First Freedom* (Chicago: American Library Association, 1960), pp. 8–14.

Chapter 11: This essay was published in the *Antioch Review,* X (Summer, 1950), 301–304, as a review-article of Professor Laski's two books, *Liberty in the Modern State* (rev. ed., New York, 1949) and *Trade Unions in the New Society* (New York, 1949). I have also commented briefly on this second work in a review published in the *Annals of the American Academy of Political and Social Science,* CCLXVIII (March, 1950), 231.

Chapter 12: This essay was originally published in *Dissent,* VIII (Winter, 1961), 78–85.

Chapter 13: This essay has not previously appeared in print.

Chapter 14: I have incorporated into this essay a number of reviews written for various journals at different times. Thus: the materials in the introductory note and in §I have been taken from my review of Viereck's *Conservatism Revisited,* which appeared in *Labor and Nation,* VI (Spring, 1950), 55; my review of Frank Lloyd Wright's *Genius and the Mobocracy* appeared in the *Saturday Review of Literature,* XXXII (September 3, 1949), 21; my review of Röpke's *The Social Crisis of Our Time* was published in the *American Political Science Review,* XLV (June, 1951), 543–545; my review of Kirk's *The American Cause* appeared in *The Nation,* CLXXXVI (April 12, 1958), 326–328; much of what I say here about Jordan has been taken from my review of his *Theory of Legislation* in the *Western Political Quarterly,* VI (June, 1953), 387–389; and for my concluding section I have borrowed some paragraphs from my review of Arthur J. Schlesinger, Jr., *The Vital Center,* which appeared in *Labor and Nation,* V (September–October, 1949), 107–108.

Chapter 15: This essay was originally published as a review of Jouvenel's *Sovereignty,* in *Dissent,* VI (Summer, 1959), 280–287.

Chapter 16: This essay was published in *Commentary,* XXVIII (October, 1959), 313–321, as a review of Walter Berns, *Freedom, Virtue, and the First Amendment.*

Afterword: This essay was first published in the *Antioch Review,* IX (Winter, 1949–1950), 495–508, and then reprinted in Paul Bixler (ed.), *The Antioch Review Anthology* (Cleveland: The World Publishing Co., 1953), pp. 37–49.

Index

Good Life, The (Jordan), 149
Gorgias (Plato), 24
Gough, J. W., 190 (n. 30)
Grand Inquisitor (Dostoevsky), 116
Great Britain; *see* England
Greece, 63
Green, T. H., 74, 193 (n. 12)
Griffin, Marvin, 93
Griswold, Erwin, 162

Hale, Robert L., 192 (n. 9)
Halévy, Elie, 189 (n. 10)
Hall, Jerome, 192 (n. 1)
Hallowell, John H., 163, 164, 166
Hamilton, Alexander, 137
Harvard University, 133
Hayek, Friedrich A., 144
Headquarters Detective, 172
Hegel, G. W. F., 41, 74, 75, 115, 194
  (n. 27)
Hegelians, 45
Henry, Patrick, 115
Hillenbrand, Martin J., 15, 16
Hillman, Sidney, 114
Hitler, Adolf, 24, 25, 26
Hitlerism, 200 (n. 5)
Hobbes, Thomas, 23, 25–27, 38, 74,
  79, 95, 111, 112, 115, 131, 193
  (n. 11), 194 (n. 28), 195 (n. 41),
  196 (n. 4)
Holmes, Oliver Wendell, Jr., 57, 170,
  190 (n. 31), 193 (n. 20), 194
  (n. 25)
Hong Kong, 100
Hoover, Herbert, 13, 115
House of Representatives, 75
Hutchins, Robert M., 196 (n. 10)
Hyde Park, London, 57

Ihering, Rudolf von, 192 (n. 9)
Index of Forbidden Books, 28, 100
Indian caste system, 46
Inquisition, 102
Italy, 176, 180, 184, 186
Izvestia, 200 (n. 5)

Jackson, Robert H., 194 (n. 32)
Jaffa, Harry V., 192 (n. 1)
Jefferson, Thomas, 43, 130, 137, 147
Jehovah's Witnesses, 76
Jeremiah, 147
Jesus, 85; *see also* Christ
Jewkes, John, 144
*John Locke and the Doctrine of
  Majority-Rule* (Kendall), 134

Jordan, Elijah, 149–151, 194 (n. 30),
  198 (n. 8)
Jouvenel, Bertrand de, 144, 153–161,
  163, 198 (nn. 1, 2)

Kahler, Erich, 119
Kant, Immanuel, 82, 118, 119
Karst, Kenneth L., 199 (n. 22)
Kendall, Willmoore, 129, 133–138,
  146, 153, 197 (n. 9)
Keynes, John M., 197 (n. 7)
Kirk, Russell, 129, 134, 146–149
Knight, Frank H., 144, 195 (n. 2)
Knowland, William F., 134
Koestler, Arthur, 38, 186
Kremlin, 116, 178; *see also* Soviet
  Union
Kronstadt sailors, 183
Kropotkin, Peter, 79

Labor government (England), 179
Lady Chatterley's Lover (Lawrence),
  172
Laski, Harold J., 73, 74, 111–114,
  153, 189 (n. 7), 193 (n. 20),
  194 (n. 25), 196 (n. 6)
Lasswell, Harold D., 15, 38
Lawrence, H. D., 172
Lecky, W. E. H., 189 (n. 3)
Left, the, 151, 175, 178–187
Lenin, V. I., 71, 177, 178, 183, 185,
  199 (n. 2)
de Leon, Daniel, 177
Leon the Salaminian, 192 (n. 1)
Leviathan, 21
Lewis, John L., 16, 114
Liberty in the Modern State (Laski),
  111
Lieber, Francis, 190 (n. 28)
Life of Reason, The (Santayana),
  36, 43
Limits of Freedom, The (Fellman),
  120
Lincoln, Abraham, 137, 194 (n. 33),
  195 (n. 38)
Lindsay, A. D., 158
Lippmann, Walter, 163, 165, 166, 169
  196 (n. 9), 198 (n. 6)
Lipset, Seymour Martin, 188 (n. 4)
Little Rock, Ark., 93
Locke, John, 5, 33, 83, 130, 190
  (n. 30)
Loewenstein, Karl, 18–22, 188 (n. 1)
Lolita (Nabokov), 90
London *Times Literary Supplement,*
  153

THE LIBERAL IDEA OF FREEDOM was typeset and composed by Tucson Typographic Service in Times Roman, a modern typeface designed in 1932 for the London *Times* by Stanley Morison. The book was printed by Arizona Lithographers on University Eggshell text paper, manufactured by Warren. Binding is by the Arizona Trade Bindery, using the "Brite Red" Joanna Parchment vellum.